BEYOND THE SALVATION WARS

WHY BOTH PROTESTANTS
AND CATHOLICS MUST REIMAGINE
HOW WE ARE SAVED

MATTHEW W. BATES

Brazos Press
a division of Baker Publishing Group
Grand Rapids, Michigan

© 2025 by Matthew W. Bates

Published by Brazos Press
a division of Baker Publishing Group
Grand Rapids, Michigan
BrazosPress.com

Printed in the United States of America

Library of Congress Cataloging-in-Publication Data
Names: Bates, Matthew W., 1977– author.
Title: Beyond the salvation wars : why both protestants and catholics must reimagine how we are saved / Matthew W. Bates.
Description: Grand Rapids, Michigan : Brazos Press, a division of Baker Publishing Group, 2025. | Includes bibliographical references and index.
Identifiers: LCCN 2024031713 | ISBN 9781540961730 (paperback) | ISBN 9781587436567 (casebound) | ISBN 9781493422012 (ebook) | ISBN 9781493422005 (pdf)
Subjects: LCSH: Catholic Church—Relations—Protestant churches. | Catholic Church—Doctrines. | Protestant churches—Relations—Catholic Church. | Protestant churches—Doctrines.
Classification: LCC BX4818.3 .B4 2025 | DDC 284—dc23/eng/20240828
LC record available at https://lccn.loc.gov/2024031713

Cover design by Chris Gilbert, Studio Gearbox

Baker Publishing Group publications use paper produced from sustainable forestry practices and postconsumer waste whenever possible.

25 26 27 28 29 30 31   7 6 5 4 3 2 1

For my sister, Annie Perkins:

My first teacher. Always positive.
When I contemplate God's justice,
I always think of you,
because you are the fairest person I know.

Contents

Introduction   1

1. Entering the Combat Zone   7
2. The More Explicit Gospel   27
3. Right and Wrong about the Gospel   48
4. Retooling the Protestant Critique of Catholicism   73
5. Is Baptism Saving?   103
6. Why Election and Regeneration Are False Starts   139
7. Once Saved, Always Saved?   172
8. Disrupting the Order of Salvation   201
9. Justification Remodeled   231
10. Beyond the Salvation Wars   256

Acknowledgments   267
Appendix: Guide for Further Conversation   269
Notes   280
Scripture and Ancient Sources Index   294

Introduction

Salvation wars have been fought throughout the church's history. Paul railed against the troublemakers in Galatia. Irenaeus fought the Gnostics. At the Council of Nicaea documents were ripped from the hands of a heretic and stomped—and medieval legend adds that jolly Saint Nicholas hit Arius in the face. Augustine grappled with Pelagius. Luther stood in for several rounds against the Catholic Church. Roman Catholics and Protestants alike ardently killed the early Anabaptists. Arminius's followers were persecuted by fellow Calvinists.

Apart from the Crusades and politically motivated conquests, these skirmishes have only rarely involved physical violence. But occasionally blood has flowed.

One reason why battles have been fought over salvation is that its stakes are high but its theology complex. What is the true gospel? What is faith? What are works? And how do they relate? Who supplies the initiative in salvation, God or us? And to what degree? Is grace timeless, or is it given at specific moments in history? Is it active via our natural capacities or as a supernatural endowment? Can grace be resisted? Is salvation a one-time event, a process, or mysteriously both? How do repentance and baptism factor into salvation, especially with regard to ceremonies or sacraments? Should infants be baptized?

Eternal life hangs in the balance. Yet the questions are endless. It is not just the complexity that makes progress toward agreement about salvation appear unachievable; there are compounding factors. After a messy divorce, church factions that previously were one family have settled into different homes. Life apart from one another has hardened into fixed denominational and institutional habit. Doctrinal statements and distinct liturgies that reinforce the separation have been designed.

All too often denominational leaders are more committed to actions and social politics that will reinforce *their brand* than they are to the truth. They are convinced that even if their denominational brand isn't entirely true, it is at least mostly right, and their brand bears witness to key truths that other brands neglect. So institutional leaders strive to preserve their own denominational slice of the pie.

Plus, pragmatic concerns come into play: denominational leaders feel duty bound to safeguard the institutions and people entrusted to their care. If the Presbyterians, Methodists, Anglicans, or Roman Catholics were to reconcile *too extensively*, then each's functionaries would no longer have a distinct purpose. Churches would close their doors. Seminaries would shut down. Pastors and priests would lose jobs. Denominational stewardship, whether intentionally or not, undercuts unity by reinforcing *the brand*.

Partisanship is the norm. Meanwhile, the doctrinal disputes seem intractable. So we must agree to disagree and maintain our separate tribal ways, right?

Mē genoito. May it never be! We must never give up on the truth. We must never give up on oneness. We must never give up on striving toward a truth-based unity for the future of the church.

While it would be delusional to think that a slender book like this one could somehow end the fighting, there is nonetheless cause for optimism. Progress toward reconciliation can and will be made. Although unity in the truth must remain a long-term hope, now is an auspicious time to make strides toward it. I'll explain why shortly.

In aiming toward a truth-based future unity, *Beyond the Salvation Wars* offers a fresh way to talk about salvation: the *gospel-allegiance model*. Then it explores this model's ability to answer controversial questions about salvation. The gospel-allegiance model seeks to expose the truth about how salvation happens according to Scripture and early Christian history, believing that in the long run this can help Protestants and Catholics move toward a healthier future.

Entering the Conversation

Since this is not my first book on salvation, new readers may be hesitant to wade in. It can be awkward to step into a conversation midstream. Should you cheer, cry, or start swinging punches?

You can relax. *Beyond the Salvation Wars* stands on its own as a complete argument. Since it fits within a multibook project, some may prefer to start with its predecessors. But that is not necessary. The topics of the books differ but relate, so whether this is the best option depends on the reader's needs and interests.

My motivation in writing *Beyond the Salvation Wars* helps to explain how it differs from my previous books, especially *Salvation by Allegiance Alone* and *Gospel Allegiance*. While I was writing these earlier books, my topic kept bumping against the restraining wall of my word-count limits. It wasn't simply that I wanted to say more. Rather, more urgently needed to be said. The gospel-allegiance model raises vital questions that demand answers. I knew that these books would be incomplete apart from a follow-up.

If you want to explore the biblical foundations of the core model thoroughly, *Salvation by Allegiance Alone* offers a wide-ranging biblical theology of salvation. Meanwhile, *Why the Gospel?* and *The Gospel Precisely* are short, noncontroversial, and written for a popular audience, making them ideal for church and group studies. *Salvation by Allegiance Alone* was followed by *Gospel Allegiance*. It is this book's prequel, and it plumbs the core model to an even greater depth.

If you are the type who prefers abundant initial proof, I'd recommend starting with *Gospel Allegiance*, which offers a more detailed treatment of the core model than does *Salvation by Allegiance*

Alone. It draws from the Bible, early Christian history, and recent scholarship in order to define and interrelate the gospel, faith, grace, and works. For example, if you wonder how to reconcile this book's content with Paul's words "For it is by grace you have been saved, through faith . . . not by works" (Eph. 2:8–9 NIV), then don't start here. I can't repeat that work, so begin with *Gospel Allegiance*. It treats that text and many others extensively, showing from Scripture how the gospel, faith, grace, and works fit together.

But it is not necessary to start elsewhere, because the big idea within the gospel-allegiance model is easy to grasp: *we are saved not merely by trusting that God's saving promises for us are true in Jesus but by bodily allegiance to him as king*. Allegiance language can help Catholics and Protestants overcome disagreements about faith and works. The introductory chapters of this book also position the gospel-allegiance model afresh by comparing it with other treatments of salvation. This will prepare readers, both the well-acquainted and the newbies, to enter the discussion.

You've already started. I hope you are excited to get up to full speed. How does this book advance the previous conversation? Like *Gospel Allegiance*, it enters more deeply into select themes than was possible in my initial book, *Salvation by Allegiance Alone*. However, this new book doesn't simply rehash old material. It goes beyond the core model to treat ongoing disputes within salvation theory.

Beyond the Salvation Wars deals with some of the most divisive issues in the church, including controversial topics such as Catholic-Protestant differences, models for baptism, election, regeneration, assurance, and perseverance. None of these topics have been covered in anything more than a cursory fashion in my previous writings. This book also treats Catholic-Protestant disputes about the mechanics of justification (models of righteousness) more thoroughly than my earlier work, featuring new topics.

Beyond the Salvation Wars is for church leaders, students, and general readers. It contains additional features to make it more practical and experiential. The appendix, "Guide for Further Conversation," includes questions and discussion prompts for groups or individuals.

But given that it offers new proposals and a novel synthesis, I trust it will prove worthwhile for scholars and professors too. This impacts my interactions and notes. Scripture and other ancient sources are given pride of place. Beyond those, the principal conversation partners are official Catholic documents and popular Protestant influencers: pastor-theologians who have written extensively on salvation, such as John MacArthur, John Piper, and R. C. Sproul. *Beyond the Salvation Wars* is also informed by academic scholarship and cites such scholarship, but I was forced to minimize the notes. I apologize to colleagues whose work deserves but has not received interaction.

Although progress toward oneness in the church is a worthy goal, I recognize that the short-term effect of a sharply pointed book like this may be more squabbling. In fact, let's get this out of the way now: readers who are inflexibly committed to a specific denomination, church confession, or systematic theology of salvation will probably hate this book. If that is you, then you have been forewarned: proceed at your own risk. But for those who love to rediscover Scripture and early Christian history, for those who are eager to reappropriate foundational truths, please read on. I trust you'll find this exploration worthwhile.

Since this book aims to cut with precision, short-term unity is an unrealistic goal. While this book affirms that both Catholics and Protestants are truly Christian and have largely modeled salvation correctly, at times it is quite critical of aspects of current Catholic and Protestant soteriology. It doesn't paper over errors with a veneer of feigned love. I am a Protestant, but I have served for over fifteen years as a theology professor in a Catholic university. I love my Catholic and Protestant sisters and brothers too deeply to offer a "let's just compromise" feel-good proposal that doesn't seek to expose and correct damaging untruths. (I love the Orthodox too, but that conversation exceeds this book's scope.) For the sake of love, this book seeks to show that dogmas, confessions, and traditional systems of soteriology must be revised. It articulates a positive proposal rooted in the unchanging truths of Scripture and early Christian history.

In short, *Beyond the Salvation Wars* is surgical: painful but lovingly aimed toward healing. It is a theological proposal with practical implications for discipleship, mission, and ecumenism. I hope that the book generates robust dialogue. But it is more of a manifesto about salvation's truths and an exhortation for the church to recover those truths over the long haul than it is an ecumenical dialogue. By way of a new gospel-allegiance model, it seeks to move beyond the salvation wars—past and present—by casting a truer vision of how salvation occurs. My prayer is that this book will help the church move beyond past denominational battles to a more unified future centered on allegiance to Jesus the victorious king.

1 Entering the Combat Zone

Near the front line, Ulrich Zwingli lay beneath the dead and wounded, trying to find air. His face was unscathed but his body wrecked. The corpses of his neighbors and friends were heaped on him. His injuries would not permit him to rise, but he continued to find pockets of air, so his shallow breathing persisted.

This battlefield scene offers a sobering reminder. More than ink was spilled as salvation wars were fought in the sixteenth century. Soon we'll explore specific reasons why the combatants were willing to lay down their lives—and why the gospel and salvation are still priceless. But with Zwingli, one of the earliest Reformers, we begin to see what is at stake.

Through preaching and public debate, Zwingli persuaded his city to become Protestant in the 1520s. Then he courageously led that city, Zurich, into battle when an alliance of neighboring Catholic cantons declared war on Zurich. Yet the Catholics won.

Zwingli fell on the battlefield. An enemy soldier who was plundering loot from the corpses found him alive, rolled him over, and shook him in an attempt to rally his breathing. The date was October 11, 1531.

What makes the drama of Zwingli's death especially fascinating is that we possess two written accounts—one Catholic, one Protestant.[1] The reports largely agree. Zwingli was found near the front line. The Catholic solider, not recognizing Zwingli, roused him and offered to fetch a priest so that he could confess his sins before dying. Zwingli refused priestly assistance.

Then Zwingli met a gruesome death. While Zwingli was still unrecognized, a Catholic officer, Captain Fuckinger—an unfortunate name that proves that truth is stranger than fiction—hacked his neck with a broadsword, ending Zwingli's life. Shortly thereafter, other Catholic soldiers gleefully identified him as their notorious enemy, Ulrich Zwingli.

Yet the differences in the accounts are instructive. In the Catholic account, when the soldiers discover that it is indeed Zwingli who has been killed, they rejoice, call him foul names, and offer thanks to God for the death of the miscreant who started "all their evils, calamities, and alarms." They express surprise that he was surrounded by soldiers rather than devils upon death.

Zwingli's downfall is God's act of justice: "He now lay there given by God's instrumentality into their hands, and he had paid the price for his wickedness. . . . By the grace of God all his schemes perished with him." The Catholic account praises God for the gift of Zwingli's death.

Meanwhile, the Protestant record casts the event in a different light. When discovered mortally wounded, Zwingli is described "with his hands together as if he was praying, and his eyes looking upwards to heaven." He looks to God alone. His rejection of confession to a priest while dying evidences his implacable conviction that the Catholic sacrament of penance has no bearing on his final salvation.

The Protestant report adds anti-Catholic elements. While Zwingli is dying but not yet recognized by the Catholics, the Catholic soldiers urge this unknown Protestant man to have "the mother of God in his heart" and to "call on the beloved saints to plead to God for grace on his behalf." But Zwingli rejects as ineffective any mediator other than Christ alone. When Captain Fuckinger thrusts his sword into Zwingli's neck, it is because he is exasperated by the obstinate refusal of this unknown Protestant man to accept Catholic norms about salvation.

8

The Protestant version stresses Zwingli's true profession of Christ and laments Catholic blindness: "There, because of his confession of the true faith in Christ, our only savior, the mediator and advocate of all believers, he was killed by . . . one of those against whom he had always preached so eloquently." For the Protestants, Zwingli dies a martyr for the cause of recovering true Christian teaching about salvation.

As modern Christians, our first reaction with regard to past salvation wars is to congratulate ourselves on our happy progress in the twenty-first century. Despite ongoing squabbles, we are no longer hacking one another to bloody bits, rejoicing at the death of our theological enemies. (Except on social media, where we stab and then gloat.) We pat ourselves on the back for our *vast* moral superiority, especially in comparison to our unenlightened forebears.

Given contemporary culture's headlong moral dive, reduced theological blood sport is probably one of the few issues about which it is correct to applaud our progress. At least church and world have made improvements on this front. No sane person wants to go back to the good ol' days when intra-Christian disputes about salvation could turn violent. I sure don't. "War is hell," as General Sherman so memorably phrased it.[2] Let's rejoice that we've left fratricidal Christian wars behind.

But some nostalgia may be warranted. If what the Bible teaches about salvation is true, then perhaps our sixteenth-century brothers and sisters were more in touch with reality than we are. In the church today we can't seem to prioritize a fervent commitment to the gospel. We nod our heads "yes" on Sunday morning: Jesus is indeed worthy. But we have more pressing concerns: Can you believe what Khloé Kardashian just posted on Instagram? Can Patrick Mahomes orchestrate another comeback win? What's on Netflix tonight? We declare our passion for the gospel but then wear out our couch cushions.

Meanwhile, Catholics and Protestants of the sixteenth century were willing to die for a correct understanding of salvation. Maybe they grasped something that we're missing. For them, this life, including its bloody battles, was merely preparation for the endless splendors or horrors of the next. War was too brief and trivial to be hell. In fact, if heretics were spreading false teachings about the gospel and salvation, fighting in a war was not hell but instead an act of generosity that might spare people from it.

The *gospel-allegiance model* can cast a long-term vision to help overcome Protestant-Catholic and Calvinist-Arminian disagreements about salvation. At least, that is this book's hope. Here are a few other things that would be nice: an end to world hunger, the demolition of the porn industry, and a winning lottery ticket. Oh, and could an apple pie float above my desk, along with a heavenly fork that will feed me a bite whenever I wish?

Progress toward church unity regarding salvation would be delicious, but surely it is not possible to get a real fork into that pie-in-the-sky crust. After all, Catholics and the Orthodox fell out of communion nearly a thousand years ago. Protestants and Catholics have been feuding for over five hundred. Given the universal church's badly fractured condition and the long-standing nature of the disputes, skepticism about ecumenical progress is understandable.

Hope for Progress toward Unity?

I'm skeptical of the skepticism. We have urgent work to do both theologically and practically to foster unity in the church. Doubtless, our short-term progress will remain fraught and choppy. But let me give five reasons why long-term progress toward Christian unity about the gospel and salvation is not only possible but certain.

1. *Jesus prayed for the church's unity.* As his death approached, Jesus interceded with God the Father for his disciples. He prayed for their unity above all else: "that they may be one, even as we

are one" (John 17:11; cf. 17:20–22). Jesus in fact prayed that "they may become *perfectly* one" (17:23).

Do you think that the Father ignored Jesus's prayer for complete unity when he uttered it prior to his death? Moreover, dare we think that Jesus is not still pleading for total unity, as he intercedes for us as priest and king at the right hand of God (Rom. 8:34; Heb. 7:25)?

Jesus's prayers for his church will be answered. Despite the sad reality of a fragmented church today, disunity will not be the church's final state. *The true church will inexorably be united in the future.* This raises questions about how we define the church and conceptualize unity.

2. *Church unity happens in the end.* We cannot explore models for church unity here. But we can affirm that God is guiding his sojourning people toward a final oneness. Scripture gives us a potent image to help us picture this future: we will be united as citizens of a single city.

If the church is fractured today, this is a temporary malady. In Revelation 21 the new Jerusalem descends from heaven. It is clear that this single city is for the *entire* people of God, because it separates God's special people from the wicked. Those who overcome by persevering in their allegiance to Jesus the king will enjoy the city and its benefits. But those who practice wickedness will experience punishment (Rev. 21:7–8; cf. 2:7–11; 3:12). This image of the entire people of God united within the bounds of a single city indicates that in the end the church will be united.

It is true that *perfect* unity will need to await the return of our Lord Jesus. Yet the new Jerusalem should not be seen as totally discontinuous with our present world. God's "new" creation is better understood as a radical renewal of the present order as it is shaken, refined, and recrafted, not an entirely new creation from nothing.[3] Thus, progress toward unity within the true church can, must, and *will* happen at some point in the future. Let's make strides today.

3. *Unity need not be hierarchical.* The image of a city reminds us that unity need not be coordinated under a single pattern of church

governance. The new Jerusalem is ruled from a single throne by God and the Lamb (Rev. 22:1). It has only one human King of kings: Jesus the Messiah (cf. 19:16).

Yet *all* of Jesus's servants now share in God's eternal rule. About the servants who worship God and the Lamb, it is said, "they will *reign* forever and ever" (Rev. 22:5; cf. 20:4–6). In other words, Jesus alone is the great divine-human king, but we come to participate in his kingship derivatively, so that we rule alongside him over the renewed earth as citizens of the new Jerusalem. As Paul puts it, speaking about all those united to the king, "If we endure, we will also reign with him" (2 Tim. 2:12).

This vision suggests that the church's final unity will not be orchestrated by a specific pattern of church governance that we can readily identify now. Certain Christians might think it wise today to be under the leadership of a specific pastoral team, body of elders, bishops, or the pope in order that unity might be safeguarded and represented. But the vision in Revelation suggests that the final oneness will involve *the co-reign of all the saints*—shared governance—coordinated within Jesus's direct kingship. Thus, if the present church desires to take steps toward the church's final reality, it must remain open to ways in which unity can be genuine apart from strictly hierarchical patterns of human or church leadership.

4. *Manuscript discoveries lead us to reconfigure ecclesial boundaries.* Ecclesial boundaries hardened in the sixteenth and seventeenth centuries. But many manuscripts have been discovered or published since that time that force us to reconfigure or soften the lines.

Let me mention a few of these discoveries. The Teaching of the Twelve Apostles (usually called the Didache), one of the earliest Christian documents that is not in the Bible, was not discovered until 1873. Its teaching is traditional, enjoying an especially close relationship to Jesus's Sermon on the Mount. Similarly, the full manuscript of Irenaeus's *On the Apostolic Preaching*, written in the second century, was not discovered until 1904. Irenaeus knew Polycarp, who knew the apostle John![4] Irenaeus's book gives insight into how the biblical gospel was received immediately after the apostles' time. Its vision of the gospel aligns with the Apostles' Creed and the model developed in *Gospel Allegiance*, which is furthered here. Meanwhile, the discovery of the Dead Sea Scrolls in 1947 has changed our understanding of what Jews in Jesus's era believed generally about salvation, helping us better understand what the New Testament teaches.

In addition to these new discoveries, other important materials were published and so made widely available for the first time. One of these collections is what is now called the Apostolic Fathers—the writings of Clement of Rome, Ignatius of Antioch, Polycarp, and others. This Christian material hails from the end of the New Testament time period and the second century. A small bit of this collection was haphazardly available to Catholics and Protestants in the sixteenth century, but it was not published or disseminated until a full century *later*, so it was essentially unknown at the time of the Reformation.[5]

The situation was only modestly better with regard to the great apologists of the second century, such as Justin Martyr and Theophilus of Antioch. The apologists were somewhat available to second-generation Protestant Reformers, such as Calvin, but not to the first generation, nor to the vital early decrees of the Catholic Council of Trent.[6] Thus the Catholic-Protestant divide was forged without pertinent information that would allow the Bible's teaching about salvation or the church's earliest doctrinal history to be fully understood. The same is true with respect to the Calvinist-Arminian disjuncture.

In other words, as the Reformation was consolidated, Catholics and Protestants alike made claims about what the universal ("catholic") church had always and everywhere believed and about Scripture's meaning, but they did so inaccurately because crucial information was totally unavailable to them—Christian and Jewish historical documents from the first and second centuries. Due to the discovery and dissemination of texts pertinent to Christian origins and its initial history, *we are in a better position today to uncover the actual beliefs of the earliest church*. While developing the gospel-allegiance model, this book seeks to capitalize on this newer historical evidence.

5. *We can build on past theological accomplishments.* New discoveries and accessible publication of ancient texts give hope that we can move beyond the salvation wars of the past to forge a healthier, truer, theological future. Realizing we can benefit from the insights of a lengthy church history strengthens this hope. If we can see beyond divisions of the past, it is only because Luther, Zwingli, Calvin, and the Catholic theologians of the Council of Trent permit us to see farther in the first place. Recent biblical scholarship has borne fruit as well. It may be cliché to say, "We stand on the shoulders of giants," but the saying is not less true for being well-worn.

In short, we have ample reason to believe that progress can and will be made toward unity. *Beyond the Salvation Wars* seeks to help the church move toward a healthier theology of salvation. Yet lasting unity can happen only in the truth. If we are to make progress beyond the salvation wars of the past toward a better future, we must begin with a *truer theological synthesis* of the church's common deposit: Scripture and early Christian history. There have been significant historical advances, even in the last twenty years, with regard to our understanding of key words such as *gospel, grace, faith, works, election, justification, holiness, sanctification, image,* and *glory.* Along with my previous books on the gospel and salvation, *Beyond the Salvation Wars* seeks to improve our understanding of such terms in Scripture and to correctly nuance how they interrelate.

Understanding the Battlefield

Although the Orthodox Church and the Catholic Church ceased communing during the Great Schism of the eleventh century, the Western church was mostly united until the sixteenth. At that time Catholics and Protestants parted company. Since the Orthodox-Catholic split is not immediately pertinent to this book's theological discussion, for simplicity's sake we'll center conversation on Catholic-Protestant relations.

In 1517 Martin Luther launched a protest against certain practices and doctrines within the Catholic Church, especially those surrounding penance, indulgences, purgatory, and the treasury of merit. He did not intend to split the church. Yet, when the Catholic hierarchy refused to reform, he would not retract his teachings. Then the church divided.

Luther's basic teaching was that humans are justified by faith alone. What Scripture teaches about justification will be nuanced and remodeled in this book. But for Luther, justification can be summarized as the state of innocence that results after a sinner attains right-standing in God's eyes. The fledging Protestant movement subsequently splintered around disagreements about baptism, Eucharist, and other doctrines, paving the way for modern denominationalism.

The Catholic Church responded to the Protestant crisis in a definitive way at the Council of Trent (1545–63). Since no ecumenical council or pope has decreed on justification in the almost five hundred years since, Trent's "Decree on Justification" remains the only truly authoritative Catholic statement about justification.[7]

Today's simplified telling of this story claims that Protestants believe in salvation by *faith alone*, but Catholics believe in *faith plus works*. Protestants typically add that Catholics deny *grace alone*. The better standard resources attempt to correct these caricatures. For example, R. C. Sproul and John MacArthur helpfully remind readers that classic Protestantism likewise believes that works are necessary by offering the following summary of the Roman Catholic versus Protestant difference:

Catholic view	faith + works = justification
Protestant view	faith = justification + works

Sproul clarifies why Protestants typically also believe in works, saying that neither Catholics nor Protestants eliminate works, but rather Protestants eliminate human *merit* when speaking about justification. As MacArthur puts it, Protestants recognize that "though works are the evidence or fruit of true faith they add or contribute nothing to the meritorious basis of our redemption."[8]

15

In other words, Sproul, MacArthur, and others are quick to correct Protestants who misunderstand their own tradition: traditionally, Protestants have always believed that works are required for salvation.[9] However, they have simultaneously argued that works do nothing to earn salvation but merely *confirm* salvation's authenticity. John Piper puts it this way: "Saving faith *gives rise to* good works."[10] Generally, within classic Protestantism works are required but serve as *evidence* of justification rather than as its basis. This is a useful starting point.

Yet while making a helpful attempt, these standard resources do not capture the full truth with precision. As we will see, the relationship between faith, works, and justification is not nuanced this way in Scripture. Moreover, these resources by MacArthur and Sproul do not go far enough in correcting typical Protestant misunderstandings of Catholicism. Catholics do not believe that they are justified strictly by faith plus works: rather, they are justified first by grace through baptism and the merit of Jesus, and only subsequently through works as humans cooperate with God's grace.[11]

Official Catholic theology straightforwardly denies that works as self-effort apart from God's enabling grace can justify. It is ironic that Protestants frequently misunderstand this, since its inclusion as the first canon of the Council of Trent's "Decree on Justification" suggests that the Catholic Church was urgent to emphasize exactly that point: "If anyone says that man can be justified before God by his own works, whether done by his own natural powers or through the teaching of the law, without divine grace through Jesus Christ, let him be anathema."[12] That is, the foremost declaration on justification by Catholics at Trent was to call accursed (anathema) anyone who says that a person can be saved by the law or by works through self-effort apart from grace.

Protestants cannot responsibly say that Catholics believe an individual is justified by good works instead of God's grace, for they certainly believe no such thing. Grace is required all along the way by both Catholics and Protestants. Grace, however, is configured differently by each.

In addition to considering grace, we must weigh how the gospel, faith, and works cohere within the Catholic sacramental system, pondering how that relates to a scriptural understanding. So also for Protestant belief. We may find that the Bible offers new things for all of us to consider regardless of our denomination or background.

I think we can blaze a path toward a better Catholic-Protestant future when we distinguish the gospel itself from very closely related concepts in the Bible. Practicing gospel allegiance can help us differentiate the *content* of the gospel from its *required response, purpose, and benefits*. Moreover, because the gospel-allegiance model untangles the fraught distinction between justification and sanctification, it may help the universal church move beyond salvation wars of the past.

More will be said on the mechanics of salvation in subsequent chapters. First, I want to help the reader quickly understand how the gospel-allegiance model relates to the universal church and what makes the model distinctive.

Gospel Allegiance and the Universal Church

In this book's prequel, *Gospel Allegiance*, I sought to elaborate and defend a new soteriological model from Scripture, offering basic engagement with traditional Protestant and Catholic positions. Although no portion of the gospel-allegiance model is unprecedented in the history of the church, collectively considered it is a fresh way for the contemporary church to recover what the Bible and the earliest Christians taught about salvation. This chapter seeks to present the essential results from a different angle in order to set the stage for fresh conversation.

So, is the gospel-allegiance model Catholic or Protestant?

The gospel-allegiance model is *catholic* (in the lowercase, not the uppercase, sense)—that is, it seeks to identify what fundamentally creates and maintains the true universal church past, present, and future. It is not (Roman) Catholic. Rather, the gospel-allegiance model seeks to describe how God's rescue through the

Christ *always* happens—including within the apostolic age—so it is a lowercase "catholic" model.

The genuine gospel has *never* been entirely missing during the last two thousand years of Christian history, for otherwise the church would have ceased to exist. In presenting a new model, I am certainly *not* claiming that either Catholics or Protestants have fundamentally misunderstood salvation or have been missing the gospel up until this blessed moment—as if such things have been heroically rediscovered only now. Quite the opposite: the universal (catholic) church has at times struggled to articulate the gospel's fullness or salvation's exact mechanics, but their essential elements have *always* been prominent in the church's teachings. Yet these elements haven't always been called the gospel, and dimensions of the gospel have at times been underemphasized or overemphasized, so the church has struggled to respond to the gospel's fullness.

I am claiming that there has been significant gospel confusion down through the ages even though the saving gospel has always been present and effective amid all God's people. Today, by studying the New Testament and earliest Christian writings, we can clarify the gospel's essential elements and slightly remodel our soteriology, so that we can speak about them with greater power and precision. Because the gospel-allegiance model claims to identify and clarify the common gospel and core soteriology that has been present in the true church from its inception until today, it is ecumenical in orientation.

Although the gospel-allegiance model is lowercase "catholic" (i.e., for the universal church), it is also decidedly Protestant. Being Protestant does not mean that one affirms everything that Luther, Calvin, or any other Reformer said. Nor is Protestantism restricted to the so-called Magisterial Reformation. Nor is it to buy into a specific systematic understanding of how faith, works, and salvation interrelate. Nor does it mean that one must affirm all the *solas* (e.g., *sola fide*, "by faith alone"). *To be Protestant is simply this: to have responded to the gospel while believing that the Catholic Church is in error about one or more matters of its authoritative teaching (i.e., its dogma)—whether about salvation,*

Mary, papal authority, or the like. I will have more to say about Catholic-Protestant boundaries later.

The gospel-allegiance model is Protestant by definition because it does not *fully* agree with what the Catholic Church *officially* teaches about salvation. Of course, Catholics and Protestants agree about many things, so the model affirms numerous dimensions of basic Christian teaching. But it disagrees with Catholicism about some fundamental matters. Moreover, the model is also Protestant for another reason: it seeks to fulfill the Protestant mandate to reform continually (*semper reformanda*) until we have completely recovered the teachings of the Bible and the apostolic church.

Even though it is Protestant, the gospel-allegiance model is distinct not only from Catholicism but also in certain regards from what I am going to term "classic Protestantism," as that developed in the sixteenth century within the Magisterial Reformation—that is, the portion of the Protestant Reformation that sought an alliance between church and state. This requires more discussion.

Gospel Allegiance versus Classic Protestantism

The gospel-allegiance model differs somewhat from both Catholic and classic Protestant articulations of how salvation works. I'll critically engage Catholicism throughout this manuscript, but readers may be interested to see immediately how the gospel-allegiance model is distinct with respect to classic Protestantism. Toward that end I offer a quick comparison below. The point is that there is widespread agreement about certain things within classic Protestantism, established in the sixteenth and seventeenth centuries—whether of the Lutheran, Reformed, Wesleyan, or Anglican variety—but the gospel-allegiance model synthesizes salvation differently.

The five *solas* are frequently used to summarize the common ground within classic Protestantism. By appealing to (1) *Scripture alone* as the final authority, Protestants contend that salvation is (2) by *faith alone*, (3) by *grace alone*, (4) in *Jesus Christ alone*, (5) for *the glory of God alone*.

The five *solas* are helpful. On the one hand, I applaud them as true. On the other, we have learned a thing or two or a thousand since the sixteenth-century Reformation about what words such as *Scripture*, *faith*, *grace*, *Christ*, and *glory* actually meant when the New Testament was being written—not to mention about the gospel and salvation. What we've learned disrupts aspects of classic Protestantism. In other words, we can better capture today than we could in the sixteenth century what words such as *gospel* (*euangelion*), *faith* (*pistis*), and *grace* (*charis*) actually meant in the New Testament era. The gospel-allegiance model embraces much within Reformation-era Protestantism, but in seeking to adhere even more closely to what Scripture teaches, it has different emphases.

What follows briefly contrasts classic Protestantism and the gospel-allegiance model. Due to its brevity, this summary cannot avoid a slight caricature of each. A caricature attempts to capture the main lines but ignores subtle shading. But we must start somewhere. I submit that such a depiction is helpful at this stage, for it flags the primary distinctions comprehensively in a short compass. For those who desire more exacting evidence—especially for those struggling with how grace, faith, and works interrelate—a nuanced biblical treatment has already appeared in *Gospel Allegiance*.

The Gospel

Classic Protestantism: The *center* of the gospel is *the cross*, with the resurrection secondarily in view.

The Gospel-Allegiance Model: The gospel includes the cross and resurrection, but its *climax* is *Jesus's reign at God's right hand as king*.

The Gospel's Theological Focus

Classic Protestantism: *The gospel is about personal atonement and justification.* The gospel is primarily about what happened on the cross, preeminently Jesus's death for a person's sins. When by faith alone an individual trusts God's promise that in Christ the atonement is effective, Jesus's righteousness is credited to that person's account so that the person attains justification (right-standing) in the presence of God.

The Gospel-Allegiance Model: *The gospel's climax is victorious enthronement.* The gospel is primarily about the victory that God won over all his enemies—including sin, death, and Satan—through the gospel events. These gospel events reached a pinnacle in the first century when Jesus, who was crucified for our sins and raised for our justification, became the ruling Christ and incorporated his people into his saving benefits.

The Gospel's Purpose

Classic Protestantism: *The gospel's purpose is the individual soul's rescue.* Salvation is primarily about forgiveness of sins so that an individual can be declared "righteous" even though sinful, avoid God's wrath, and grow in holiness. Then the individual's soul can go to heaven rather than hell after death. When a person is eternally saved for heaven or passed over for damnation, God alone is glorified.

The Gospel-Allegiance Model: *The gospel's purpose is the holistic rescue of God's image bearers, through which creation, humans, and God are glorified.* Salvation is not about souls getting into heaven but rather is purposed toward the recovery of human flourishing right now and then forevermore. The gospel's purpose is to enable all the nations (inclusive of individuals) to give allegiant obedience to Jesus the king—having experienced his forgiveness, victory, and transformative new-creation power—so we can reign with him now and in the resurrection age. Allegiance to King Jesus not only eternally saves *from* punishment and death but also is *for* the restoration of glory for humans, creation, and above all God.

Saving Faith

Classic Protestantism: *Saving faith is mental trust in God's saving promises.* Saving "faith" (*pistis*) is an inward confidence aimed away from one's own works or self-righteousness and instead at the truthfulness of God's promises in Jesus Christ. Saving faith is

21

trusting that by faith alone Jesus's death for your sins and his priestly mediation on your behalf are personally effective for your salvation.

The Gospel-Allegiance Model: *Saving faith is faithfulness, trusting loyalty, or allegiance to the king heralded in the gospel.* Although inclusive of it, saving faith is not primarily trusting that God's saving promises in Jesus are true. Nor is it trusting that faith alone is effective. Rather, faith is a relational way of life, bodily and communally expressed, from start to finish. For personal faith to be saving it must be relationally externalized bodily as enacted *allegiance* to Jesus in his capacity as *the rescuing and victorious king* announced in the gospel.

Works

Classic Protestantism: *Works confirm salvation.* Our works are good but hazardous because we tend to trust our deeds rather than Jesus's accomplished work on the cross on our behalf. Works are excluded from personal *justification* and cannot in any way serve as the basis for meriting final salvation. Yet once justifying mental "faith" is in place, good works will invariably follow if a person is genuinely saved as part of that person's *sanctification* or growth in holiness.

The Gospel-Allegiance Model: *Works are foundationally saving as an embodiment of allegiance.* We cannot earn salvation through works of the law (works-righteousness or legalism), but good works have a foundational positive saving function because they are part of *pistis*, the word traditionally translated as "faith." Good works are saving as part of allegiance ("faith/fidelity") to the king from the ground up. The individualized distinction between justification and sanctification within classic Protestantism is false. That is, the division between a person's justification and sanctification has an insufficient scriptural warrant and obscures how Scripture actually describes the salvation process.

Saving Grace

Classic Protestantism: *Saving grace is God's timeless unmerited favor in Jesus Christ.* Grace is God's unmerited favor in providing personal salvation in Jesus Christ. It is usually understood as given before creation to those elected or predestined for salvation. Since each person is born guilty and cannot perform any deeds to merit forgiveness, each *individual* must be saved by grace, a free gift originating in God's timeless will, entirely outside each person's own future efforts, abilities, or foreseen merits. Saving grace means that God always acts to save individuals before and apart from anything they might do to merit salvation on their own. Many aspects of grace—such as its effectiveness, scope, and resistibility—are understood in diverse ways by Lutherans, the Reformed, Anglicans, Methodists, and other Protestant traditions.

The Gospel-Allegiance Model: Saving grace is multifaceted. It is unmerited, enormous in size, benevolent, and timely. *Yet the premier saving grace is the gospel itself, which was given by God in the first century as an unmerited, allegiance-demanding gift.* Within the gospel-allegiance model, when we are talking about the grace required for ultimate salvation, it must not be abstracted away from *the gospel* as *the specific undeserved grace* that God has already opted to give humanity *collectively* within *history*. Above all, saving grace means this: humans, considered as a whole, did nothing to earn or merit God's specific grace of the gospel when it was given approximately two thousand years ago, but King Jesus's people now enjoy the gospel's powerful gifts and special saving benefits.

This gospel-grace is for everyone, but it is not effective for an individual (i.e., no saving benefits are enjoyed) unless he or she reciprocates by giving a return gift to God: bodily allegiance to King Jesus. After yielding allegiance initially, a person must produce Spirit-led good works, however imperfectly, as part of the embodiment of that allegiance for final salvation to result. To perform bodily allegiance in serving the king, including good works, is to accept saving grace (the gospel and its benefits) by giving a return gift to the king through the Spirit's help, not to violate grace.[13]

It is essential to appreciate the basic differences between classic Protestantism and the gospel-allegiance model because this book will deepen the conversation about each. To present their gist at this stage is risky because it is impossible to avoid oversimplification. The gospel-allegiance model will be further explained in what follows, so there will be ample time to add nuance.

In summary, the gospel-allegiance model departs from Catholicism in significant ways that will be explored. While it is a Protestant model, the gospel-allegiance paradigm also differs from classic Protestantism regarding what words such as *gospel*, *faith*, *works*, *grace*, *glory*, and *salvation* actually meant in the New Testament time period and how they interrelate. This book will extend, refine, and deepen the gospel-allegiance model by applying it to some of the most controversial aspects of salvation—topics that still divide Christians today. The result is *salvation remodeled*.

Martin Luther and Ulrich Zwingli were the earliest Protestant Reformers; they acted simultaneously and initially with relative independence. This chapter opened with Ulrich Zwingli's bloody demise. As we begin to rethink salvation today, let's go back to an earlier moment in Zwingli's story so that we can better understand the initial Protestant-Catholic fracture.

The city council of Zurich was impaled on the horns of a dilemma. Ulrich Zwingli's popular preaching from entire books of the Bible rather than from the approved lectionary had stimulated sweeping reforms. Citizens had eaten sausages even though this violated the Catholic Church's Lenten fasting regulations—the law of the land. Since fasting from meat is a form of penance associated with the merit necessary to gain final salvation within Catholicism, many felt that not only was it criminal to eat the sausages, but it also jeopardized the salvation of souls.

But Zwingli was causing even more controversy. He had disrupted a public sermon by shouting, "Brother, this is where you err!" when a homilist was championing the role of Mary and the saints. Again, salvation was in view, as the validity of the Catholic indulgence system depends on the excess merit that the saints have purportedly accrued in Christ. Going farther, Zwingli had explicitly repudiated the authority of Catholic bishops regarding church order and gospel proclamation on account of their corruption. But equally troubling, at least from the city council's standpoint, Zwingli had preached that tithing was not God's absolute law, threatening the city's tax revenue.[14] The situation was precarious.

The council decided to hold a public discussion to decide between Zwingli's faction and his opponents. The date was set for January 29, 1523. The Catholic bishop of Constance was invited, but he opted instead to send a delegation. Zwingli drafted what are today called the "Sixty-Seven Articles" in preparation. Some six hundred people, an enormous crowd given the setting, gathered for this "First Zurich Disputation."

After taking the floor, Zwingli and the Catholic bishop's primary representative, Johannes Fabri, shared a lively exchange. Fabri wanted to move locations from the public setting. He claimed that only a council or university scholars could decide such weighty theological matters. Zwingli would have none of it:

> Since reference is made to judges which my Lord Vicar thinks cannot be found outside the universities, I say that we have here infallible and unprejudiced judges, that is the Holy Writ, which can neither lie nor deceive. These we have present in Hebrew, Greek and Latin tongues; these let us take on both sides as fair and just judges.[15]

Zwingli took his stand on Scripture, appealing to the Bible in its original languages of Hebrew and Greek, as well as the customary Latin translation. He wanted to debate Fabri about specific doctrines then and there on the basis of Scripture alone. Zwingli pointed out that the town hall was full of learned men, but more importantly, these men were taught by the Holy Spirit. Thus, they were perfectly capable to "decide which party produces Scripture on its side."[16]

After Zwingli's resounding appeal to Scripture and the Spirit's ability to assist the audience, silence fell. The burgomaster arose, asking if anyone cared to speak further. No one, including Fabri, dared. Zwingli took the floor again, urging anyone who wished to denounce his views to come forward. A buffoon shouted, "You can all boast over your wine, but here no one stirs."[17] Everyone laughed, and conversation eventually resumed. But at this point it was clear that nobody dared to wrangle with Zwingli.

The dispute arrived at an amusing grand finale when Zwingli challenged Fabri: "If you can . . . prove one of my articles false by means of the Gospel, I will give you a rabbit cheese. Now let's hear it. I shall await." Apparently, Fabri was as perplexed as we are about the offer. He retorted, "A rabbit cheese, what is that? I need no cheese."[18] ("Rabbit cheese" was a Swiss idiom for a "remarkably fine cheese.")[19] Yet Fabri was unable to procure any cheese because he continued to evade Scripture-based discussion of Zwingli's articles. Hence the town council arrived at a verdict rapidly, issuing it during the noon break: "Master Zwingli shall continue to proclaim the Holy Gospel as hitherto, according to the spirit of God."[20] So Zwingli's reform marched onward.

Zwingli soon abolished the Mass in favor of an evangelical worship service, collaborated in destroying images of the saints, and became embroiled in controversies about baptism. Zwingli's disciples would break ranks with him over infant baptism. One of them, Felix Mantz, was drowned, with Zwingli's approval. All of this gives us a glimpse into the practical ways in which Scripture, church authority, the sacraments, and saving works were under intense negotiation in the sixteenth century.

The battle continues still. A true understanding of the mechanics of salvation is no less pressing today. I hope that the gospel-allegiance model can advance the conversation.

(As a reminder, prepared questions can be found in the appendix, "Guide for Further Conversation.")

2 The More Explicit Gospel

The true gospel is worth it. Because it is priceless, we must be precise. We need to press beyond vague imprecisions or pop-culture Christian distortions in order to be exacting about the gospel's true content and boundaries.

The gospel is of utmost importance because it is how God is bringing about salvation. If we misunderstand the gospel, we misunderstand how God is rescuing us, what it means to participate in his mission, and what it means for the church to be the church.

But that does not mean a study of the gospel is easy. This chapter may prove especially challenging for three different types of readers. *The-gospel-is-simple reader* believes that all that needs to be said about the gospel can be said in a sentence or two. They are convinced that the gospel is well-known already and that analyzing it hinders rather than helps the church's mission, because it clouds the gospel's simplicity and adds unnecessary baggage. This reader may be tempted to give a cursory read, but I especially encourage this type to wrestle with the framework and nuance of the gospel as presented here.

A second type, *the-gospel-is-easily-corrupted reader*, tends to feel nervous about any attempt to reappraise the gospel. They are suspicious of any results that do not align with their preconceived notions about the gospel or of departures from what they've heard others teach. I sympathize because false teaching is an ever-present danger. I encourage this reader to recognize that our finest professional Bible scholars—N. T. Wright, Scot McKnight, Michael Bird, Michael Gorman, and many others—use Scripture to describe the gospel along the same lines as I do.[1] I encourage skeptical readers to read this chapter (or *Gospel Allegiance*) several times and to follow up the Scripture references with care.

A third type, *the avid reader*, may be tempted to skip this chapter entirely because they've read a great many books on this topic already, including some by the aforementioned authors and perhaps one or more of my other books. Since what Scripture says about the gospel is unchanging, it is inevitable that portions here will overlap with what others have said and what I've written previously. Yet I encourage even those already familiar with a King Jesus approach to read this chapter to reacquaint themselves with or gain mastery of the material. I've freshly articulated the material and have made additions beyond my earlier work.

Regardless of whether you are one of the three types described above, I hope that all readers fit into a fourth category: *the excited-to-be-equipped reader*. The gospel is foundational to the church's evangelism, mission, and everything that follows in this book. This chapter presents what Scripture says about the gospel's content, purpose, and power, and it nuances what it means to receive the gospel's benefits.

Yet, given that the church is plagued by gospel imprecision and confusion, what method can we use to ensure that we discover the real gospel, and with exactitude? Let's start here: the actual gospel is the one we find in the Bible. It is the one written down by the apostles in Scripture in the first century.

We can work from seven angles to make sure we are recovering the genuine gospel of Jesus, the apostles, and Scripture.

1. *Gospel in its ancient culture.* Before the Jesus movement, "gospel" and related terms *already* had an intelligible meaning in the first century. Prior and contemporary

28

usage of *gospel* among Jews and pagans necessarily informed earliest Christian usage.

2. *Raw gospel content.* This is the most important angle. We must prioritize Bible passages that explicitly give the gospel's content. The most important include Mark 1:14–15; Luke 4:18–19; Romans 1:2–4; 1 Corinthians 15:3–5; and 2 Timothy 2:8.

3. *Gospel proclamation patterns.* We have records of what the apostles proclaimed about Jesus in the earliest days of the church (e.g., Acts 2:14–36; 3:11–26; 5:27–32; 10:34–43; 13:16–47; 17:22–31). Motifs that appear repeatedly can be identified as core elements of the gospel.

4. *Other gospel texts.* Although only a few Bible passages intentionally express the content of the gospel, many add nuggets in passing. To get the fullest picture, these must be integrated.

5. *Gospel titles.* Beginning with our earliest ancient manuscript evidence, "The gospel according to Matthew"—and Mark, Luke, and John—was named such for a reason by early Christians. Any definition of "the gospel" must be able to account for this.

6. *Gospel purpose.* We must pay attention to scriptural passages that describe the gospel's purposes, goals, and aims.

7. *Gospel power.* Although the gospel contains specific content, it is not inert. "The gospel" is "the power of God for salvation" (Rom. 1:16). The gospel's purpose and power are also closely related to its benefits. We must distinguish between the gospel's content, its benefits, and how those benefits are personally received.

Using this method, when we inspect what the Bible says about the gospel, we discover that what the Bible emphasizes *the most* about the gospel is something that far too many Christians do not consider to be part of the gospel at all: *Jesus's kingship.* Let's explore the evidence together.

Gospel in Its Ancient Culture

The earliest Christians were Jews living in the Greco-Roman world. Their language was drawn from their broader cultural matrix. Since theirs was an outward-reaching movement, key terms needed to remain transparent even when referring to fresh Christian realities.

The word *euangelion* ("good news," "gospel," "glad tidings") was intelligible to insider and outsider alike. Pagans and Jews who lived before and after Jesus, as well as early Christians, used the word. *Euangelion* sometimes appears in the singular within this wider culture but was often plural, *euangelia*, with no appreciable difference in meaning. (For a comparable situation in English, do you consider the word *news* to be one thing or many things?)

In the broader culture, *euangelion* could refer to any sort of positive news. Here are some ancient examples: *euangelion* refers to a fish sale; tidings of victory in a theater competition brought by a messenger to a ruler; a favorable verdict in a lawsuit; gaining an advantageous political alliance.[2]

But *euangelion* frequently intended significant *political news*—official reports pertaining to battle victories or the downfall or rise of a ruler, king, or emperor. For example, the death of Philip of Macedon and ascension of Alexander the Great was received by some individuals as *euangelia*—"glad tidings"—good news worthy of celebration by offering sacrifice to the gods.[3]

Moreover, when bringing "good news" (*euangelion*) to public officials, messengers expected a reward. The first-century writer Plutarch reports, "After the battle at Mantinea . . . the one who first announced the victory had no other reward for his *euangelion* than a piece of meat sent by the magistrates from the public mess."[4] This particular prize is mentioned because it was stingy and insulting; ordinarily, a messenger could expect more as a reward for bringing "good news" than a lump of meat from the public mess. This example from Plutarch is especially relevant because a reward for political news is also the context for the first appearance of the word *gospel* in the Bible.

The verb *euangelizomai* ("to proclaim good news") appears numerous times in the Greek Old Testament. It is especially prominent in Isaiah when the prophet speaks of the restoration of God's rule over his people (Isa. 40:9; 52:7), the nations praising God (60:6), and benefits brought by a messiah (61:1).

But the noun *euangelion* appears only six times in the Greek Old Testament.[5] In every case it concerns news of kingdom-wide concern, but it is usually about the kingship or royal succession. The word's first occurrence in the Old Testament, as in the example from Plutarch above, plays on a messenger anticipating a reward for bringing *euangelion*, but here the expectation is even more dramatically reversed.[6] Speaking about his actions prior to becoming king, King David reports, "When the messenger told me, 'Saul is dead,' I seized him and killed him in Ziklag, the very one, [so he thought,] I was required to reward for *euangelia*" (2 Sam. 4:10 AT).

Notice that here *euangelia* pertains to glad tidings about a change in the royal regime: Saul's death meant that David could now become king. This messenger thought that he'd be rewarded for bringing this gospel. But he badly miscalculated. He was killed because David's respect for the messianic office did not allow him to receive this "good news" about Saul's death with the self-serving glee that the messenger had anticipated. Even though it resulted in the death of the man who brought it, it was still called gospel in this passage of the Bible because *euangelion* ordinarily refers to national good news irrespective of personal outcomes or benefits.

Outside the Bible, we find *euangelion* ("gospel") used similarly to describe changes in imperial rule at the time of Jesus. The caesar who reigned when Jesus was born, Octavian, is described by an inscription written in 9 BC as a savior—indeed, a god—because he brought peace, order, and greater public benefits than any of his predecessors. The day of his birth is hailed as "the beginning of the gospel [*euangelion*] for the world that came by reason of him" primarily because he brought an ugly period of civil war to an end. "Gospel" language here connects to the emergence of a new emperor.

31

Later, about forty years after Jesus's death, Rome was racked by civil wars again. But eventually Vespasian brought stability and founded a new dynasty. The Jewish historian Josephus reports that upon securing the title of emperor, "Vespasian was greeted by *the good news* [*euangelia*] from Rome and by embassies of congratulation from every quarter of the world."[7] The gospel coming from Rome was that Vitellius was dead and that Vespasian had been acclaimed the new emperor. When Vespasian arrived in Alexandria, so many embassies arrived announcing this gospel that the city couldn't contain the throng.

In the ancient world *gospel* (*euangelion*) often refers to kingdom-wide good news irrespective of whether the arrival of a new king will ultimately prove to be good news for this or that individual. As we will see, when we situate New Testament *gospel* language within Jewish and Greco-Roman norms, we find robust support for the gospel as a *royal announcement: Jesus is the Messiah.*

Yet, when we compare, it is striking how the early Christians make this announcement *the unique good news.* That is, in our outside sources, we find that *euangelion* pertains to good news but is not *the singularly definitive gospel* akin to what we find in Mark, Paul's letters, and the rest of the New Testament.

In sum, on the one hand, early Christian deployment of *euangelion* is fully intelligible within its social world as a royal proclamation. On the other hand, the New Testament writers see this gospel about Jesus the king as unique and ultimate, compelling them to absolutize the word to an unprecedented degree. Viewing Jesus's attainment of the kingship as part of the prophetic promise that God would bring radical renewal as he himself began to rule from Zion, they identified Jesus as sharing in the good news of that rule, because he was seated on the throne at God's right hand (e.g., Ps. 110:1; Isa. 52:7; Mark 14:62; Acts 2:33–36; Rom. 10:15).

The writers of Scripture are stretching the boundaries of their culture's *gospel* language, pressing it to convey something more: *The gospel is that Jesus is the Messiah!* But wait, he is not an ordinary king. You must understand, this is *the ultimate good news* because this ruler and his reign are unprecedented: *Jesus's kingship is how the one God's decisive rule is now being accomplished on earth as in heaven.*[8]

Raw Gospel Content

Jesus Is the Christ

Surprisingly, neither Jesus's death nor the cross is what the Bible most emphasizes when it describes the gospel's content. The resurrection is mentioned more frequently than the cross, but even it doesn't get top billing in Scripture. Rather, it is Jesus's present reign as the Christ or king:

- "Every day in the temple and at home, they did not cease teaching and gospeling [*euangelizomai*], 'The Christ is Jesus'" (Acts 5:42 AT).
- "Now those who were scattered went about gospeling [*euangelizomai*] the word. Philip went down to the city of Samaria and proclaimed to them the Christ" (Acts 8:4–5 AT; cf. 9:22).
- "Paul . . . reasoned with them from the Scriptures, explaining and proving that it was necessary for the Christ to suffer and to rise from the dead, and saying, 'This is the Christ, this Jesus, whom I am proclaiming to you'" (Acts 17:2–3 AT; cf. 18:5, 28).

This affirmation, Jesus is the Christ (Messiah), is by far the most common way to summarize the gospel or gospel activity in the Bible. In fact, the New Testament frequently qualifies the gospel simply by describing it as "the gospel of the Christ" (Rom. 15:19; 1 Cor. 9:12; 2 Cor. 2:12; 9:13; 10:14; Gal. 1:7; Phil. 1:27; 1 Thess. 3:2).

The King and His Kingdom

In some of the passages of Scripture that give explicit gospel content, we find that the word *gospel* (*euangelion*) relates to *the kingdom of God*. Jesus heralds the gospel:

Now after John was arrested, Jesus came into Galilee, proclaiming the gospel of God, and saying, "The time has been fulfilled, and *the kingdom of God* has drawn near; repent and believe in *the gospel* [*euangelion*]." (Mark 1:14–15 AT)

Notice that Mark locates Jesus's words about the gospel immediately after Jesus's baptism and testing. It was at his baptism that Jesus's office as Messiah was historically realized. He was chosen by God as the king before ordinary time began (Eph. 1:4), but Jesus's becoming *the Christ* was a historical process.

First, the eternal Son had to be sent by the Father to become incarnate in the first century. But *historically considered*, it was his anointing that initialized *the becoming-the-king process*. That is what the title "Messiah" or "Christ" actually means: "anointed one." Subsequent to his anointing, Jesus would tread the path of the cross, be raised, *attain the sovereign throne within history*—and then begin *to reign* as king and high priest in a powerful new way.

When the Spirit comes down upon Jesus at his baptism, he is set apart as the future king. Only then does Jesus proclaim that the kingdom of God has drawn nigh. Because he has been anointed, he now knows that his attainment of the throne is rapidly approaching. The "gospel of God" (Mark 1:14) is a royal proclamation that pertains to the inevitability of God's rule breaking in through the rule of God's Messiah.

This is why when Jesus goes to Nazareth, he unrolls the scroll of the prophet Isaiah and begins to read:

The Spirit of the Lord is upon me, because he has *anointed* [*echrisen*] me *to proclaim good news* [*euangelisasthai*] to the poor. He has sent me to proclaim liberty to the captives and recovering of sight to the blind, to set at liberty those who are oppressed, to proclaim the year of the Lord's favor. (Luke 4:18–19, citing Isa. 61:1–2 and 58:6)

Because he has been *christ-ed* or *messiah-ed* (from the verb *chriō*), Jesus is now in a position to *herald the gospel* (from the verb

34

euangelizō). What is this gospel? That God is orchestrating a regime change in and through him that will benefit the poor, the sick, and the oppressed (cf. Luke 7:22).

Make no mistake: *the gospel is political and has social implications*, even though it must never be reduced to a mere social program. Indeed, Jesus says that the "proclamation of the kingdom of God" was why he was sent by God (Luke 4:43). From a biblical standpoint, any definition of the gospel is inadequate that can't make sense of Jesus's own proclamation of the kingdom—including how he brought physical healing and good news to the poor as he was in the process of attaining his full kingship.

Yet the good news that Jesus is becoming king is couched in paradox, for what the world considers the antithesis of kingly glory—the cross—looms before Jesus and any would-be follower: "And calling the crowd to him with his disciples, he said to them, 'If anyone would come after me, let him deny himself and *take up his cross and follow me.* For whoever would save his life will lose it, but whoever loses his life for my sake and *the gospel's* will save it'" (Mark 8:34–35).

The gospel demands that all of Jesus's followers tread a cruciform path if they are to obtain life after judgment when the Son of Man rules in the age to come (Mark 8:38). The cross is essential to the gospel and central to it. But this does not make the cross uniquely *the center* of the gospel. Jesus takes up the cross as part of his larger becoming-the-king vocation.

To understand Jesus's words about cross-bearing, we must keep the overarching framework in view. In context, Jesus is explaining the true meaning of Peter's confession, "You are *the Christ*" (Mark 8:29). The implication is that the gospel is about how Jesus is becoming king, and the cross is essential to that process but is not its sole purpose or final goal. The final goal beyond the cross and resurrection is the Messiah's rule on God the Father's behalf: "For to this end Christ died and lived again, *that he might be Lord both of the dead and of the living*" (Rom. 14:9). This is why the gospel reaches its zenith after Jesus ascends to the right hand of

God to reign. Kingship is the bigger gospel category within which we locate the cross.

Paul's Gospel Summaries

When the apostle Paul details the gospel, he also speaks above all about Jesus as the Messiah-King. That is, Jesus's kingship has a centrality to the gospel—as its overarching framework and context—that the cross, even though it is essential, lacks. Although there are other pertinent texts, Paul offers two expanded descriptions of the gospel's content: Romans 1:2–4 and 1 Corinthians 15:3–5.

In Romans, Paul begins by identifying himself as the king's slave and ambassador (1:1). Then Paul expands on the gospel:

> the gospel of God that *he promised beforehand* through his prophets in the holy Scriptures concerning his Son, who as it pertains to the flesh *came into being* by means of the seed of David; who as it pertains to the Spirit of Holiness *was appointed Son-of-God-in-Power* by means of the resurrection from among the dead ones—Jesus the Christ our Lord. (Rom. 1:2–4 AT)

In this presentation of the gospel's content, Paul places special emphasis on three actions: (1) God's *advance promises* about his Son; (2) the Son's fleshly *coming-into-being*, or incarnation; (3) God's *appointment* of the Son to a new ruling office as Son-of-God-in-Power. Previously he was only the divine Son. Now he reigns as the divine *and human* Son. We need not merely a divine savior but a human king too. Jesus rules in both capacities as the Son-of-God-in-Power.[9]

Other gospel details in Romans 1:3–4 add support (cf. 2 Tim. 2:8). Paul mentions the agency of the seed of David in bringing about the incarnation, the resurrection as that which triggered Jesus's exaltation to the ruling office, and the role of the Spirit. The Holy Spirit demarcates the functional boundary where Jesus's kingship is specially realized. When Paul details the gospel's content in Romans 1:2–4, the cross is not even mentioned. Here the gospel is about how God's promises in Scripture have come to fruition in the Son's incarnation and enthronement.

Paul's emphasis on certain actions that define the gospel continues in what is doubtless its most famous presentation:

> For as a matter of primary import I handed over to you the gospel I also received: that the Christ *died in behalf of our sins* in accordance with the Scriptures, and that he *was buried*, and that he *has been raised on the third day* in accordance with the Scriptures, and that *he appeared* to Cephas [Peter], then to the Twelve. (1 Cor. 15:3–5 AT)

This passage tempts us to think that Paul's gospel is exclusively Jesus's death, burial, resurrection, and postresurrection appearances. Indeed, these are all essential to the gospel in its fullness.

However, Paul says not that *Jesus* died but rather that *the Christ* died. We absolutely must not lose sight of the royal-messianic framework that houses this whole gospel presentation by Paul. The kingly structure shows to what the death, burial, resurrection, and appearances pertain. The climax of the gospel is Jesus's enthronement as *the Christ*—to such a degree that Jesus's present kingship is already presupposed in 1 Corinthians 15:3–5 as the box into which the gospel fits.

"Jesus Christ" is not a name. It is a claim. It is a name with an honorific title appended that makes a claim: Jesus *the messiah*.[10] Or, in our idiom, *King Jesus*. A king represents his people. And if the king is over all, he represents all people, indeed all creation.

Moreover, collective forgiveness is in view in 1 Corinthians 15:3–5. In his description of the gospel, Paul says not that *Jesus* died for *my or your personal sin* but rather that *the Messiah* died in behalf of *our sins*. The emphasis is not on Jesus's death for your or my personal sins but rather on the king's death for collective sins. This passage is about *what the king has done for an entire group of people*. Here the gospel is about collective or corporate representation and substitution, not about what God has done to forgive you or me personally. The gospel truly brings about your individual forgiveness and mine, but only when we enter the "he died for our sins" group.

The Climax of the Gospel Is Enthronement, Not Atonement

In contemporary Christianity the gospel has become a "me"-centered story about how an individual can trust God for forgiveness and heavenly bliss. When we make personal atonement or forgiveness the framework and center of the gospel, we distort the Bible's presentation of the gospel in serious ways.

We've lost sight of Jesus's kingship as the core gospel message. Christian culture—from late antiquity, through the Reformation, and right up to the present time—has made forgiveness rather than Jesus's kingship the framework. The result for the church's mission and the world has been disastrous.

The gospel proper does include the Christ's objective atoning work for the whole group ("he died for our sins"), but Jesus's established kingship is thereby presupposed and highlighted. Meanwhile, as subsequent chapters will show, *personal appropriation* of the atonement is a *benefit* of the gospel that is conditioned on individual response, not an objective part of the gospel itself.

Gospel Proclamation Patterns

In the previous section we explored the most explicit descriptions of the gospel's content given in the Bible. But what the apostles proclaim about King Jesus serves as a supplement to our gospel description: Acts 2:14–36; 3:11–26; 5:27–32; 10:34–43; 13:16–47; 17:22–31.

When we work through Acts, we see that many of the gospel proclamations reach a pinnacle with the announcement that Jesus has become the King or the Lord. For example, Peter's Pentecost sermon: "Let all the house of Israel therefore know for certain that God has made this Jesus whom you crucified *both Lord and Christ*!" (Acts 2:36 AT). Likewise, consider the emphasis on the

Christ's forthcoming royal visitation at the end of Peter's sermon at Solomon's portico (3:20–23) and the exaltation motif in Peter's speech before the Sanhedrin (5:31). Meanwhile, gospel activities are repeatedly and explicitly summarized as proclaiming or demonstrating that "Jesus is the Messiah" (5:42; 8:5; 9:22; 17:3). It is clear from Scripture that the gospel's primary framework is Jesus's kingship, even though other elements are essential to the gospel's entirety.

When we bring together the statements of gospel content and the repeated patterns of gospel proclamation, we can best summarize the biblical gospel as follows:

The gospel is that Jesus the king

1. preexisted as God the Son,
2. was sent by the Father as promised,
3. took on human flesh in fulfillment of God's promises to David,
4. died for our sins in accordance with the Scriptures,
5. was buried,
6. was raised on the third day in accordance with the Scriptures,
7. appeared to many witnesses,
8. *is enthroned at the right hand of God as the ruling Christ,*
9. has sent the Holy Spirit to his people to effect his rule, and
10. will come again as final judge to rule.[11]

These ten elements are an attempt to summarize the one biblical and apostolic gospel. This is what I mean by "a more explicit gospel," or, as I have termed it in another book, *The Gospel Precisely.*

The ten events are descriptive, not prescriptive. That is, one could package the content accurately in different ways or expand on these elements. For example, Jesus's taking on human flesh could be expanded to include his remarkable activities during his years of public ministry. Yet it is a reasonable summary, since, as I have shown elsewhere, each element appears as part of the gospel in multiple biblical texts.[12]

My framing of the whole is intentional. The gospel is first and above all the claim that *Jesus is now the Messiah or King*. Within that King Jesus scaffolding, the gospel details how the Messiah was sent, took on human flesh, died an atoning death for our sake on the cross, was buried, raised, appeared, was enthroned, sent the Spirit, and will come again to judge decisively and to reign publicly. To reinforce that Jesus's present kingship is the climax of the biblical gospel, it is italicized in the list of ten.

Other Gospel Texts

In addition to the texts already discussed, numerous passages augment our understanding of the gospel. Let me offer a few tidbits even though I can't discuss all the relevant texts here.[13] We discover that Scripture announces the gospel in advance to Abraham, "All nations will be blessed through you" (Gal. 3:8 NIV), meaning that through Abraham's seed, the Messiah-King, redemption would be accomplished and the nations would experience the Spirit (3:13–14).

We also learn that even though the gospel was attested by the Old Testament prophets, it was a mystery long hidden. Yet now, by God's command, it has been disclosed (Rom. 16:25–26). The gospel was directly revealed to Paul by the Messiah-King himself (Gal. 1:11–12). Yet Paul still can say that he received the gospel from others via human tradition (1 Cor. 15:1–3; cf. Gal. 1:18). How can this be?

Paul doubtless learned portions of the ten elements of the gospel elsewhere, but the appearance of the *now-living, glorified king* to Paul was so foundational that Paul can speak about the gospel as directly revealed to him. For he received this portion of the gospel by divine revelation from Jesus himself (cf. Acts 9:3–8; 22:6–10; 26:12–18; 1 Cor. 9:1). In fact, he can go farther, calling it "the gospel of the glory of the Messiah, who is the image of God"

(2 Cor. 4:4 AT). The gospel is about how God is in the process of restoring his glorious rule over creation through the installation of his king. Paul makes the present rule of the glorified king the premier gospel fact that summarizes his apostolic preaching: "Jesus the Messiah as Lord" (4:5 AT).

The rule of King Jesus is not nonpolitical, nor is it purely future. The profession of Jesus as king creates a citizen body immediately when he is professed as king. When any two or three gather in his name, he is there and he is actively presiding to govern and correct behavior (Matt. 18:18–20). This is why Paul can exhort the Philippians, "Order your life as citizens [*politeuesthe*] in a manner worthy of the gospel of the Christ" (Phil. 1:27 AT). As Michael Gorman puts it, "Already in the first century the apostle Paul wanted the communities he addressed not merely to *believe* the gospel but to *become* the gospel and thereby to *advance* the gospel."[14] Profession of the gospel of the Christ inscribes the gospel's moral norms and virtues onto the citizen body as that profession persists, so that individuals are transformed.

Gospel Titles

Nearly all scholars, whether Christian or otherwise, agree that Mark's Gospel was first, penned less than forty years after Jesus's death. Its opening words are of special interest because "gospel" (*euangelion*) is deployed in a puzzling way: "Beginning of the *gospel* of Jesus the Christ" (*Archē tou euangeliou Iēsou Christou*, Mark 1:1 AT). The puzzle is resolved and we learn something vital about the gospel when we attend to subtle language differences.

The first words do not say, "The beginning of the Gospel *of Mark*," as if this story is about Mark himself and his authorship of a "Gospel." Nor does it say, "A beginning of the Gospels about Jesus the Christ," as if Mark were overtly signaling to future readers that he was trying to pioneer a new literary genre. (Even though others eventually did follow Mark's lead by writing "Gospels.") Nor does Mark write, "Beginning of *a* gospel about Jesus the

Christ," suggesting that there could be many different gospels and that his is merely one offering.

Rather, Mark tellingly writes, "Beginning of *the* gospel of Jesus the Christ." Mark firmly asserts that there is only *one definitive gospel*. And he proceeds to tell a story about how Jesus was sent, was anointed as the king, proclaimed his forthcoming rule as king, and died as a ransom for many, and then his tomb was discovered empty. The other canonical Gospels have a similar storied shape. *The good news* about *Jesus the Messiah* is singular, definite, unique, and has a narrative structure. This conclusion is reinforced in ancient manuscripts of the Gospels.

Our earliest surviving manuscripts of the four Gospels—physical texts written by hand in the Greek language that can be viewed in libraries and museums today—are not titled in the way that contemporary convention might lead us to expect. They aren't titled "Matthew," "Mark," "Luke," "John," although these are popular abbreviations today. Nor "The Gospel *of Matthew*," and so forth. Rather, we find "The gospel *according to* Matthew."[15] The small difference between "of" and "according to" shows that the gospel was viewed as *one* narrative about Jesus the Messiah. The four are different versions of the one gospel because Matthew, Mark, Luke, and John authoritatively bear witness to *the singular gospel* about Jesus the Messiah. As part of our Christian mission, we should bear witness to it today too.

The point is this: from the vantage point of the earliest church, *there can only and ever be one true gospel*, although it is described by diverse witnesses. This reinforces the conclusion drawn above about Paul's gospel. (See especially 1 Cor. 15:1–11 on the gospel as a single narrative held in common by the twelve apostles, James, Paul, and other Christians.)

We can safely conclude the following: any attempt to define the gospel that does not take seriously a kingdom framework and the basic narrative pattern found in the four Gospels fails. At the same time, it is false to the New Testament witness to claim that there were many apostolic "gospels" rather than one true gospel—even though that one gospel is variously attested. The significance of this is clarified in view of the gospel's purpose in Scripture.

Gospel Purpose

The gospel is God's premier gift, his ultimate grace. But why did he give it? After two thousand years of church history, it is nearly impossible to avoid foisting our own ideas about salvation onto the texts prematurely. If we answer, "So that we can go to heaven when we die," we are simply wrong from a biblical standpoint. If we answer instead, "Salvation," or, "So that we can have resurrection life," we are closer to Scripture's emphasis (see Rom. 1:16; Eph. 1:13; cf. 2 Tim. 1:10). But we are still considerably short of the most precise answer.

Immediately after detailing the content of the gospel—the fulfillment of God's promises in the Son's incarnation and enthronement—Paul speaks about the gospel's purpose: "Jesus the Christ our Lord, through whom we received grace and apostleship for the obedience of *pistis* in all the nations" (Rom. 1:4–5 AT). What is the *exact purpose* of the gospel? It is for all nations to come underneath the banner of Jesus the Messiah by practicing "the obedience of *pistis*."

The royal context makes it highly probable that *pistis*, traditionally translated as "faith," is better understood as fidelity, loyalty, or allegiance here. (And this is true for all the occurrences of *pistis* in Rom. 1:1–3:26.)[16] That is, Paul is emphasizing not mental trust in Jesus's ability to effect forgiveness but rather external behavior—"the obedience characterized by fidelity": embodied, allegiant obedience to a king.

We cannot seriously doubt that this is the fundamental purpose of the gospel, because Paul, in describing the gospel in Romans 16:25–26, repeats himself, indicating again that its purpose is "the obedience of *pistis* in all the nations." Paul speaks similarly in Romans 15:18–19, saying that he has "fulfilled the ministry of the gospel of the Messiah" by bringing about "the obedience of the nations" (AT). Allegiance and the obedience of the nations to King Jesus embody the most explicit purpose of the gospel in Scripture.

The danger of hasty generalizations about the gospel's saving purposes should now be apparent. When we tell ourselves or others that the purpose of the gospel is salvation, we should not have postmortem existence in heaven in view. For we have a clearer vision of what salvation with regard to the gospel primarily looks like: *people from every nation are gathered under King Jesus in a posture of loyal obedience*, both now and in the resurrection age to come.

Allegiant individuals from these nations are living by the Spirit as servant-kings in the new era that the ultimate Servant-King, Jesus, has inaugurated. Final salvation above all involves a radical sociopolitical restructuring of the world, a new creation ruled by humans, restored so that they fully image God's glory via God's Son. This is why Paul speaks of "the gospel of the glory of Christ, who is the image of God" (2 Cor. 4:4). The gospel is purposed toward glory's restoration—that is, the recovery of the fullest honor and dignity for humans, creation, and ultimately God.

Much more could be said about the gospel's purpose. Indeed, I have penned a separate book, *Why the Gospel?*, that weaves together Scripture's many strands.[17] But at the very least we must say this about the gospel's purpose: God's *love* for all creation motivates his rescue operation. Jesus the king restores God's glory to the world, because by gazing on him we come to be conformed to his image. The nations are gathered under the kingship of Jesus in the new Jerusalem, and those united to the king reign with him.

Gospel Power

When King George V of England died in 1936, the members of the Privy Council were hastily summoned. Wearing regalia, the councillors and assisting dignitaries issued an official proclamation to all citizens of the realm: "We . . . do now, hereby, with one voice and consent, publish and proclaim that the high and mighty Prince Edward Albert . . . is now, by the death of our late sovereign of happy memory, our only lawful Liege Lord, Edward VIII."[18] *The proclamation itself served to officially ratify and install a new king.* After issuing the proclamation, the dignitaries and councillors embodied their allegiance. They kissed King Edward's hand and swore oaths of fealty.

A proclamation is also an event, because the very act of proclaiming can cause monumental changes in the world. Official proclamations are speech-acts that bring into being new social and political realities.

The Christian gospel is a similar speech-act. The gospel is not just historical *content*. It is not merely a true story about how Jesus became king. The gospel is a powerful *event*. "I am not ashamed of the gospel," Paul declares, "for it is the power of God for salvation for everyone who performs the *pistis* action" (Rom. 1:16 AT). In other words, the gospel unleashes God's saving power into the world. Yet Paul indicates that the ultimate saving power connected to the gospel is circumscribed, so that it reaches only some humans. Its fullest saving advantages are "for" only all doers of the *pistis* action.

Paul explains why the gospel is God's saving power yet is bounded in this way: "For in it [the gospel] the righteousness of God is revealed" (Rom. 1:17). We can infer that the principal manner in which the gospel is *the power of God for salvation* is that it *reveals the righteousness of God*—and this saving righteousness is not available apart from humans performing the *pistis* action. That is, righteousness is one of the special benefits of final salvation that marks off the church from humanity in general. There is much more that needs to be said.

It is enough for now to note that Paul does not say that the gospel itself *is* or *includes* the righteousness of God. Nor does he say that the gospel *contains* it. Thus, even if the righteousness of God does indeed refer to our justification (a disputed point), nevertheless Paul does not include our justification by faith within the gospel in this passage. In fact, neither Paul nor any other New Testament writer straightforwardly includes the realization of personal justification by faith as part of the gospel's content in any passage of Scripture.

Because Luther made it foundational, the inclusion of personal justification by faith as part of the gospel is a common misunderstanding among scholars and pastors. But if Scripture is our standard, the gospel is not personal justification, nor does the gospel proper include it. But the gospel does *reveal* "the righteousness of God." This is a small but crucial difference. And it thrusts us into the heart of Catholic-Protestant debates about justification. In subsequent chapters we'll explore this more.

Paul has indicated that the gospel is not inert content but rather God's saving power since it unveils the righteousness of God. But Paul is not finished: "For in the gospel the righteousness of God is revealed by *pistis* for *pistis*, as it is written, 'But the righteous one will live by *pistis*'" (Rom. 1:17 AT, citing Hab. 2:4). Here Paul gives crucial information about how the righteousness of God is made manifest: by *pistis* for *pistis*. And he offers proof from the Old Testament prophet Habakkuk. The most important results of a close reading of this text are as follows:[19]

1. Both the Old Testament covenantal context in Habakkuk and the royal context in Romans suggest that the phrase "by *pistis* for *pistis*" (*ek pisteōs eis pistin*) intends "by fidelity for fidelity," or "by allegiance for allegiance."

2. For Paul, the "by allegiance" refers to *the king's faithfulness or loyalty* in his obedience even unto death (cf. Rom. 5:17–19; 2 Cor. 4:13). The righteousness of God is unveiled by means of King Jesus's faithfulness or loyalty to God and to us, especially in taking the path of the cross.

3. The "for allegiance" indicates purpose, explaining why the king was allegiant. Jesus was allegiant to God so that we would have the opportunity to be loyal to God too by giving allegiance to Jesus as the Christ. "For allegiance" refers to how the king's allegiant actions were purposed toward facilitating *our allegiance to him as the king* (cf. Rom. 3:22). The righteousness of God is revealed in the gospel by Jesus's allegiance to God and our allegiance to Jesus the king.

4. In the phrase "the righteous one will *live* by allegiance,"
   the righteous one who lives by allegiance is first of all
   Jesus the king, and secondarily the righteous one is each
   human who gives him allegiance. The kind of *life* in view
   is life on the other side of death and vindicating judgment.
   It is *resurrection life*.

In short, the gospel is not individualized justification by faith.
Rather, the gospel is the power of God for salvation, because it
announces the reign of Jesus as king. This king provides benefits for his people, such as forgiveness, life, and justification. The
offer of benefits provided by this victorious king is good news for
humanity as a whole regardless of whether this or that individual
has come to share in them yet. Jesus displayed allegiance in order
to bring about our allegiance. He is the justified one who lives by
allegiance so that we can be justified by allegiance too, and in so
doing tap into his resurrection life.

3

Right and Wrong about the Gospel

The previous chapter explored what Scripture teaches about the gospel's content, purposes, and power for the sake of evangelism and mission. Since Protestants and Catholics frequently accuse one another of compromising the gospel, it was also necessary to establish an accurate baseline for our aims in this book.

Here is the most important idea that I want to communicate in this chapter: *All major streams and Christian denominations agree about the actual biblical, apostolic gospel and hence are fully Christian.* Yet this truth has been obscured by faulty articulations of the gospel in Catholicism and among Protestants. We need to identify and to correct inaccurate *gospel* language so that we can begin to take tangible steps together toward unity. I want to show that, in ways that matter, both Catholics and major Protestant leaders and denominations are both right and wrong about the gospel.

The Real Gospel Is Affirmed by All Major Groups

Scrutinize it, please. Catholics, Protestants (the major denominations), and Orthodox all affirm the truthfulness of these ten events. They always have.

48

The gospel is that Jesus the king

1. preexisted as God the Son,
2. was sent by the Father as promised,
3. took on human flesh in fulfillment of God's promises to David,
4. died for our sins in accordance with the Scriptures,
5. was buried,
6. was raised on the third day in accordance with the Scriptures,
7. appeared to many witnesses,
8. *is enthroned at the right hand of God as the ruling Christ*,
9. has sent the Holy Spirit to his people to effect his rule, and
10. will come again as final judge to rule.

Is there anything among the gospel's ten events with which a Catholic, Orthodox, or major Protestant denomination—past or present—would disagree? *No.* Is there anything here that Bible-oriented Protestant pastoral leaders who write on salvation would fail to affirm as true—folks like John Piper, R. C. Sproul, John MacArthur, and Paul Washer? *No.* Would the pope, metropolitans of the Orthodox Church, or the archbishop of Canterbury disagree with the truthfulness of any of these events? *No.* Are there any Lutheran, Reformed, or Anglican doctrinal confessions that would fall afoul of these ten? *No.*

Thus, even if these streams, denominations, or individuals within them don't realize it—because they call things gospel that are not part of it or misspeak about it—they *all* affirm the real gospel. There doubtless are rogue individuals or minor denominations within these streams that would deny some of the items above. But that simply reinforces my assertion. All these streams identify any such rogues as deviant—even heretical—precisely because these ten events are agreed-upon truths within all major Christian bodies.

If you've come to appreciate my claim above, you're ready for the next question: If Catholics and Protestants affirm the actual biblical gospel—such that neither has abandoned or hopelessly compromised it—then why do Catholics and Protestants still accuse one another of infidelity to the gospel?

Now, that's an interesting yet complicated story.

I'll discuss Protestant gospel problems soon too. But let me start with Catholicism.

The Catholic Gospel Problem

Once we recognize what the gospel in Scripture actually is—the ten events—we discover that official Roman Catholic theology upholds the actual gospel faithfully. It always has. The Orthodox have too. This is especially difficult for Protestants to acknowledge. There is a lot of emotional and intellectual baggage to work through.

Yet while Catholic teaching does affirm the true gospel, this is not to say that there are not significant errors in Catholic soteriology writ large when judged in light of the Bible and early Christian history. We'll get to those in subsequent chapters. But here let's start with how Catholics have contributed to our current gospel muddle. While affirming that Catholicism has not abandoned the true gospel and thus is fully Christian, I'd like to highlight three ways that Catholic teaching about the gospel has obfuscated it.

The Sacramental Eclipse

The first problem is the most serious: within Catholicism the gospel is eclipsed by the sacramental system. That is, within Catholicism there is little official interest in the gospel in its own right except inasmuch as it is felt to be mediated through the authority of the bishops and the sacramental life (e.g., baptism, confirmation, reconciliation, ordination, Eucharist).

The urgent good news of Jesus's *kingship* is obscured and personal evangelism eviscerated. For within Catholicism the decision that purportedly launches your salvation is ordinarily made *for you* by those who may or may not actively confess Jesus's kingship. Your parents and godparents, who may or may not be allegiant disciples of King Jesus, opt for you to receive the sacrament of baptism as an infant. The only salvation decision that an individual ever needs to make afterward is to continue along the sacramental path.

Moreover, broadly speaking, Catholic sacramental teaching does not emphasize Jesus's kingship or loyalty to him in his royal capacity. Thus there is significant risk that a baptized and observant Catholic may be led through the sacraments to believe that Jesus is the Lamb of God who takes away his or her sin but may never give allegiance to him as king.

There is scarcely any interest in the gospel per se within official Catholicism. By official Catholicism I mean documents issued by the Catholic teaching office, also called the magisterium. For example, if you look for a section on the gospel in the definitive everyday teaching tool for the Catholic Church, the Catechism, you will be looking in vain. You'll find a brief mention of the formation of the four Gospels (§§125–27) but no explanation or exposition of the gospel itself akin to that undertaken in chapter 2 of this book or, more extensively, in like-minded resources. The most you'll find in the Catechism is a very brief statement about the center of the good news:

> The Paschal mystery of Christ's cross and Resurrection stands at the center of the Good News that the apostles, and the Church following them, are to proclaim to the world. God's saving plan was accomplished "once for all" by the redemptive death of his Son Jesus Christ. (§571)

That's it. My edition of the Catechism has 688 pages. *The gospel gets only two sentences.* To say that "the gospel" is woefully underemphasized by official Catholic teaching understates the magnitude of the problem.

Yet, notice, the sacraments do get front billing. In the brief statement about the center of the gospel in the Catechism, the bit about the "Paschal mystery" is exceedingly important to Catholics. It signals that the *real import* of Jesus's once-for-all death and resurrection is mediated through the sacraments. The "once for all" language may be confusing to outsiders, because within Catholicism the *once-for-all historical* Christ events correspond to *eternal* heavenly mysteries that are participated in *repeatedly* during each eucharistic celebration of the Lamb of God mystery (i.e., during the Mass). In other words, for Catholics each celebration of the Mass reactualizes the Lamb's eternal sacrifice and Jesus's ongoing priestly mediation.

Want further evidence that the sacraments radically overshadow an emphasis on the gospel in everyday Catholic teaching? In comparison with the two sentences on the gospel in the Catechism, the sacraments of baptism, confirmation, and Eucharist get 144 pages in my edition. The gospel is eclipsed by the sacraments.

The situation improves little when you look at official papal documents. Efforts toward a "New Evangelization" that promised to restore an emphasis on the gospel, launched by previous popes and brought to a climax by Pope Benedict XVI in *Porta Fidei* (2011), were a step in the right direction. Benedict urged Catholics to travel "the highways of the world to proclaim his [Christ's] Gospel to all peoples of the earth" and called this proclamation of the gospel "a mandate that is ever new" (§7). But Pope Benedict never quite got around to saying what the gospel that should be shared actually *is*. Moreover, this "New Evangelization" energy has largely dissipated under Pope Francis.

The Missing King

There is a second problem beyond the overemphasis on the sacraments at the expense of plain teaching about the gospel within Catholicism: when the gospel's content is explicitly discussed in the Catechism, as in popular Protestantism, the Catholic articulation skews toward the Paschal mystery—heavy on the cross, with some resurrection sprinkled on top—but it does not adequately front Jesus's kingship. (Protestants and Roman Catholics should pause here to applaud the Orthodox for more consistently stressing Jesus's kingship than the Western church.) Of course, the Catholic liturgy recognizes that Jesus is the Christ. I'm speaking about emphasis. The sacramental focus in the Mass is on receiving forgiveness through Jesus's merit as the eternal Lamb of God and high priest and his presence in the bread and wine via transubstantiation, not on Jesus's kingship.

And yet what I've said about the Catholic gospel problem is not the whole story. Problem one, the sacramental eclipse, and problem two, the missing king, are genuine failures. But if I made that the whole story, it would be grossly misleading. The gospel's true content—the ten events—is in fact amply taught by the Catholic Church. It is just rarely called *the gospel*.

The Gospel Proclaimed but Renamed

The third problem with the gospel within Catholicism is a good problem to have. Mostly. The true gospel according to Scripture—the ten events—is taught in the Catholic Church, but Catholicism tends to call it *the faith* or *the creed* rather than what Scripture prefers: *the gospel* or *the kerygma*. In other words, in Catholicism *the gospel is proclaimed but renamed*. This damages the Catholic Church's ability to effectively evangelize and causes needless ecumenical confusion.

In Catholicism the gospel is frequently called *the creed* or *the faith*. For instance, in *Porta Fidei*, when Pope Benedict XVI advocates for "vigorous adherence to the Gospel," he has especially in mind "a public profession of the *Credo*" (§8) and "the celebration of *the faith* in the liturgy, especially in the Eucharist" (§9). What Benedict intends is the Niceno-Constantinopolitan Creed as that encapsulates and expands the earlier Apostles' Creed. Benedict is typical of Catholicism in using *the Creed* or *the faith* for what the Bible calls *the gospel*. As a Protestant who has spent twenty years within Catholic higher education, I can attest that this causes widespread miscommunication in Protestant-Catholic dialogue.

Because the gospel as described in the Bible—the ten elements—is very close in content to the Apostles' Creed, the biblical gospel certainly is taught and believed within Catholicism. In fact, all of part I in the Catechism (264 pages!) is a detailed exposition of the Apostles' Creed as supplemented by the Niceno-Constantinopolitan Creed (§196).

These creeds implicitly but faithfully bring out the true gospel's trinitarian substructure. Unsurprisingly, the Catechism's exposition of the creeds sometimes moves into speculative territory—making assertions about Mary and the like—that Protestants (myself included) do not welcome. Nevertheless, the Catechism certainly does amply cover and affirm the ten events. The actual content of the biblical gospel is thoroughly taught in the Catholic Church. It is just rarely called the gospel.

Yet the creeds are not good stand-alone teaching tools about the gospel without an intervening reframing. The biblical and apostolic gospel relentlessly emphasizes Jesus's messianic kingship—and this is muted in the creeds. Furthermore, creeds are doctrinal statements that invite intellectual affirmation—belief—more than allegiance. Response to the true gospel is weak in Catholicism, because apart from an intentional reframing, the creeds do not naturally promote a royal gospel and an allegiance response.

In summary, like the major Protestant denominations, Catholicism, broadly considered, upholds the apostolic gospel's content (the ten events) with remarkable fidelity. But Catholic teaching obscures the gospel by its sacramental system, by not emphasizing Jesus's kingship, and by conflating the language of *gospel*, *creed*, and *faith*. Beyond the gospel, deep soteriological disagreements between Catholics and Protestants remain. I will have more to say about a possible path forward later.

Now I want to switch the focus by spotlighting gospel problems within Protestantism.

Protestant Gospel Problems

Protestants pride themselves to be, as a matter of self-definition, those who have recovered the gospel over against Catholicism. It is difficult for Protestants—myself included—to admit that we might have a gospel problem.

I'll be candid. For those steeped in classic Protestantism, the gospel-allegiance model comes with horse-sized pills that may prove difficult to swallow. But if the gospel-allegiance model proves to be a healthy corrective, then Protestants must admit that it is not only Catholicism that has erred. Their gospel has been less than fully accurate too.

In this book's prequel, *Gospel Allegiance*, I developed the gospel-allegiance model at length using Scripture and compared it to classic Protestantism. I sketched the results in chapter 1 of this book. This should be sufficient, at least, to demonstrate a possible Protestant gospel problem. I cannot repeat that analysis here. Moreover, subsequent chapters will expose additional imprecisions within classic Protestantism.

But here I can highlight certain implications that follow from my previous treatments because they directly relate to common Protestant misperceptions about the gospel. These misperceptions continue to weaken Protestant evangelism, discipleship, and mission.

The following are common *wrong ways* of describing the gospel within classic Protestantism:

- The gospel is primarily about how an individual person can get saved.
- The gospel is that Jesus has done it all for you so that you don't have to do anything yourself for salvation.
- The gospel can be accurately summarized as Jesus died for your sins so that you can be forgiven when you die.
- The gospel is the Romans Road: God is righteous, humans are sinners, Jesus Christ is the savior, so repent and believe.
- The gospel is uniquely centered on the cross.
- The gospel is Jesus's death, burial, and resurrection. Period.

I'm glad you haven't stopped reading. Some quit in the middle of the list above. In identifying these as faulty descriptions, I am probably saying something different about the gospel than what you're used to hearing from prominent Christian leaders. For example, Matt Chandler, in *The Explicit Gospel*, primarily describes the gospel by using the Romans Road template. Greg Gilbert, in *What Is the Gospel?*, does the same and devotes a chapter to "Keeping the Cross at the Center."

I have already given evidence in the previous chapter that these *misconstrue* the gospel—and I've made a much fuller case in *Gospel Allegiance*. These are both leading pastor-scholars whom I respect because they are teaching the Bible and taking care of people. But I am singling them out here because they are widely respected as Scripture-based teachers, and hence they illustrate well the present landscape of gospel confusion among Protestants.

Here are two additional typical Protestant *errors* that I'd like to add on the basis of the discussion that follows:

- The gospel includes the *personal* receipt of justification by faith.
- The gospel does not include social and political action.

The remainder of this chapter will explore these two common misunderstandings of the gospel among prominent Protestant leaders.

Recent Protestant Gospel Conversations

The goal in focusing on recent Protestant mistakes about the gospel is to add nuance so that as this book unfolds we can remodel our understanding of how the gospel saves for Protestants and Catholics alike. In my judgment, John Piper and Greg Gilbert illustrate the first error, that of making the personal receipt of justification by faith part of the gospel. Meanwhile, John MacArthur and others make the second error when they say that the gospel does not include social and political action. There is much at stake practically for the church's life and mission in such discussions.

Is Personal Justification Part of the Gospel? Weighing Piper's and Gilbert's Claims

The question is whether it is accurate to call "Jesus is king" gospel on its own or if instead it is necessary to say that "Jesus is king" can be termed gospel only if it includes personal forgiveness or justification. I discussed this briefly in *Gospel Allegiance*, but since then the conversation has moved forward. Greg Gilbert, Scot McKnight, and I engaged in a back-and-forth dialogue hosted by *Christianity Today*'s blog series and by 9Marks. Furthermore, John Piper has responded to portions of my book *Gospel Allegiance*. I'll attempt to bring the reader up to speed and then offer three proposals that I think can advance the discussion.

Entering the conversation. When Martin Luther launched the Protestant Reformation, he identified "justification by faith" as the essence of the gospel. Thereafter, Protestants have tended to follow suit. For example, in various books John MacArthur, John Piper, and R. C. Sproul—the list could be multiplied—all claim that justification by faith is the heart of the gospel. MacArthur calls justification by faith "the core and touchstone of the gospel according to Paul" and summarizes, "Justification by faith is the linchpin of Paul's teaching on the gospel."[1] R. C. Sproul states, "Justification by faith alone is essential to the gospel."[2] John Piper is even more effusive: "I am thrilled to call justification the heart of the gospel."[3]

But scholars of Scripture have not always been convinced that justification by faith is as central to the gospel as these folks believe. In the last fifty years, especially, there has been a significant reappraisal of what the New Testament teaches about salvation.[4] The reason why a great many Bible scholars have not been persuaded by Luther's claim that justification by faith is central to the gospel is simple: *the Bible never clearly claims that justification by faith is part of the gospel at all, let alone its center or its essence—not even once.*[5]

This doesn't mean that justification by faith has been rejected. It means that justification by faith, while remaining a true doctrine, finds a better fit in our overall understanding of salvation within rearranged categories. In terms of the pastoral discussion on these issues, N. T. Wright blazed the trail. He claimed that our final justification will be based not simply on our trust in God's promises in Jesus Christ but on a person's whole faith-life journey in relation to Jesus as Lord.[6] In 2007 John Piper wrote *The Future of Justification* as a critique, asserting that apart from the receipt of personal forgiveness first, "the lordship of Jesus is terrifying, not good news."[7]

While this wrestling about justification was unfolding, pertinent work on the gospel continued apace. In 2009 Greg Gilbert wrote *What Is the Gospel?* In it he follows Piper's lead. Gilbert asserts, "'Jesus is Lord' is not the gospel" and "'Jesus is Lord' is really not good news at all if we don't explain how Jesus is not just Lord but also Savior."[8] Scot McKnight's *King Jesus Gospel* (2011) showed how a narrow soterian gospel had inadvertently replaced the original royal gospel of the New Testament, and he chose Gilbert's book to illustrate this error.[9] Meanwhile, books by Michael Bird, N. T. Wright, and Michael Gorman helped reinforce a King Jesus approach to the gospel.[10]

Recent developments. In 2020 Greg Gilbert preached a published sermon for T4G ("Together for the Gospel") with the title "What the Gospel Is and Is Not."[11] Gilbert opens by affirming that "the beating heart of the gospel is Jesus's penal substitutionary atonement for us and our justification by faith alone in him." He expresses surprise that what he regards to be the straightforward truths of his *What Is the Gospel?* have not received uniform affirmation. "Believe it or not," he says, "that book—and it's definition of the gospel . . . has not been without its detractors." Gilbert then quotes my work and McKnight's, suggesting that we "take the story of Jesus's kingship and divorce it from the realities of personal salvation, forgiveness, atonement, and justification," and that we claim that "'Jesus is king' is the gospel, and that personal salvation, atonement, and justification *are not*." Gilbert proceeds from there to affirm a King Jesus gospel and a kingdom focus, provided that we remember that Jesus is a king who saves by bearing the sins of his people.

Both Scot McKnight and I felt that Gilbert had misrepresented us but had also raised wider issues that deserved public discussion. So I penned "Good News? Are T4G/TGC Leaders Starting to Change Their Gospel?"[12] The article caused an eruption on social media. McKnight followed up with "King Jesus Gospel: Mere Kingship? No," which also found a huge readership.[13] Gilbert replied—for which McKnight and I were grateful—but his choice of title, "'Jesus Is King' Is Not Good News," was telling and unfortunate. Gilbert put the matter even more starkly in the body of his article: "The proclamation 'Jesus is King' is not good news at all."

Gilbert's title and language were lampooned on social media. Folks wondered: If "Jesus is the Christ," which means "king," is good enough for the Bible to use repeatedly as a summary of the gospel, why isn't it good enough for Gilbert and Piper? The backlash was so severe that Gilbert (or his editor) changed that article's title several days later to the bland "A Response to Scot McKnight and Matthew Bates."[14] Finally, in "Why T4G/TGC Leaders Must Fix Their Gospel," I critiqued Gilbert's and Piper's position using Scripture and Greco-Roman evidence while seeking to articulate a positive path forward.[15]

Proposals for Advancing the Discussion

I've reviewed a dialogue that began with books and emerged in a social-media skirmish not because anyone is still actively monitoring a debate that ended five years ago but because the issues are timeless and point to unresolved tensions in Protestant soteriology. Controversy around these issues will keep occurring until they are resolved by Scripture and articulated with theological exactness. I've had several years to ponder the debate. Below I offer three points that I hope can advance future conversation as it is carried out by others. The goal is unity in the truth.

1. Must "Gospel" Include Personal Forgiveness?

John Piper and Greg Gilbert claim that *euangelion* must include *personal* rescue by Jesus as savior or else the word can't properly mean "gospel." Yet evidence has already been presented to the contrary in the previous chapter. In the New Testament and its world *euangelion* frequently refers to a royal proclamation—such as news of a new emperor—for the general citizen body *apart from whether that proclamation would result in good for any given individual personally*. For example, when Vespasian became emperor, this was called "good news" because it was empire-wide good news, even though it was bad news on a personal level for Vespasian's enemies. When the word is used by native speakers in the New Testament era, the "good" in "good news" is primarily a *communal good*, not intrinsically a personal good.

Let's consider Jesus. He is described as proclaiming the gospel, even when his proclamation does not result in the reception of a *personal* good for the majority of individuals who hear him. For example, after visiting Nazareth and Capernaum, Jesus says that his primary purpose is *"to proclaim the good news [euangelisasthai] . . . to the other towns also,"* and he says this *after* the people have just heard the good news and have *rejected* it (Luke 4:43 NIV; cf. 4:18–19, 29, 37; 10:13–16). *Jesus proclaims "gospel" ("good news") for those in Nazareth and Capernaum just as much as for the other towns, even though the bulk of individuals in these towns had personally rejected him and therefore lacked individual forgiveness.* Similar examples abound. Later Jesus sends his disciples out "to proclaim the gospel" (Luke 9:6 AT) and to announce that "the kingdom of God has drawn near to you" (10:9 AT), even though he indicates that many towns and individuals will not receive this message favorably (10:10–16). Similarly, Jesus "heralds the gospel" to the people in the temple, even though many of these very people unrepentantly reject him and support his crucifixion a week later (20:1 AT).

Here is the point: *Jesus consistently uses "gospel" language to describe his emerging kingship with reference to people who explicitly reject his kingship and who lack personal forgiveness, and he does this even while warning such people that they are under God's judgment.* In such circumstances, Jesus does not say, "I would like to use the word *gospel* when speaking to you, but the language doesn't apply because you are personally rejecting my offer of forgiveness." Instead, he uses "gospel" to describe the whole situation that attends his emerging kingship despite outcomes of personal forgiveness for this or that individual.

It is the same for John the Baptist, Paul, and others. John the Baptist's proclamation is summarized as "proclaiming the good news," even though the crowd to whom he was speaking included *both* those who would be gathered into the barn and the chaff that would be burned up with unquenchable fire (Luke 3:17–18). Paul describes the saving message that "Jesus is Lord" as good news while in the same breath saying that "not all have obeyed the good news" (Rom. 10:9–16 NRSV). Notice that Jesus's lordship is called "good news" (*euangelion*) in Scripture *even with respect to those who have entirely rejected it such that they personally stand condemned.*

In sum, we cannot artificially restrict *euangelion* ("gospel") by forcing it to carry the meaning of *individual* or *personal* good news, for it was not restricted in this way in the New Testament or the ancient world. Piper and Gilbert's claim that the "gospel" of Jesus's kingship cannot mean "good news" unless it includes the good news of *my* or *your* personal salvation is not based on accurate biblical or historical research.

2. Clarifying "Our"

I wonder about how ambiguity in the word *our* in the phrases "our justification" and "our forgiveness" might be bedeviling this conversation and other like-minded discussions of salvation. I claim that the gospel does not include *our* personal justification by faith. Piper and Gilbert claim the opposite. Here is the issue: the word *our* is capable of an individual-first meaning or a group-first meaning within ordinary language.

"Our" as individual first. At times *our* has in view individual experience first. Let's say that three friends and I join the army. We are each issued boots, but we separately discover that the glue is separating from the sole and discuss the problem. Then I tell the sergeant, *"Our* boots are defective." What makes the phrase "our boots" accurate is prior individual experience that has served to create a group. The correct use of *our* in such a context is based on the experience of each individual first and subsequently on the discovered commonality.

"Our" as group first. At other times *our* has in view the preexisting group's reality apart from individual experience. For example, an army general might say, "The president is *our* leader." In this use of *our*, the army's reality as a group comes prior to the experience of any current soldier. For this statement to be true, it doesn't matter who is in the army currently or whether each individual actually affirms the president's leadership. Groups can have properties that extend beyond their individual members. *Our* can describe a group's reality prior to and apart from the experience of any single individual who subsequently joins a group.

So, when attempting to describe what Scripture teaches about salvation, is it more accurate to use the language of individual first or of group first? *Group first is more accurate.* After Jesus's enthronement and the outpouring of the Spirit at Pentecost, the justified church as a group always exists prior to the justification of any individual.[16] So Scripture prefers to use *our* in a group-first sense when speaking about *our forgiveness* and *our justification*.

For example, when Paul says that the gospel includes the Christ's death "for *our* sins" (1 Cor. 15:3) or that the Christ was raised "for *our* justification" (Rom. 4:25), Paul uses *our* in a group-first sense, not individual-first. Paul is not talking about how Jesus died and was raised for the sins of Peter, Paul, and Mary individually—and then on the basis of each one's individual experience of personal rescue from private sins, they talked about it together, and then came to acknowledge its group reality. Rather, on the basis of the Christ's saving work that culminated at Pentecost, *the forgiven or justified group exists prior to the individual's experience, so that when any individual by faith commits to Jesus as Lord, they enter the justified community.* Thus, if we desire to track the Bible's theology with the greatest accuracy, it is best if we give the phrase "*our* justification" a group-first meaning.

Of course, this is not to deny that justification is personally or individually experienced. It most certainly is. For example, Paul speaks of his own attainment of personal justification in Philippians 3:9, saying he received it "not by law" but "through the loyalty [*pistis*] of the Christ—the righteousness that is from God and is based on loyalty [*pistis*]" (AT). But it is vital that we recognize that in speaking about his personal attainment of justification in this way, Paul never identifies the attainment of *individualized* justification *to be part of the gospel itself per se.* Nor does any other New Testament writer do so. Rather, as we will see more fully in the next chapter, in Scripture personal justification is a result or *benefit* of the gospel when an individual is united to King Jesus and his body via the Spirit.

Let me clarify what language Scripture prefers in describing how the gospel interfaces with *our* justification or forgiveness: it is accurate to say that "*our justification*" *is part of the gospel when using "our" in a group-first manner to speak of justification as a benefit that the Christ has objectively won for himself and his church as a collective body; but it is inaccurate to say "our justification" is part of the gospel when using "our" in an individual-first manner.* It is likewise incorrect to say that "my justification" or "your justification" or "personal justification" is a part of the gospel per se, because *personal justification is better described as a benefit that results from the gospel.*

3. Conditional and Unconditional

I wonder if this whole debate could be sharpened in the future by distinguishing what is *unconditional* and *conditional* with respect to the gospel and its benefits. For future dialogue, I propose that theologians distinguish between the gospel's *unconditional promise* and *potential* for the justification of each individual and its *conditional fulfillment, realization,* or *actuality.*

I submit that the gospel's content includes *the promise* that any individual can be justified by faith. In this sharply qualified *promissory sense*, the gospel includes personal justification by faith. That is, I hold that *the potential* justification of each and every individual is within the gospel's purview, but that each and every individual's *realized* justification is not part of the gospel. In my judgment, Piper and Gilbert, if I am reading them correctly, wrongly include the realization of personal justification within the gospel by failing to nuance these matters.

The distinction that I am proposing—the distinction between potential gospel benefits that are based on a promise and their conditional realization—is made in Scripture. After preaching the gospel in Acts 13:16–37, Paul concludes, "I want you to know that *through Jesus the forgiveness of sins is proclaimed to you* [plural]. Through Jesus *everyone who has faith is justified from every sin*, a justification you were not able to obtain under the law of Moses" (13:38–39 AT). Paul then warns them not to scoff and disbelieve and so come under God's judgment (13:40–41).

Notice that Paul first presents forgiveness and justification as possible benefits that have been supplied to a group, *you* (plural), as part of the gospel unconditionally. Next, the *promise* that *each individual* ("everyone who has faith") can obtain justification is associated with the gospel's goodness somehow, but only *if one responds* to the gospel. In other words, *personal receipt* of justification is a *benefit of the gospel that is conditioned on adequate personal response to it.* This means that an individual does not obtain the gospel benefit of forgiveness or justification until the faith condition is met, until she or he yields trusting loyalty to Jesus as king.

Why Does This Debate Matter?

I opted to revisit the Piper-Gilbert versus Wright-McKnight-Bates debate in order to offer theological proposals that I believe can advance present and future conversations. A more exacting use of language can help the church move beyond salvation wars present and future. As part of the gospel, corporate justification has already been won by King Jesus for himself and whoever happens to be part of his church. *The gospel itself does not include personal justification by faith but does include the promise that a person can be justified by faith if that person meets the condition of faith.* Personal justification is a conditional *benefit* of the gospel that comes through union with the king and his body as facilitated by the Spirit, not an already realized actuality within the gospel.

Why does a proper nuancing of personal justification with respect to the gospel matter practically? First, the gospel-allegiance model gives God more glory for the gospel, because otherwise the gospel *itself* depends on human response for its goodness. When we get the gospel right, we are reminded that it is about what God has done within history to save a people for himself—God's triune saving actions alone. Therefore, God gets all the honor for gifting us with his very good gospel. To assert with Greg Gilbert and John Piper that your personal response or mine is required for God's "good news" to count as *fully good* takes away from what God has accomplished in establishing a saved community through it. Ironically, because it is the opposite of their intentions, Piper and Gilbert's version of the gospel's content significantly detracts from God's glory by making it depend on each individual's justifying faith for its fullness.

Second, a proper nuancing protects us from making salvation self-centered. Piper and Gilbert's position inadvertently taints the gospel with our culture's narcissistic individualism: the gospel can't count as good news unless *I* personally get something out of it. Their misarticulation reinforces the misguided notion that salvation is primarily about *me*—about my personal need to escape wrath so I can enjoy heaven. The true gospel is purposed toward God's rescue of Jesus the king and his body in such a way that anyone who confesses allegiance to this king can join it, so that with God's assistance this liberated group can help restore God's whole creation project.

Third, a proper nuancing reminds us that God's saving goals are achieved in community for community. God's gospel is purposed toward creating a people who practice loyal obedience to Jesus the king (Rom. 1:5; 16:26). This happens through *a communal process of glory refreshment* as we gaze on the king, building one another up and welcoming others into the king's love. This is why Paul calls the good news "the gospel of *the glory* of *the Christ*, who is the image of God" (2 Cor. 4:4).

The Gospel and Social Justice? Weighing John MacArthur's Position

We have just explored one current gospel debate among Protestants. When we realize that the gospel does not automatically include my personal forgiveness *but that the gospel's forgiving benefits are for a community that can include me*, then God receives more glory, our individualistic culture is undermined, and the church is strengthened.

But there is another, quite different reason why we need to reinstall King Jesus at the forefront of gospel proclamation. Consider what happens when we leave kingship out: we end up with a vision of salvation focused on a savior who rescues us from sin so that we can escape to an otherworldly heaven. We have no king and no kingdom and hence no vision for how salvation might connect to today's Christian social and political activity. This is what is at stake in a second current conversation among Protestants about the gospel's relationship to social justice.

The Statement on Social Justice and the Gospel, recently issued by leading evangelicals, seeks to separate the gospel from social actions. John MacArthur is the leading signatory of the statement, with initial cosigners such as Voddie Baucham, Phil Johnson, and James White. A study of the royal gospel in Scripture clarifies why the statement misunderstands the biblical gospel. Consider the following excerpt from the statement:

> WE AFFIRM that the gospel is the divinely-revealed message concerning the person and work of Jesus Christ—especially his virgin birth, righteous life, substitutionary sacrifice, atoning death, and

bodily resurrection—revealing who he is and what he has done with the promise that he will save anyone and everyone who turns from sin by trusting him as Lord.[17]

There is much that is good and accurate in this MacArthur-affiliated statement. But notice what is missing in its attempt to define the gospel, because this is where the problem begins. *The statement's definition of the gospel makes no mention of the kingdom of God, Jesus's enthronement, or his attainment of the kingship.* The Statement on Social Justice and the Gospel mishandles Scripture and erodes the gospel's power for the church and the world in at least three ways.

1. If No King, Then No Politics

Is Jesus a "this world" king? First, the MacArthur statement empties Jesus's present kingship of its authority, but Scripture makes it clear that Jesus is a real-world king right now. By ignoring Jesus's present kingship as gospel, the statement fails to correctly describe the inescapable political and social dimension of how Jesus saves each person. Truly, Jesus's kingdom is not "of this world" inasmuch as it does not *derive* its source or power *from* our world (cf. John 18:36). But this is not to say that it lacks on-the-ground actualization in our present world, for that would deny the gospel's "Jesus is the Christ" climax altogether and the legitimacy of Jesus's sovereign authority over the church as a real-world sociopolitical body. The apostle Paul urges, "Live as a political-body [*politeuesthe*] of the gospel of the Christ worthily" (Phil. 1:27 AT).

Is Jesus's kingship an ongoing event within history? The MacArthur-backed statement leaves out of its gospel definition what the New Testament says is most characteristic of the gospel. The gospel is not merely *content* to be proclaimed but is a *power-releasing event* that moves unjust individuals into a righteous community (Rom. 1:16–17; 1 Cor. 2:4–5; 1 Thess. 1:5 [see chap. 2]). As Graham Twelftree puts it in his major study of Paul's gospel, "God's saving drama in Christ is not only gospel but it is experienced as gospel in a saving event."[18] Scripture teaches us that *the gospel is an ongoing event that includes Jesus the king's reign over his people, especially their social and political life.*

When we make the gospel profession "Jesus is king" or "Jesus is Lord," we are constituted as a citizen body under Jesus's real-world political and social authority, so that we must live in a cruciform manner if indeed we are to continue to profess him to be our king. When Paul says, "No one can say 'Jesus is Lord' except in the Holy Spirit" (1 Cor. 12:3), he is describing how this confession makes Jesus's reign present in the real world by manifestations of the gifts of the Spirit, as each person builds up others in the midst of the king's body (12:4–27).

Does the statement ignore kingship as gospel? I want to make sure that my assessment of the Statement on Social Justice and the Gospel is fair. One might argue that Jesus's kingship is included as part of the gospel in the statement's affirmation that we need to trust Jesus as Lord. But it is implausible that trust includes a loyal response to Jesus's kingship within this statement, because any on-the-ground reality that would involve the Lord Jesus acting as king—that is, exercising social or political sovereignty over a person's body—is deliberately excluded from the gospel as the statement continues:

> WE DENY that anything else, whether works to be performed or opinions to be held, can be added to the gospel without perverting it into another gospel. This also means that implications and applications of the gospel, such as the obligation to live justly in the world, though legitimate and important in their own right, are not definitional components of the gospel.[19]

The statement's call to trust Jesus as Lord is coupled with a unilateral denial that the gospel proper can include the demand to live justly in the world—"whether works to be performed or opinions to be held"—as part of that response to Jesus.

What should we make of this claim? On the one hand, the statement is wildly off base in what it assumes about what the words *gospel*, *trust* (*pistis*), and *Lord* mean in the New Testament, because it defines them in ways that suggest these words can be cordoned off from sociopolitical actions and bodily obedience. On the other hand, ironically, the statement does not go far enough here: it would be more accurate to say that the gospel proper is about what King Jesus has done and does not include any specific individual's "trust" response to the gospel at all! To be exact: the statement errs by making personal salvation by trusting in Jesus as Lord intrinsic to the gospel proper, when in Scripture personal rescue is one of the gospel's *benefits* and faith is not part of the gospel proper but merely how a person should *respond* to it.

In sum, the statement's most basic failure is that it eviscerates Jesus's kingship by ignoring the this-world social and political reality of his present reign. It rests on a deficient faith-is-mental-but-works-are-bodily construct that illegitimately decouples faith and allegiance.[20] The statement reduces faith to trusting in Jesus as Lord for salvation rather than allowing faith to also include allegiance to Jesus in his present reign as king of the world.

2. The Gospel Necessarily Benefits Non-Christians

There are some additional problems with the statement. Not only is Jesus's present rule as king emptied of its significance, but the statement also fails to distinguish between *special benefits* of the gospel that belong only to the church and *general benefits* of the gospel for non-Christians and creation. Contrary to the statement, in Scripture the gospel's *general benefits* include social justice.

It is true, as the statement points out, that the most important benefits of the gospel, such as finding God's full forgiveness and final salvation, are ultimately only for Christians. This is helpful, and we must never lose sight of such bedrock truths. But the statement acts as if these special saving benefits for the church are the *only* benefits that attend the gospel.

Scripture tells us otherwise. Passages such as Luke 4:16–21 and 7:22 prove that authentic heralding of the Jesus-is-king gospel will *necessarily* be attended by acts of social justice—Jesus's gospel will

69

be good news for the poor, blind, oppressed, and captives—and that these liberating expressions of the king's goodness are made available to the *general* population as part of the gospel.

General benefits for *all humans* are *inescapably* made available when Jesus is authentically given kingship. How? Jesus's kingship is always present in the world but is especially operative in the midst of his outward-reaching people. As crucified and risen, Jesus is given space to rule by his ambassadors. His cross-shaped, self-sacrificial love brings relief for the poor, the unhealthy, and the oppressed as a sign that the king's cross-and-resurrection life is now at work. Because the gospel is marked by the cross and the resurrection, authentic gospel proclamation inscribes the gospel communally—word and deed—in the form of just social actions that benefit all humanity. The king's justice is one of the *general social and political benefits* of the gospel that insiders and outsiders alike will necessarily experience through authentic gospel proclamation.

3. Evangelists Are Part of the Gospel

Third, here is a different but related way to see the matter. Contra the MacArthur statement, when we get the climax of the gospel right—Jesus is the king—we discover that social action on behalf of the poor is not merely an application of the gospel. Rather, *the king's virtues come to be inscribed within the king's citizen body* because he rules there. Messengers who are being transformed by gospel allegiance inescapably become part of the cruciform gospel message itself. *In any act of communication—including the proclamation of the gospel—the messenger is invariably part of the message.* Paul describes how the authentic evangelist is part of the gospel message in this way:

> Because we loved you so much, *we were delighted to share with you not only the gospel of God but our lives as well.* Surely you remember, brothers and sisters, our toil and hardship; *we worked night and day in order not to be a burden to anyone while we preached the gospel of God to you.* (1 Thess. 2:8–9 NIV)

When Paul's missionary team preached the gospel, their actions were part of the gospel message. Their love for the Thessalonians expressed God's gospel love. Their willingness to take a lowly, self-sacrificing posture—working night and day—was a cross-shaped social activity that reflected their king's values. As Graham Twelftree puts it for Paul, "The gospel becomes Christ himself, expressed and experienced" so that it is "embodied and lived" by those who participate in it.[21] Here's the upshot: *Because the true gospel is a sociopolitical proclamation that emerges from and attends to Jesus's present reign as king, when the king's citizens authentically proclaim the gospel, a sociopolitical vision and its enactment will necessarily be part of the gospel's liberating message.*

I've spent time on the question of the gospel and social justice because this MacArthur-backed statement is symptomatic of larger trends that have dominated evangelicalism. The Statement on Social Justice and the Gospel places the gospel in its own heavenly cul-de-sac, pristinely set apart from social and political realities. If, with the statement, we wrongly determine that the gospel is primarily about personal trust in Jesus, so that an individual can be forgiven and attain heaven, should we be surprised if the gospel's earthly sociopolitical demands are left at the curbside? Should we be surprised if the gospel's power to create and sustain sociopolitical action in favor of the poor and oppressed tends to be ignored, *especially within sociopolitical groups that already hold significant this-world power*? The true gospel inescapably creates, includes, and effects a social and political lifestyle commiserate with the king's just rule.

Right and wrong about the gospel. That is how this chapter presents the current Catholic and Protestant situation. Once we understand what the gospel actually is, we discover that official Catholic doctrine readily affirms its truthfulness. Jesus's kingship is happily professed. Yes, there is confusion in official Catholic doctrine about the gospel. It isn't even usually called *the gospel* by Catholics but instead *the faith* or *the creed*. There are also problems regarding the boundaries of what it means to appropriately respond to the gospel and in delineating how we come to enjoy its benefits.

The same is true for the vast majority of Protestant leaders, pastors, and scholars past and present. While they affirm the true gospel—what I've summarized as ten events—they also misarticulate the gospel's authentic boundaries. In terms of current gospel conversations, in particular John Piper and Greg Gilbert claim that the gospel of Jesus's kingship can't be called the gospel unless it includes *personal* forgiveness or justification. Meanwhile, John MacArthur and others have asserted that the gospel can't be defined in terms of social or political action in behalf of the poor or oppressed without compromising it. Both of these definitions of the gospel fail in light of what Scripture teaches. They are shortsighted and need to be corrected for the sake of the church and the world.

If Scripture is our standard, then we see that Catholics and Protestants are both right and wrong about the gospel. Moreover, this rightness and wrongness is not merely trivial but touches upon foundational issues of practical, pastoral, and ultimate theological concern. We've made a good start, but if we hope to move beyond the salvation wars of the past, we need to go deeper.

In the next chapter we'll explore the classic Protestant criticism of Catholicism with regard to the gospel and see why it is mistargeted. Then we'll re-aim it.

4

Retooling the Protestant Critique of Catholicism

Protestantism and Catholicism, broadly considered, uphold the apostolic gospel's content with remarkable fidelity, even if there is confusion on both sides of the aisle when it comes to delineating the gospel proper. So both are fully Christian. Chapters 2–3 have sought to establish this. Yet deep disagreements between Catholics and Protestants remain.

What Paul teaches in the Letter to the Galatians about salvation remains at the heart of the conflict. Accordingly, Galatians has the potential to correct *both* classic Protestantism and Catholicism. Exploring *how* is our task in the present chapter. Progress will come not by glossing over differences but rather by articulating the truth in the service of future unity.

I will argue that Galatians does forcefully critique Catholic soteriology, but not in the way described by classic Protestantism. Meanwhile, a close reading of select portions of the letter also shows why Protestants have been misapplying justification by faith. An exploration of the leading issues in Galatians will also put us in a better position to reappraise the true relationship between justification and sanctification—and other matters too—when we seek to build an alternative model in chapters 8–9.

Galatians can lead the church to a healthier place if we are willing to hear afresh what it says about the gospel and justification. That is my claim. But in speaking this way, I know that this chapter will do little to end Protestant-Catholic disagreements on its own; indeed, it may sharpen the dispute in various camps. My hope is that in the long run the ideas in this chapter, as they are discovered here or independently by other scholars, can be deepened, refined, confirmed, and articulated afresh, so that they eventually contribute toward a broader allegiance-to-the-king movement.

Misuse of Galatians

Because Paul's language is so sharply pointed in Galatians, summaries of its argument have become the quintessential Protestant description for what ails Catholicism.

In Galatians, Paul expresses frustrated astonishment that troublemakers have infiltrated the churches, convincing some to abandon the one true gospel in favor of a non-gospel: "I am astonished that you are so quickly deserting him who called you in the grace of Christ and are turning to a different gospel—not that there is another one, but there are some who trouble you and want to distort the gospel of Christ" (Gal. 1:6–7). Paul goes on to express a wish-prayer: if anyone preaches a gospel contrary to the one that was initially preached by Paul's missionary team, "let that person be an anathema"—that is, cursed and cut off from God's people (1:8 AT). Paul uses the strongest possible language.

The surface logic of Paul's argument in Galatians is especially alluring to traditionally minded Protestants.[1] They tend to follow this line of thinking:

1. the gospel is being perverted in Galatia by certain troublemakers (1:6–9; 2:5, 14);
2. the principles of grace alone and justification by faith alone were being compromised by the troublemakers who

were seeking instead to be justified by works (2:16; 3:11; 5:2–4);

3. these troublemakers were seeking to be justified by works, since they were trying to earn personal salvation by keeping the law perfectly (3:10; 5:3);

4. but personal faith is uniquely and exclusively saving (5:6).

In light of 1, 2, 3, and 4, the temptation to conclude the following is powerful:

5. personal justification by faith alone is the gospel or at least central to it.

Once this conclusion is drawn, another becomes inexorable:

6. Catholics are preaching a different gospel because they violate the principle that a person is justified by grace alone through faith alone, so they are cursed and cut off from Christ by Scripture's own standard.

Since the gospel defines the boundary for authentic Christianity, when this final deduction is made by Protestants, they feel assured of their own status and have legitimized the exclusion of Catholics from the Christian family.[2]

But hold on. Leaps have been made. Several considerations problematize the traditional Protestant logic, showing that while the Protestant critique remains weighty, something has gone awry.

Retooling the Language of Salvation

To reassess the classic Protestant critique, we need to be exacting about how the gospel, justification, and faith interface theologically.

Paul describes the gospel otherwise. The conclusion that "justification by faith" is central to the gospel is an inference drawn from a certain customary way of reading Galatians. It probably is a false one. When Paul and other New Testament authors actually describe the gospel's *content*, they never mention personalized justification by faith, let alone make that the centerpiece. Instead, they consistently give a royal narrative (akin to the ten events in part or in whole [listed in chap. 2]) about the Messiah (e.g., Rom. 1:2–4; 1 Cor. 15:3–5).

Thus, it is highly probable that Paul's intent with his "gospel" language in Galatians is a royal proclamation too. After all, Paul identifies himself as an ambassador of the resurrected king (Gal. 1:1). Then he narrates this king's self-donation: "He gave himself in place of our sins in order to deliver us from the present evil age" (1:4 AT). Furthermore, if we use Romans to help interpret Galatians, Paul says not that justification *is* the gospel but rather that the righteousness of God is *revealed in* (or through) the gospel (Rom. 1:17). The difference is crucial.

The differences between *revealing* the gospel and *being part of* the gospel are significant. Consider an analogy. I've secretly bought you, as my friend, a new wristwatch. I tell you, "Your birthday gift will be revealed at the party tonight." We would be making a category mistake if we were simply to equate the gift and the party. The party is *the occasion* or *event* for the gift's disclosure; it is not the gift itself. Meanwhile, the watch is a *benefit* occasioned by the party but should not be confused with the party proper.

In this analogy, the gospel is an event—like the party. Meanwhile, the righteousness of God is a gracious benefit fully revealed for the first time during the event—like the watch. Here's the main point: the gospel is not the righteousness of God (or justification) but rather the event that reveals it. *The righteousness of God is a benefit occasioned by the gospel—a benefit that is revealed in and through the gospel's arrival within human history. But the righteousness of God is not the gospel.* (For a fuller discussion of "the righteousness of God," see chap. 9.)

Personal forgiveness/justification are not included. The gospel's true *content* is all about what Jesus the king has done with the Father and the Spirit in accomplishing salvation. The gospel itself is the Christ events, which I've summarized in ten parts in chapter 2.

As we saw in chapter 3, the gospel includes benefits for the church and the world collectively considered but does not include our personal "faith" response or any of the benefits we individually receive. Let me give a few more examples from Scripture.

A person's realization of forgiveness or justification is not part of the gospel's objective content but instead depends on adequate response. For example, in Acts 10 Peter shares with Cornelius's family and friends the good news about how Jesus has become the saving king. When he does this, Peter states that personal receipt of forgiveness is *conditioned* on an adequate response: "all those who give faith unto him receive forgiveness of sins through his name" (Acts 10:43 AT). Potentially all can receive it, but only those who perform the "faith" (*pistis*) action actually attain personal forgiveness. Performance of the *pistis* action is the condition.

Or consider Paul's statement about how the righteousness of God is revealed in the gospel (Rom 1:17) as it is subsequently clarified by Paul: "the righteousness of God" is "for all those who perform the *pistis* action" (3:22 AT). Again, the righteousness of God is available to everyone, but it is conditioned on performing the "faith" action. Personal forgiveness or justification is not part of the objective content of the gospel but is a subjective conditional benefit of the gospel.

Allegiance alone? Protestants champion *faith alone* as the only saving response to the gospel. Among other texts, Galatians 5:6 does show that *pistis* is uniquely saving: only "faith *itself* working through love" avails. Yet famously Scripture also explicitly denies three times that *pistis* alone effects justification: "a person is justified by works and not by faith alone" (*ex ergōn dikaioutai anthrōpos kai ouk ek pisteōs monon*, James 2:24; cf. 2:17, 26). What does *pistis* mean?

I contend that Protestant-Catholic wrangling has been plagued by overly restrictive understandings of "faith." How *faith* is used today or how related terms were used at the time of the Protestant-Catholic split in the sixteenth century may or may not correspond to the Greek word *pistis*. What matters is the meaning of the ancient word *pistis*.

Pistis is a wide-ranging word. Recent scholarship has shown that its range includes trust, trustworthiness, faith, and loyalty, and that covenant fidelity is an especially important meaning in relevant literature.[3] But when talking about the *pistis* necessary for ultimate salvation, "faith" is best summarized as *trusting loyalty directed toward King Jesus* or *allegiance to the Christ*. I've offered extensive evidence for this claim at both the popular and the scholarly level.[4] Faulty ideas about faith include the following:

- Reducing saving faith to *belief in* (or mental assent to) the truthfulness of certain saving facts, like Jesus's death for sins and his resurrection from the dead.
- Reducing saving faith to *trust* (confident assurance) in God's saving promises. Saving faith cannot be systematically defined in the New Testament as merely inward confidence that Jesus has paid it all for me, or the like.
- Not aiming saving faith at the proper object. The proper object is Jesus as the *Christ-king*, who reveals the triune God, as he is described in the ten gospel events.
- Radically misconstruing the character of the king or God. That is, if your Christ permits theft, sexual immorality, greed, or other acts that Scripture calls sinful as an acceptable ongoing lifestyle under his rule, then your loyalty is to an idol of your own making, not the true king (1 Cor. 6:9–11; Gal. 5:19–21; Eph. 5:5–6; Rev. 22:15).
- Disconnecting saving faith from bodily enactment. "I have been crucified with the Christ and I no longer live, but the Christ lives in me; *the life I live in the flesh* I live by *pistis* [faith, loyalty] to the Son of God, who loved me and gave himself for me" (Gal. 2:20 AT). True *faith* is lived out *in the flesh* and necessarily turns away from habitual sinning to enact good deeds.

In fact, James denies that *pistis* alone can save precisely because saving faith can never be disconnected from good deeds that we perform with our bodies: "Faith by itself, if it does not have works, is dead" (James 2:17). This is true because saving faith is made *complete* by our deeds. In speaking about Abraham's justifying faith, James says, "You see that his faith and his actions were working together, and *his faith was made complete by what he did*" (2:22 NIV).

Since *pistis* in the New Testament can mean "loyalty," "fidelity," or "faithfulness"—all of which ordinarily presuppose inward "trust" yet focus on relational externalization with the body—to bring together what the New Testament holistically teaches, it is preferable to speak about salvation by "allegiance alone." The royal gospel invites an allegiant response.

Having gained a greater appreciation for the language of gospel, justification, and faith, we are in a better position to see why the traditional Protestant critique of Catholicism remains forceful yet partially misses the mark. I hope to offer a truer critical engagement here (see also chaps. 8–9).

Re-aiming the Protestant Critique

With these distinctions about the gospel, faith, and justification in view in a preliminary fashion, let's return to Galatians. The surface logic of Galatians wrongly leads Protestants to believe Catholics have abandoned the gospel. The aim here, drawing primarily from Galatians, is to expand these insights to correct the classic Protestant model and offer a more accurate critique of Catholicism.

Part-for-Whole

Regarding the troublemakers who have twisted the gospel in Galatians, what if classic Protestant interpreters have wrongly assumed that Paul is speaking about perversion to *the content* of the gospel, but Paul is after something different? Instead, what if Paul is pointing at how the troublemakers have twisted the gospel's *response* and its *effect*? This is called a part-for-whole reference, variously called *synecdoche*, *metonymy*, or *pars pro toto* by language experts. This use of language is very common.

We use part-for-whole all the time in everyday communication without thinking twice about it. Let's say we're eating lunch together. If you say, "My chicken tastes bland," I might reply, "Try this bottle." What I intend to communicate is "Take this bottle of barbeque sauce, extrude some of the sauce, and eat it on your chicken so that it will taste better."

With my "Try this bottle," I've referred to the bottle alone. But I'm not interested in the bottle per se—as if the plastic shell could improve the chicken. "Bottle" was just the easiest referent for evoking a holistic nexus of related associations. My reference to *the part*, the bottle, is a shorthand way of speaking about the significance of *the whole*, its special sauce-filled *content* and its taste-altering *effect* or *result*.

If Paul is doing the same, then the *content* of the gospel proper (the ten elements) is not under dispute in Galatia. Paul mentions the gospel because it is the easiest way to refer to a network of close associations that connect to the gospel: *response (pistis)* and beneficial *result* (justification).

Here's my proposal: in Galatians *pistis* as response and the attainment of justification as benefit are under dispute, but the content of the gospel itself, the ten events, is not. Paul's use of part-for-whole with *gospel* elsewhere in Galatians makes it highly probable that part-for-whole is in play too when Paul speaks of a "different gospel" in Galatians 1:6–7. As we will see below, Paul indisputably uses part-for-whole multiple times with regard to the gospel in Galatians, so it can't be said that this solution is unwarranted or a sleight of hand.

For example, consider part-for-whole with *gospel* in Galatians 2:7. What Paul actually says is "the gospel of the foreskin" (*to euangelion tēs akrobystias*). But in so doing, he is using part-for-whole thrice in a single phrase. First, the *foreskin* is merely a portion of the penis, but for Paul, by part-for-whole, it refers to the man who retains the foreskin (*the uncircumcised male*). Second, for Paul, *the uncircumcised male* refers by part-for-whole to a class of people, both male and female, outside of Judaism (*the gentiles*). Third, Paul's imagery evokes *the gentiles* as a part-for-whole to refer to a division of labor within the whole Christian mission: *Paul's mission to the gentiles* over against Peter's to the Jews. The words of Scripture actually say "the gospel of the foreskin," but Paul uses a chain of part-for-whole references to speak ultimately of the gospel of his gentile mission over against Peter's to the Jews. Here's a summary of Paul's implicit part-for-whole chain of reasoning:

> The "gospel of *the foreskin*" →
> the gospel of *the uncircumcised male* →
> the gospel of *the gentiles* →
> the gospel as that pertains to my gentile mission.

In sum, Paul is not announcing that the *content* of the gospel is about the penis. Yet that is what we might conclude if we were to fail to pay attention to his part-for-whole intentions. By "gospel of the foreskin," Paul actually intends the gospel as that pertains to his mission to the gentiles, and we know this because he directly compares it to Peter's mission to the Jews. Paul is so comfortable using part-for-whole that he uses it in a triple way to qualify his "gospel" language in Galatians 2:7.

Straight toward the Truth of the Gospel

Consider further Paul's part-for-whole use of "gospel" language in Galatians 2:14. When Paul for the first time discusses justification, he speaks about "the truth of the gospel" (2:14). Paul first describes Peter's table-fellowship behavior. Namely, as a Jew, Peter's initial practice had been to avoid dining with gentiles; yet after God's revelation to him (see Acts 10:28–29), Peter had begun to dine with uncircumcised gentiles (Gal. 2:12). In the eyes of at least some, this was to fail to uphold the "works of the law" (2:16). Yet when certain men came from James, Peter reversed course and began to eat only with the circumcised (2:12–13).

What Paul says about "the truth of the gospel" in Galatians 2:14 supports a part-for-whole interpretation. Specifically, Paul says, "But when I saw that *they were not walking straight toward the truth of the gospel*, I said to Cephas in front of them all . . ." (AT). Notice! Paul does not say that Peter and his associates were violating the *content* of the gospel. He says something different: Peter and his associates "were not walking straight toward the truth of the gospel" (*ouk orthopodousin pros tēn alētheian tou euangeliou*). Nor, contrary to Luther, Calvin, and their heirs, does Paul say that justification (or faith) *is* the gospel or even part of it. In actuality, justification pertains to something obliquely yet closely related: living in alignment with *the gospel's truth*.

Peter's *behavior* wasn't moving toward or in alignment with the truth of the gospel. This suggests not a compromise in the gospel's content but a compromise of the gospel's *lived effect*, *actualized benefits*, or *practical results*. Peter had compromised not the gospel's raw content but its theological truthfulness as this pertained to its behavioral outworking. In Galatians 2:14 Paul uses "the gospel" in a part-for-whole fashion to refer to *behavior that results* from the gospel's truth that affects the wider community.

In other words, in Galatians *Paul aligns justification (by faith) with correct practices that safeguard the gospel's truth but does not identify justification as part of or equivalent to the gospel's content*. This is exactly what we would expect if a person's justification is a benefit that results from the gospel and is conditioned on giving allegiance to the king but is not part of the gospel itself.

As further evidence that this interpretation is correct, we find the same in Galatians 2:5, where "the truth of the gospel" refers not to the gospel's content but to Titus's *behavior*. Specifically, "the truth of the gospel" in 2:5 refers to Titus's *refusal to accept circumcision when pressured by the troublemakers* (2:2–5). These references in 2:5 and 2:14 not to the gospel directly but to behavioral norms that pertain to "the truth of the gospel" are exactly what we would expect if Paul sees the personal attainment of justification as a result, effect, or benefit of the gospel rather than part of the gospel's essential content.

Peter's works-of-the-law table-fellowship activities did not deny the gospel of Jesus's kingship directly. None of the ten elements were compromised. But Peter's behavior did not accord with *the truth of the gospel* in its one-family purpose or effect. Hold this thought.

The One-Family Gospel Purpose

The most precise statements of the gospel's purpose indicate that it is for "the obedience of faith"—that is, allegiant obedience to Jesus the king among all the nations (Rom. 1:5; 16:26). However, within this gospel purpose the nations are joined to Israel, becoming one body in the Messiah. Paul says that the mystery "is that the gentiles are coheirs with Israel, co-bodied, and co-sharers of the promise in the Christ, Jesus—*through the gospel*" (Eph. 3:6 AT).

Paul speaks about this in Galatians when he says, "The Scripture, foreseeing that God would justify the gentiles by faith, preached *the gospel* in advance to Abraham, '*All nations will be blessed in you*'" (Gal. 3:8 AT). In Galatians 3:8 the gospel that Scripture announced in advance to Abraham is not justification by faith but expressly *all nations will be blessed in you*. The gospel here pertains to the arrival of the Messiah as a fulfillment of God's promise to Abraham regarding his singular seed (3:16).

For Paul, "by faith" in Galatians 3:8 refers first to the faith (loyalty) of the king, through whom the blessing of Abraham has come to the gentiles via the Spirit (3:14). It is probable that it secondarily includes all who give loyalty to the king (3:11; cf. Rom. 1:17). The result is that we are "all *one* in the Messiah, Jesus" (Gal. 3:28 AT). Once again Paul does not say that the gospel *is* or *includes* our justification by faith; rather, the justification of the gentiles is a *result* of the gospel, and "by faith" describes the instrumental means by which the blessing comes to them. But if the key gospel purpose is to create one allegiant worldwide family under the rule of the one and only King of kings, then Paul's "justification" language makes sense:

> We know that a person is not justified by works of the law but through the loyalty of Jesus the king, so we also have given loyalty

to the king, Jesus, in order to be justified by the loyalty of the king and not by works of the law, because by works of the law no one will be justified. (Gal. 2:16 AT)

Through the king's loyalty to God and to God's people the gospel creates one worldwide family out of the many nations. That is, the gospel does this when people give their allegiance to the king as a response to it. In Galatia, table-fellowship rules that reinstituted distinctively Jewish "works of the law" practices were splitting that one people into Jew and gentile factions, *denying the truth of the gospel in its one-family purpose and result.*

In other words, justification by *pistis* is not the gospel (nor part of it) but rather a key doctrine that safeguards the unity of the one true church. It shows that those who create false dividing walls, such as Jew and gentile, within the one true Jesus-is-king church are massively and dangerously in the wrong.

The Sad Irony of Justification

It is a tragic irony. Justification by faith is true. We can even say that justification by faith alone is true if faith includes embodied loyalty per Scripture. But those who make justification by faith alone the centerpiece of the gospel—whether Reformers like Luther and Calvin or contemporary pastor-leaders like Piper and MacArthur—have created *precisely the dividing wall* in the church that Paul's doctrine of justification seeks to avoid.

R. C. Sproul's words express the typical Protestant sentiment: "The Reformers concluded that when Rome rejected and condemned sola fide, it condemned itself, in effect, it ceased to be a true church."[5] As Sproul's example indicates, justification by faith alone has always been the main weapon that Protestants use to declare that Catholics have not responded to the gospel, are not justified, and therefore are not part of the true church.

Meanwhile, historically speaking, the Catholic Church has wrongly insisted that justification is by the instrumentality of its sacraments of baptism and penance alone and has formally excommunicated those who disagree. Thankfully and importantly, the Catholic Church has now softened this position. In its most recent ecumenical council, Vatican II, Catholicism weakened its sacramental absolutes for personal salvation without explaining how to understand its previous absolutes. In a document issued by Pope Paul VI, Christians outside the Catholic communion are now said to be "in some real way . . . joined with us in the Holy Spirit."[6]

In short, on both sides of the Protestant-Catholic aisle, the theology and rhetoric around justification has tended to alienate and harden. As we shall see, this is especially tragic, because if Scripture is our standard, then the building of walls between gospel-affirming Christians is precisely *the opposite* of how the doctrine of justification by faith is supposed to function in the church. To justify means "to declare righteous," but its purpose is not personal or even communal right-standing before God as an end unto itself. Justification's practical ethical and pastoral aim is to safeguard *the unity* of the one "declared righteous" church as that is constituted when we confess allegiance to the one king together.

In Scripture, a primary function of justification by faith (allegiance) is to guarantee that the one true church can never be divided into we-are-more-righteous-than-you-in-God's-eyes parts or tiers. Whether Peter eats with the uncircumcised or the circumcised does nothing to alter the status of both groups as fully "declared righteous" within one family in God's eyes; yet it does in the eyes of humans who can easily be misled into thinking those who perform "works of the law" are righteous but others are not.

The irony would be funny if it weren't so tragic. During the course of church history, we've managed to flip upside down how God intended the doctrine of justification to function practically within the church. We've allowed justification to split the one and only Jesus-is-king professing church into Protestant versus Catholic factions, each declaring that they are truly righteous in God's sight while the other is not. Since there is only one God, who gives only one gospel that is centered on only one victorious king, *one and only one worldwide justified church is indivisibly created as allegiance to the king is confessed.*

85

On both sides of the Catholic-Protestant divide, the Western church has mobilized the doctrine of justification pastorally in precisely the opposite way God intended for it to function. Justification is supposed to safeguard unity, not create and reinforce dividing walls. When we recognize that justification is not part of the gospel but rather a communal *benefit* of the gospel first, and a personal benefit only secondarily, the church might begin to experience ecumenical healing.

Toward a Better Reading of Galatians

In the next subsection I'll propose a more accurate reading of Galatians. But in order to prepare the way, let's work through a few common questions.

What about Works?

In my experience teaching this material, I've noticed a common obstacle to understanding: a failure to distinguish between *works* and *works of the law*. Classic Protestantism assumes that Paul objects to *all works* with regard to justification. But Paul's concern is not with *works in general* (any and every deed) but more precisely with *works of the law*.[7]

Works of the law were mandatory practices that functioned to show which Jews were maintaining God's old covenant faithfully and which were not. They were not merely social boundary markers. They were still laws amid other laws that needed to be performed. But their primary function was to divide insiders from outsiders—faithful Jews from unfaithful Jews and gentiles.

Paul describes works of the law. He associates circumcision, the observance of special sacred days, and table-fellowship rules with "works of law" (Rom. 3:27–30; Gal. 2:16; 4:9–10; Col. 2:16). Here is the key point: *Paul rejects the saving value not of all good works but only of works of the law*. Misunderstandings to the contrary involve a failure to notice or accept that Paul sometimes abbreviates "works of the law" as "works" (e.g., Rom. 3:27; 9:32), which also explains key texts like Ephesians 2:8–10.[8]

Doing is required. In fact, for Paul, good works consistently form part of the basis for final salvation (e.g., Rom. 2:6; 2 Cor. 5:10; Gal. 6:7–10; 2 Tim. 4:14; cf. Matt. 16:27; John 5:28–29). It is "the *doers* of the law who will be justified" (Rom. 2:13) as the Spirit assists us, so that those who are allegiant to the king perform deeds that fulfill the law's deepest intent (2:29; 8:4; 8:13). Moreover, Paul's earliest interpreters who weigh in on the matter—second-century Christians such as Ignatius of Antioch, Justin Martyr, and Irenaeus—interpreted Paul to be saying that good works in general have a saving value as an expression of faith but that works of the law as an independent system have no saving value (e.g., circumcision, food laws, and observing special days).[9] The earliest church's understanding of Paul's theology was that works of the law had no independent saving value, but within an allegiance-to-the-Christ framework, good works formed part of the basis for final salvation.

How Can Works Be Required, Since Our Works Are Imperfect?

This question betrays a partial misunderstanding. Perfection in performing the law or "good works" was never required for final salvation within the Mosaic covenant. Hence Jews in Paul's day did not believe that perfect obedience was required for participation in the blessed age to come.

This shows that the timeless fundamental human problem cannot possibly be the "doing of deeds" to try to please God as opposed to trusting in him. There has been a Protestant tendency to oversimplify on this point. God's people *were commanded to perform works of the law* in the Old Testament, including offering sacrifices for worship and participation in the atonement system. Part of the reason why Jews in Paul's day did not believe that God required sinless perfection for salvation was that their covenant contained a God-given sacrificial system designed to facilitate forgiveness (e.g., Lev. 1–7; 16). In the Old Testament sinless perfection was neither expected nor required for salvation, and "works" were required for forgiveness.

Yet Paul requires perfection. But the question is only a partial misunderstanding because Paul came to believe something different from what his fellow Jews believed. Paul came to believe that perfect obedience to the law was absolutely required for those who would seek justification by the terms of the Mosaic covenant. Since this almost certainly departs from what Paul believed when a Pharisee prior to his encounter with the risen Lord, it is best to conclude that Paul's new convictions about the Christ changed his mind.

Paul says that anyone who seeks to be justified by works of the law is guilty if he or she does not keep *everything* in the *entire* law. He says this explicitly twice and implies it elsewhere (Gal. 3:10; 5:3; Rom. 2:25; cf. James 2:10). Yet this is not because the old-covenant law demanded perfect righteousness with no possibility for forgiveness. *We must conclude that Paul was convinced that the covenantal arrangement itself had fundamentally altered with the coming of the Christ.*

The simplest solution is that Paul believed that the old covenant was no longer able to effect forgiveness. For Paul, the sacrificial system embedded in the Mosaic law had reached its "end" (*telos*— i.e., goal and completion) in the Christ events that constitute the gospel (Rom. 10:4). Thus, anyone now seeking to be justified by the Mosaic law is required to maintain its demands perfectly or be liable for the whole (Gal. 3:10; 5:3). Although the old covenant previously was effective in its sin-atoning capacity, inasmuch as it anticipated the king's atonement (Rom. 3:25), the old covenant no longer atones. If we are in the king, we have been delivered out of the old epoch (Gal. 1:4), even though we should still be instructed by it (Rom. 15:4; 1 Cor. 9:9). We participate in the new creation (Gal. 6:15).

Why Was the Old Covenant Unable to Justify?

This deliverance from the old covenant was necessary because the old covenant was part of the old epoch of creation. Within this old epoch, not only were we in bondage to evil spiritual powers, but the very structure of the old order was also arrayed against us. Paul calls this fundamental structuring of the old order the *stoicheia* (see Gal. 4:3, 9; Col. 2:8, 20).

Sin was operative in a parasitic fashion, piggybacking on this old order, making use of the *stoicheia* to infect us. In other words, the old-covenant law itself was God-given and good, but it was structured within the old creation, so that sin consistently resonated with the old order, crossing over through its elements to enslave humanity (e.g., Rom. 7:7–13).

But with the Messiah's advent, a *new creation* has already broken into the midst of the old. We are liberated from sin's domineering tyranny. We've been given a new covenant (Gal. 3:15–17; 4:21–31; cf. 2 Cor. 3:6) as the hallmark of this new creation in the king (Gal. 6:15; cf. 1 Cor. 7:19; 2 Cor. 5:17). Universally binding terms of loyalty within this new covenant can be spelled out or met not through a written code but only by the Spirit (2 Cor. 3:3–6, 12–18).

Speaking specifically about justification, Paul explains why the old covenant is no longer effective for forgiveness: "If I rebuild what I tore down, I prove myself to be a transgressor" (Gal. 2:18). Paul is speaking about what it would mean to rebuild the "works of the law" (2:16). To do so would be to turn back to the dysfunctional old order. It would be to turn away from the liberated new creation that is constituted by the king's reign via the Spirit's presence. Any person who reinstalls that *stoicheia*-based old system proves to be a violator of its regulations. Since the old-covenant system has reached its goal and end, forgiveness can no longer flow through it.

Here's the upshot: *Anyone who attempts to reinstate the old covenant or any other written-rule system of salvation, whether in whole or in part, will violate God's law, incurring the same guilt as someone who has violated every regulation within it.* The written regulations of the old covenant no longer function as universally binding mandates, for God's Spirit guides humans to obey the deepest intentions of the law in the Christ. The terms of true allegiance to the king cannot be defined or dictated by any written-rule system, for the Spirit alone can dictate how to fulfill the intent of God's law in the Christ.

A Better Reading of Galatians

In a previous section we explored the surface logic that fuels the traditional Protestant critique of Catholicism. Now that we've sharpened the conversation, the root issues have been exposed.

I suggest that this alternative logic more faithfully captures the spirit of Paul's criticism of the troublemakers in Galatia and its applicability to Protestant critiques of Catholicism:

1. Paul uses "part-for-whole" language with regard to the gospel frequently in Galatians, and this best explains his reference to gospel compromise. Although the gospel was being corrupted in Galatia (Gal. 1:6–9), it was not the *content* of the gospel that was being twisted but rather the gospel's *means* and *results*. The perversion pertained to a failure to walk correctly with regard to "the truth of the gospel" (2:5, 14). This referred to *correct practices that display and safeguard the gospel's **result** of one justified family* (3:29).

2. The troublemakers certainly were committed to Jesus as the Christ, but they believed that right-standing with God came through *pistis* toward the king *plus* works of law, such as circumcision (Gal. 5:1–6).

3. These troublemakers were seeking to be justified not by *works*—moral effort, or good deeds in general—but rather by *works of the law* (Gal. 2:16; 3:2, 5, 10). That is, they believed that circumcision, kosher observance, and keeping sabbath/festivals (as a supplement to "faith") could delineate who *truly* had right-standing before God.

4. Personal justification is neither the gospel nor part of the gospel but is a result or benefit of the gospel. Justification's logic is *group first* (see chaps. 2–3). The Jesus-is-king community was justified together first when the Spirit was poured out at Pentecost. Subsequently, any individual can receive "justification" as a gospel benefit too. When a person repentantly declares allegiance to Jesus as the Christ, the king's justified body obtains a new member as the Spirit applies the benefits of salvation to that individual.

5. Good works are included within faith. The idea here is that bodily faith is the primary cause and works the secondary cause

within faith's purview. There are a number of classic Protestant theologians in the Reformed tradition who have identified faith as the primary cause of justification but works as a valid secondary instrumental or effective cause.[10] My view adds nuance inasmuch as saving faith is not merely mental but also bodily.

Saving faith is relationally externalized so that it includes deeds of loyalty, but a list of required specific good works can't be universally mandated as part of a rule-based system of salvation without morphing into a species of works of the law. Works of the law are different from works in general. Works of the law are ineffective for salvation because the foundational elements within the old order (the *stoicheia*) allow sin to dominate humans who rely on such systems. A works-of-the-law system demands universal conformity to a binding list of regulations, but it does nothing to empower obedience, because it necessarily functions within the old order.

Yet in the king a new creation blossoms in the midst of the old creation, supplanting it. The church has resurrection life and Spirit empowerment. Within the new creation, God's law is personally fulfilled not because the letter dictates it but because the individual heart, as it is being transformed by participation in the Spirit-guided community, desires it.

Applying Galatians to Catholicism

I've sought to expose aspects of Paul's doctrine of justification in the preceding sections. How might such insights from Galatians inform Catholicism? It is well-known that Protestants prioritize Scripture in formulating doctrine, while Catholics give more space to the church's tradition and the authority of the pope. But to what degree? How exactly does Scripture function theologically for Catholics?

Scripture, Tradition, and Authority in Catholicism

If Catholicism eventually reforms its official teaching about justification, it will be because, by Catholicism's own standards,

Paul's doctrine in Galatians, Romans, and elsewhere *must* inform its theology as part of Scripture alongside tradition and authority.

Catholics believe that three divinely revealed entities exist and must coordinate: *the teaching office* (the pope in conjunction with the bishops), *sacred Scripture* (the Bible), and *sacred tradition* (authoritative traditions that developed during church history). For Catholics, the church's teaching office was established by Jesus. Meanwhile, sacred Scripture and sacred tradition flow "from the same divine wellspring" as God reveals himself to humans.[11] For Catholics, the teaching office, Scripture, and tradition all originated through God's special revelation within time, because God ordained them to be mutually supporting and interdependent. When the Catholic teaching office, headed by the pope, fixedly determines a meaning within Scripture or tradition, it is expressed as a *dogma*—a statement of mandatory belief or practice. This new dogma becomes authoritative in its own right as part of the growing tradition.

Catholics do not believe that individuals have the right to authentically decide for themselves or others what the Bible means. As the Catholic Church's most authoritative statement, *Dei Verbum*, puts it, "The task of authentically interpreting the word of God, whether written or handed on, has been entrusted exclusively to the living teaching office of the Church."[12] This means that the current pope alone, in consultation with the living bishops, has the right to determine what the Bible and church history mean.

This puts the individual who is trying to assess the truthfulness of Catholicism in an awkward place. From the Catholic vantage point, no individual can make Catholicism's fidelity to Scripture or history a criterion when testing Catholicism's truthfulness, since neither that individual nor any other has the right to authoritatively interpret Scripture or tradition in order to determine whether Catholic doctrine is in fact true. For Catholics, private individuals—whether laypeople, priests, Catholic, non-Catholic, or professional scholars—have no right to decide what Scripture, tradition, or Catholic doctrine truly means.

But here is the important part for our purposes: for Catholics, this does not mean that the pope or bishops should allow tradition to override the Bible. *Dei Verbum* states, "This teaching office is not above the word of God, but serves it, teaching only what has been handed on, listening to it devoutly, guarding it scrupulously and explaining it faithfully."[13] By Catholicism's own standards, the Catholic teaching office is *"not above the word of God,"* which includes Scripture, in formulating dogma. The Catholic teaching office is not allowed to contradict the Bible but must serve, heed, and teach *"only what has been handed on"* with respect to Scripture's doctrine.

The rub, of course, is that within today's Catholicism, only the current pope (in consultation with the living bishops) can rightfully determine what Scripture means so as to determine whether current Catholic dogma is in fact faithful to Scripture's doctrine. I leave it for the reader to decide whether this circular reasoning process is virtuous or vicious for individuals who are trying to discover the truth. Whatever the case, *if the Catholic Church is to remain true to its own dogmatic standard, then the doctrine found in Scripture must be heeded and faithfully transmitted by its teaching office.* The actual Catholic view is that Scripture's doctrine cannot be scrubbed out or overwritten by later tradition. The Catholic Church must faithfully hand on the witness of Scripture and the earliest church. In light of this, I submit that the truths of Scripture presented here should pressure the Catholic teaching office to reform its dogmas.

Galatians and Catholicism

The good news is that official Catholic doctrine acknowledges allegiance to Jesus the king. This is true even if it is neglected in its official teaching. Since the confession "Jesus is the Christ" creates and constitutes the authentic church, practicing Catholics are certainly part of the one true church under ordinary circumstances. For it is this confession that summarizes the gospel and actualizes its saving power. This is why I regard Catholics as my brothers and sisters in the king, and I celebrate and honor them as full family members.

Despite the rhetoric of classic Protestantism, the Catholic system is not wrong because it requires "doing"—works, effort, or good deeds—for salvation in general. After all, Paul says that good works are required for salvation and calls us to work out our salvation. Catholicism is not wrong because it fundamentally fails to appreciate grace. Nor is the problem necessarily that individual Catholics do not trust Jesus alone, since their good works—including personal sacramental efforts—may genuinely be empowered by the Spirit. Participating in the sacraments is not in and of itself problematic except inasmuch as they are made mandatory for salvation in ways that contradict the doctrine of Scripture and the church's earliest traditions.

I love my Catholic brothers and sisters, so I offer the following remarks as strong medicine based on the unchanging testimony of Scripture and earliest Christian history. These remarks are offered in the charitable hope that Catholicism will ultimately reform its dogmas. If Scripture is part of the unyielding standard—and it is for Catholics and Protestants alike—then there are errors in current Catholic teachings about salvation.

Much like the troublemakers in Galatia, Catholicism legislates what sacramental deeds must be completed for salvation for every person. This written code creates an old-creation false boundary akin to works of the law within the one family of God. *A central Catholic error regarding salvation is the belief that the terms of true allegiance can be universally and officially mandated through a list of must-do and must-not-do commands via the sacraments for everyone.*

As Paul says with reference to works of the law as a system of justification, "For if what I tore down, I again rebuild, I establish myself to be a lawbreaker" (Gal. 2:18 AT). Paul is saying that works of the law cannot save and that *any attempt to introduce an alternative written-regulation system of salvation similar to "works of the law" will only serve to prove that we are rule-breakers in need of salvation from that alternative system.* To create a salvation system with required enumerated commands is to turn back the clock to the old order, to allow sin to resonate with the *stoicheia.*

Sacraments in general can be celebrated as helpful for the Christian life when their performative terms are not made mandatory for salvation. The traditional Catholic position is that the sacraments are absolutely mandatory, but as noted above, *Lumen Gentium* has undermined this position by affirming that other Christian communions are somehow really "joined with us in the Holy Spirit" (§15).

In what follows I will criticize the mandatory position, with the understanding that there is tension in Catholic dogma over this issue presently. To the degree that it *requires* specific regulations of sacramental performance for *everyone* for salvation, the Catholic position wrongly and very dangerously asserts that the one true church can successfully be defined by something other than gospel allegiance and the Spirit. But Catholicism has officially softened this position without fully correcting or explaining—and this is a hopeful sign! Accordingly, Catholics do not belong under the anathema that Paul describes in Galatians but are justified, part of God's one worldwide family.

Mandatory Activities among Catholics

While expressing "faith" as essential, Catholics have universally binding mandates that everyone must perform or risk damnation. If it is to be a faithful servant of God's word per its own standard, the Catholic Church should reconsider its current dogmas, testing whether they deny the *only-one-body result* of the gospel as described in Galatians. In my view, Catholic dogma wrongly suggests that the community of the justified (and any individuals therein) must be marked out by things other than Spirit-led allegiance to the king in at least four ways: penance, holy days, acceptance of the whole dogma, and baptism.

Penance. Catholicism asserts that if you commit an intentional, serious sin after baptism, you have forfeited the justifying righteousness that you obtained at baptism. The Council of Trent declares that if anyone who has sinned after baptism claims to be able to recover righteousness "by faith alone without the sacrament of penance," then that person is cursed and separated from

Christ.[14] This is to impose an old-order "works of the law" type rule and to make it a mandatory requirement for allegiance— exactly what Paul opposes in Galatians. For Catholics, the only recourse for regaining justification is to confess one's sins to a priest in hopes of acquiring an absolution.

Yet for Catholics, even within absolution there is still a lingering and unresolved effect of sin that makes penance necessary. Penance involves undertaking a disciplinary penalty in association with a sin. Although Catholics believe that "absolution takes away sin," at the same time "it does not remedy all the disorders sin has caused." So in order for a person to recover "full spiritual health," *penance* is imposed by the priest in accordance with "the gravity and nature of the sins committed." The purpose of penance is expressly to *"make satisfaction for"* or *"expiate"* *the sin.*[15]

Although Catholicism claims that Christ alone has expiated our sins, it also, for reasons that are not fully explained, affirms that it is nevertheless necessary for the sinner to suffer with Christ in penance (while accepting his assistance) in order to become a coheir with him. Common forms of penance include agreeing to pray a Hail Mary sequence, undertaking a fast, performing a work of mercy, or serving a neighbor.

Yet these dogmas about penance do not accord with Scripture or the teachings of the apostles. The Catholic bishops at Trent wrongly believed penance to be biblical because commands in the Bible to "repent" (Greek *metanoeō*) had been mistranslated in Latin as "do penance." The Council of Trent's "Decree on Justification" cites Matthew 3:2, Acts 2:38, and Revelation 2:5 in support of "do penance," but the original Greek, as opposed to the Latin Vulgate, actually says "repent" in these places. The meaning "do penance" is not possible for the Bible in the way Trent intends, since the system of penance and absolution by a priest was not in place until after the Donatist crisis in the third century. Jesus and the apostles lived in the first.

When making observations about the tensions between Scripture and Catholic doctrine, here and elsewhere, I am not advocating that the church should believe in Scripture alone—I believe in molecules, pianos, and rockets, and so should you. Along with other traditionally minded Protestants, I contend that *sola scriptura* means that the Bible should serve as the final court of appeal over tradition and church authority. *Sola scriptura* allows for valid traditions to develop beyond what is explicit in the Bible. For example, the doctrine of the Trinity is not explicitly articulated in Scripture, but its fourth-century expression does emerge from and accord with the Bible.[16] Valid theological traditions can develop, but they must accord with Scripture.

My concern with Catholicism's use of Scripture and tradition as it pertains to salvation is much more specific: when the Catholic Church claims that the restoration of justification has *always* required the sacrament of penance via priestly mediation, such that the Catholic sacrament of penance (reconciliation) today continues apostolic practices and teachings about salvation, this is a faulty claim in light of Scripture and earliest Christian history.[17]

There is no evidence that Jesus or the apostles commanded penance or absolution by a human priest within the framework of the new covenant—especially since, apart from Jesus as the high priest, *there is no evidence for human priests of the new covenant at all* in the earliest Christianity represented by the New Testament writings.[18]

Catholicism asserts that during the sacrament of penance (reconciliation) the forgiveness is offered by Christ himself in the person of the human priest. This assertion rests on the notion that human priests, when validly ordained, participate in Jesus Christ's unique high priesthood—although there is no genuine scriptural support for such an idea. For Catholicism, a mortal sin is not absolved until the person seeking reconciliation and the priest perform the sacramental action, for as with baptism, the forgiving grace is dispensed by God only by the performance of the sacrament itself (*ex opere operato*). Under normal circumstances, for Catholicism, a person who opts not to participate in the sacrament of reconciliation is not justified by God and is in danger of hell.

Catholic theology here is also difficult to reconcile with Hebrews 10:10–14, in which Jesus's high priestly sacrifice of his own body is said to be perfectly efficacious *ephapax* ("once for all") and *eis to diēnekes* ("for all time"):

> And by that will we have been sanctified through the offering of the body of Jesus Christ once for all [*ephapax*]. And every [old covenant] priest stands daily at his service, offering repeatedly the same sacrifices, which can never take away sins. But when Christ had offered for all time [*eis to diēnekes*] a single sacrifice for sins, he sat down at the right hand of God, waiting from that time until his enemies should be made a footstool for his feet. For by a single offering he has perfected for all time [*eis to diēnekes*] those who are being sanctified. (Heb. 10:10–14)

The "once for all" and "for all time" description of the perfect efficacy of the Christ's heavenly offering and high priestly mediation is difficult to square with the Catholic claim that the Christ's sacrifice must be made effective through new covenant earthly priests mediating that one sacrifice *repeatedly through the flow of time* during the Catholic Mass.

By making the sacrament of penance and absolution by a priest to be a mandatory practice for salvation, the Catholic Church excludes the apostles and their heirs from the church, for they never carried out such practices.

Holy days. Beyond the sacraments, certain fasts, holy days, and Sunday Mass are also obligatory for Catholics. To knowingly fail to observe these days without a valid reason, according to Roman Catholic teaching, is a mortal sin that forfeits a person's innocence (justification) in God's sight.[19] If an obligatory fast or holy day is wrongfully missed, absolution and penance as described above are required for the restoration of justification.

Paul indicates that it is impossible to maintain justification by keeping commands within a written-regulation system, such as the command to observe holy days and fasts. To say that Paul is not friendly toward mandatory holy days for justification is a considerable understatement. Paul says to the Galatians,

> But now that you have come to know God, or rather to be known
> by God, how can you turn back again to the weak and worthless
> elementary principles [*stoicheia*] of the world, whose slaves you
> want to be once more? You observe days and months and seasons
> and years! I am afraid I may have labored over you in vain. (Gal.
> 4:9–11; cf. Col. 2:14–17)

To reinstate universally required holy days—as Catholicism
does—is to reinstitute an old-order written-rule system, to turn
back to the *stoicheia*. This plays into sin's hand. Such rules create
false walls in the one true church, and those who rely on those walls
rather than or in addition to allegiance to the king compromise the
one-justified-family *benefit* and *result* of the gospel. Only Spirit-
based allegiance to the king allows the flesh to become obedient
to the deepest intentions of the law of God.

Acceptance of the whole dogma. Another false boundary pertains to Catholic dogma. A common contemporary reaction to
the Catholic-Protestant dispute is to believe that one should join
whichever captures more of the truth. This is not, however, a genuine option with regard to Catholicism.

To be Catholic you must consent to *all* that the Catholic Church
officially teaches—its entire dogma—or you are by default a heretic or schismatic. (Officially Catholicism regards Protestantism
as both schismatic and heretical.) You must agree not just about
justification, faith, and works, but about *everything*—to the degree
that it is understood—or you are outside the Catholic Church.
This is a false boundary because both Scripture and experience
show that a person can be united with the Spirit while disagreeing
with Catholic dogma.

As a test case, consider Mary's immaculate conception. Catholicism claims that when Mary was conceived by her parents, she did
not receive the stain of original sin, so that she subsequently remained sinless and perpetually a virgin. Let's say a practicing Catholic investigates the scriptural basis and historicity of this claim.

There is no evidence that Mary's immaculate conception was
held by Jesus, the apostles, their immediate successors, or the

ancient church in general. It was a minority view until the late Middle Ages and became a dogma less than two hundred years ago.[20] Mary's perpetual virginity is explicitly denied in Scripture: "Joseph did not know Mary *until* she had given birth to a son, and he named him Jesus" (Matt. 1:25 AT). Since this indisputably refers to sexual knowing, Matthew straightforwardly indicates that Joseph did indeed have sexual intercourse with Mary *after* Jesus was born. Catholic dogma about Mary's perpetual virginity contradicts Scripture.

Moreover, Mary certainly appears to have sinned when she opposed Jesus's ministry (Mark 3:21–31), which conflicts with Catholic claims about her sinlessness. When told that his mother and brothers are outside trying to stop him, Jesus explicitly indicates that Mary and his brothers have *failed to do God the Father's will* (3:35). By normal Christian standards, Mary's behavior was both *a sin of commission*, by actively opposing Jesus's obviously beneficial ministry, and *a sin of omission*, by failing to do the Father's will.

Mary's immaculate conception is not described in the New Testament. In terms of history, its first intimations appear in the late second- or early third-century document the Protoevangelium of James. Scholars agree that the Protoevangelium of James as a whole is replete with historical impossibilities and inaccuracies.[21]

From the official Catholic vantage point, a person who stops believing essential Catholic dogma is outside the church. If a Catholic stops believing in Mary's immaculate conception or perpetual virginity or, while struggling to understand how they could be true, ceases to believe or trust what the Catholic Church teaches regarding these dogmas, then this person has been *instantly excommunicated*—even if the church takes no official action subsequently. (Technically this person has become a schismatic by their own action, incurring a *latae sententiae excommunication*.[22]) With regard to Catholicism, individuals cannot pick and choose which doctrines should be believed and which should be rejected. A professing Catholic who does not consent to *the whole dogma* is not in fact Catholic—even if they insist otherwise—because that person has already been excommunicated from the Catholic Church.

Baptism. A final obstacle should be mentioned. Within Catholic dogma, it is impossible to be justified apart from baptism because it is the one and only instrument (tool) that God uses to cause justification. Yet this disregards what Scripture teaches. The next chapter will discuss why.

Under ordinary circumstances Catholics are fully Christians because they make the key gospel confession that Jesus is the Christ. This means Catholics are justified, part of God's one worldwide family.

Protestants frequently draw upon Galatians to accuse Catholics of compromising the gospel. As the Reformers tried to correct soteriological errors in the sixteenth century, however, they read Galatians imprecisely. Justification by faith was wrongly treated as part of the gospel in the Protestant polemic against Catholicism. Then justification by faith was wielded to claim that Catholics have abandoned the gospel and hence are outside the church.

A close reading of Paul's letters shows that personal justification is not part of the gospel but rather one of its leading benefits. Faith is not part of the gospel either. Saving faith is best understood as an allegiant response to the King Jesus gospel. Paul's doctrine of justification by faith is purposed to show that there is one, and only one, righteous family and that this family is the family that gives allegiance to King Jesus.

I'm persuaded that Catholics, Orthodox, and Protestants are not equally and fully correct in their doctrinal determinations. I've sketched common Protestant problems and have also shown how the doctrine of justification in Galatians should pressure the Catholic Church toward specific reforms in dogma. Nevertheless, each is equally and fully Christian inasmuch as each upholds and responds with allegiance to the royal gospel. In our overall attempt to move beyond salvation wars of the past and present, in this book's final chapters we will return to the question of how justification is presently modeled among Catholics and Protestants, and then we will seek to *remodel* it.

But if our remodeling is to help the church in some small way move beyond past salvation wars, we must examine how other key pieces of the puzzle might (or might not!) contribute to the overall picture of salvation: baptism, election, regeneration, and perseverance. The next three chapters will seek to navigate these tricky and controversial topics, showing how they fit into the overarching gospel-allegiance proposal.

5 Is Baptism Saving?

Salvation wars of the past have colored even the pure waters of baptism red. "All who take the sword will perish by the sword" (Matt. 26:52). Jesus's words proved true for Ulrich Zwingli. Zwingli died battling Catholics, but previously Zwingli had wielded violence against his own.

Zwingli was so persuasive in his reforming efforts that his most eager students surpassed him. When the magistrates of Zurich ordered all infants to be baptized within eight days, key Reformation leaders met to determine a course of action:

> It came to pass that Ulrich Zwingli and Conrad Grebel, one of the aristocracy, and Felix Mantz . . . recognized that infant baptism is unnecessary and recognized further that it is in fact no baptism. Two, however, Conrad and Felix, recognized in the Lord and believed [further] that one must and should be correctly baptized . . . since Christ himself says that whoever *believes* and is baptized will be saved.[1]

Zwingli reportedly was persuaded against infant baptism, but he failed to advocate against it because he feared an uprising and persecution. Instead he sided with the city's magistrates.

But Grebel and Mantz determined that only upon "recognized and confessed faith," while having achieved "the union with God of a good conscience," should a person receive baptism.[2] A former Catholic priest, George Cajocob (Blaurock), requested that Grebel baptize him, and in turn he baptized Grebel and Mantz. The Anabaptist movement was born.

The Anabaptists were fiercely persecuted for teaching that baptism must be voluntary, yet their ranks swelled. The Zurich authorities issued an ultimatum: anyone caught rebaptizing would be drowned. Mantz continued, so the magistrates drowned him in the city's river. He was the first to receive this gruesome "third baptism." Despite the bloodshed, the Anabaptist movement grew.

The church is divided—past and present—over different understandings of whether, why, and how baptism is saving. Yet historical inquiry has now put it beyond reasonable doubt: the earliest Christians held a strictly *voluntary* theological position with respect to baptism. This can be shown not only from Scripture but also secondarily by evidence from early Judaism and early Christian documents that were not available in the initial phases of the Reformation. *In the New Testament and during earliest Christianity (through AD 200), baptism was deemed effective for personal salvation only on the basis of voluntary personalist repentance and expressed loyalty to King Jesus.*

When desiring to be extra precise, I will use the word *personalist* as distinct from *personal* to stress that, in terms of social norms, the majority of individuals in Jesus's era found their identity amid a collective. This chapter also shows that an *ex opere operato* interpretation of baptism is disallowed by the evidence. *Ex opere operato* means "by the work worked." It asserts that God graciously confers a promised benefit whenever a sacramental action is correctly performed. An *ex opere operato* view of baptism is held by Catholics, Orthodox, and some Protestants.

Since the apostles and their heirs uniformly held to a voluntary personalist theology of baptism that excluded an *ex opere operato* interpretation, this means that even if infants were baptized in the first two centuries (contrary to the evidence), the apostles would not have regarded it as initializing salvation. This chapter presses the church toward a new, sharper precision in its doctrinal statements: rather than paedobaptism (infant or child baptism) or credobaptism (believer's baptism), we should instead advocate for voluntary *allegiant or loyalist baptism*. I will conclude the chapter by suggesting—perhaps surprisingly—that although infant baptism is unwise, it is not *entirely* incompatible with God's saving purposes within the gospel-allegiance model.

Baptism as Saving? Yes and No

Is it necessary for a person to be baptized before we can say that person is saved or justified? On the one hand, it would seem that the answer must be yes.

Peter indicates that repentance followed by baptism is for the forgiveness of sins, exclaiming, "Repent and be baptized, every one of you, in the name of Jesus Christ for the forgiveness of your sins" (Acts 2:38). Elsewhere Peter affirms, "Baptism saves, not by the removal of filth from the flesh, but by the pledge of a good conscience toward God, through the resurrection of Jesus the Christ" (1 Pet. 3:21 AT). There it is: *baptism saves*.

Paul indicates that baptism buries us with the Christ so that we are united with his death and resurrection life (Rom. 6:3–4). He further asserts that we are saved by God's mercy, "by the washing of regeneration and renewing by the Holy Spirit" (Titus 3:5). It is probable that Paul thinks that baptism, regeneration, and the receipt of the Spirit normally coincide.

So, yes, baptism is saving. Right?

On the other hand, baptism is not saving in the New Testament. When Jesus asks, "Who do you say that I am?" Peter boldly declares, "You are the Christ, the Son of the living God" (Matt. 16:15–16). In response, Jesus calls Peter "blessed" and says, "I tell you, you are Peter, and on this rock I will build my church" (16:17–18). Jesus says that the church has been launched when Peter confesses him to be the Christ *entirely apart from Peter receiving baptism.*

When Jesus says, "On this rock I will build my church," he is referring to Peter, yes, but Peter in his *professing* capacity. Peter is identified as the rock not because there is a distinctive Petrine office associated with Rome—at least our text suggests nothing of the sort—but because Peter has just made the foundational gospel declaration that constitutes the church.[3] The church will be built—that is, others will enter it—by that same profession of Jesus's kingship.

Furthermore, as Peter's example makes clear, this declaration of Jesus's kingship can be made *at any moment* without formal participation in baptism or any other sacrament. Peter founded the church within history (and was the first to enter it) by his declaration *entirely* apart from undertaking baptism. Peter may have participated in John's baptism, but we have no evidence that Peter ever received baptism with water into the name of Jesus as the Christ.[4] In any case, Peter's personal cleansing from sin was achieved not by water baptism but only when his initial declared allegiance was ratified via Spirit immersion at Pentecost.

That cleansing from personal sins can happen *entirely apart* from baptism is confirmed not only by Peter's foundational example but by others too. It is striking that we have no evidence that any of the twelve apostles underwent baptism into Jesus's name. The same can be said for the thief on the cross. The thief only confesses that Jesus is the true king and shows his willingness to yield allegiance to him in the future: "Remember me when you come into your kingdom," prompting Jesus to reply, "Today you will be with me in paradise" (Luke 23:42–43). God can cleanse sins without baptism.

Similarly, the apostle Paul says that it is by *professing* "Jesus is Lord" that we are saved when that is combined with *believing* that God raised Jesus from the dead (Rom. 10:9). Paul is emphatic when explaining, "For it is with your heart that you believe and are justified, and it is with your mouth that you profess your faith and are saved" (10:10 NIV). Paul says nothing here about the necessity of baptism. Elsewhere he indicates that his mission is to preach the gospel, not to baptize (1 Cor. 1:14–17). The one true church is constituted by declaring "Jesus is king" and then persisting in that confession.

A different example in Acts that features faith alone demonstrates that baptism is not saving. Those at Cornelius's house hear the gospel, respond with faith, and receive the Spirit—all of this *before* and hence *apart* from baptism (Acts 10:44–48). It was because they had already been cleansed directly by God that Peter baptized them: "Can anyone withhold water for baptizing these people, who have received the Holy Spirit just as we have?" (10:47). God can take the initiative in supplying the Spirit to initialize salvation apart from baptism or the laying on of hands.

Cornelius and his guests are subsequently baptized, but that baptism was *not* to cleanse sins or bring about union with the Spirit. We know this with certainty because later at the council in Jerusalem, Peter explains what happened: "God, who knows the heart, bore witness to them, by giving them the Holy Spirit just as he did to us, and he made no distinction between us and them, *having cleansed their hearts by faith*" (Acts 15:8–9). According to Peter's testimony, these gentiles *had already been cleansed by God by faith as the sole instrument in such a way that Spirit union was achieved before and hence apart from baptism.* Peter is urgent that the council know that God accomplished this cleansing by faith prior to and thus apart from Peter's subsequent baptismal actions.

Why did Peter baptize Cornelius and his guests, then? We don't know. Given what we'll discover in this chapter, it is reasonable to guess that it was to devote the physical body to God. But whatever its purpose, Peter's interpretation forbids us from saying that their baptism was required in any fashion as part of the instrument of personal forgiveness, cleansing, or justification. Peter is emphatic when explaining: union with the Holy Spirit—and the cleansing of sins that attends it—had already happened by faith alone before and apart from baptism.

Is Baptism Saving? Too Imprecise!

The reason why it is difficult to answer the question of whether baptism is saving or justifying is that the question is too imprecise, for three reasons.

One moment in a sequence. First, the question "Is baptism saving?" frequently assumes that a person's salvation can be reduced to an initial event. But on the level of biblical theology, it is indisputable that salvation has past, present, and future dimensions with respect to a person's entire life (Rom. 8:13–19; Phil. 3:7–14). Because baptism occupies only a moment in a person's lifelong journey, it could potentially initialize, advance, ratify, or complete a person's salvation, but making baptism salvation's totality is simplistic. In other words, *baptism can fit in only one location in the chronological sequence of a person's lifelong salvation process.*

This chapter shows evidence that in the New Testament and early Christianity *baptism is never the very first step in a person's salvation process.* I will not have an extended discussion of this point, but there are always preliminaries to baptism, such as hearing the gospel, arriving at initial faith, and repenting from sins. Nevertheless, for a person's life journey toward final salvation, baptism is ordinarily within the initial phase of entering it decisively. After baptism, it was required that a person *persevere* by continuing to respond to the gospel in order to reach final salvation (for further discussion, see chap. 7).

Baptism's meaning before Jesus. Second, baptism had a meaning within Judaism before Jesus arrived on the scene. When assessing whether baptism is saving, people often simply assume that baptism is what someone does in response to the good news of Jesus's death for sins and resurrection to enter salvation. But this ignores its earliest context. *When baptism is first happening in the New Testament, it is not a Christian initiation ritual at all.* It is *a Jewish practice* being carried out for forgiveness of sins by John the Baptist among those who had no initial interest in Jesus. This will require extended discussion.

Baptism is a multipart event. Third, not only does the question of whether baptism is saving ignore where baptism fits in the sequence of a person's salvation journey and baptism's Jewish roots, but it also frequently assumes that baptism is a homogeneous saving event, when in fact *any single baptism is a complex process that consists of numerous smaller events.* When we read in Scripture that baptism is saving, we must consider that a specific part or parts of the process could be uniquely definitive for actualizing salvation, whereas other parts may be merely customary or optional. In other words, to say that baptism is saving is imprecise with regard to baptism as a complex, multipart event that may have essential and inessential subparts.

To discern to what degree baptism is saving in the New Testament, we will press into baptism's *Jewish context* further and will attend to its nature as a *multipart event* that may have essential and inessential saving features.

Baptism as a Jewish Practice

Jesus, the apostles, and John the Baptist were Jews. Jesus and several apostles emerge publicly within John's ministry. Moreover, Jesus's apostles eventually conduct baptisms in parallel with John, eventually surpassing and superseding his efforts (John 3:23–26; 4:1–3). To discern how baptism fits into salvation within earliest Christianity, we must begin with John's intentions. We know that John ultimately pointed toward Jesus. What more can we say?

Immersion. That baptism ordinarily was done by immersion follows from John's location at the Jordan River. Moreover, Paul describes baptism as burial and resurrection—imagery that suggests submersion followed by emergence (Rom. 6:3–4). Immersion also follows from the word itself: *baptizō* or *baptō* is to "dip, immerse, or dunk," whereas baptism (*baptisma*) is the result of that action. Baptizing or baptism was not particularly religious in the New Testament era: fingers, garments, metal, and ships are all described as having been "baptized"—that is, submerged—as part of everyday nonreligious life.[5]

Ritual washing and impurity within Judaism. What was the purpose of baptism within Judaism before Jesus? Some Jews in Jesus's day were rigorously committed to immersive washing in conjunction with ritual purity. Ritual washing did not always require an immersive bath. However, archaeological evidence shows pools for baptismal purification (*mikvot*) extant from the second century BC onward. Purifying baptismal pools were increasingly common in Jesus's day, and they are described in the New Testament (e.g., John 5:1–7; 9:7).[6]

To be ritually impure was not ordinarily to be sinful. Impurity became sinful only if it was not eradicated before spreading inappropriately or encountering holiness. For example, when a woman menstruated or a man had an emission, these were not sinful acts. But they did cause ritual impurity or uncleanness, so the priests were commanded to remove impurity, lest a person endanger themselves by defiling holy space or objects (e.g., Lev. 15:31).

A person's impurity might serve as a threat to contaminate the holy, but, importantly, the direction of movement could be reversed. Holiness (or purity) could radiate outward from God's presence, serving as a risky threat to the impure should they contagiously contract holiness when in an impure state. When Achan seizes plunder at Jericho that has been devoted to a holy God, the devoted things have a contagious holiness. Thus Achan becomes devoted too and was liable for destruction (Josh. 7:11–12). He had contracted holiness inappropriately, so he was stoned to death.

In order to control the threats posed by impurity and holiness, the Pharisees and the community at Qumran had elaborate rules. Prescribed rituals maintained the purity of vessels, fluids when poured, food, human bodies, and other objects.[7] Jesus was critical of the Pharisees for being obsessed with what enters the body via unwashed hands and vessels but indifferent to the contaminating evil that erupts from the heart (Mark 7:3–4, 14–23).

Repentance, not water, cleanses. There were men who opted to live near the Dead Sea at Qumran. Any man who wanted to join them had to demonstrate self-discipline through a year of rigorous testing. This allowed him to enter their pure water. Upon subsequent testing of character, two years later, he attained full membership.[8]

As further attested by the Dead Sea Scrolls, we find that *repentance came first* at Qumran, and on its basis *the immersive water was purified.* Community members, the Men of Holiness, took a ritual bath before the common meal. The following command governed life at Qumran: "None of the perverse men is to enter purifying waters used by the Men of Holiness and so contract their purity."[9] Note well: the baptismal waters do not contract impurity as they cleanse the men, but instead the water contracts *purity* from the Men of Holiness. A comment clarifies why: "Indeed, it is impossible to be purified without first repenting of evil, inasmuch as impurity adheres to all who transgress his word."[10] Repentance was the cleansing agent prior to the baptism.

In other words, the men at Qumran and any seeking to join them had to first repent from sins against the Lord's commands. They were then clean. Subsequently, their repentant purity made their water pure when they baptized themselves in it. It was deemed dangerously inappropriate for the nonrepentant to enter the pure water afterward because they would contract holiness when in an unholy state, much like Achan.

We might expect the immersive water to be the cleansing agent in baptism, but at Qumran *it is not the water at all but prior repentance that is the cleansing agent.* Repentance has created a pure body *before* baptism, so during baptism a person is not being cleansed from sins by virtue of the baptismal act itself. An *ex opere operato* interpretation of baptism at Qumran as that which cleanses a person's impurity is impossible. Instead, a penitent person's already pure body contagiously transferred *purity* to the baptismal *water* during the baptismal event, *purifying the water, not the person.*

Josephus on John's baptism. We are now in a better position to understand John's baptism. We tend to read Christian ideas into John's baptism prematurely, as if it intends commitment to Jesus or his entrance into the church. John was preaching his message *before* he was aware that Jesus was the Messiah or the Lamb of

God. John was looking forward to the revelation of a coming one, but John's message was not cross-shaped before Jesus was revealed to John, only afterward (John 1:26; cf. 1:29).

In Scripture, John's baptism is described as "a baptism of repentance" (Matt. 3:11) or as "a baptism of repentance for the forgiveness of sins" (Mark 1:4; Luke 3:3). *John thought that repentance for forgiveness was possible prior to the Messiah's emergence* and that it also connected in some way to the baptism that John was offering.

Did you know that the Jewish historian Josephus speaks about John's baptism in greater detail than Scripture does? Josephus shows us that John's baptism—a baptismal ministry that Jesus and his apostles took over—initially had meaning for Jews that had nothing to do with initiation into Jesus's death and resurrection:

> But to some of the Jews the destruction of Herod's army seemed to be divine vengeance, and certainly a just vengeance, for his treatment of John, surnamed the Baptist. For Herod had put him to death, though he was a good man and had exhorted the Jews to lead righteous lives, to practice justice towards their fellows and piety towards God, and so doing to join in baptism. In his view *this was a necessary preliminary if baptism was to be acceptable to God. They must not employ it to gain pardon for whatever sins they committed, but as a consecration of the body implying that the soul [psychē] was already thoroughly cleansed by right behaviour.* When others too joined the crowds about him, because they were aroused to the highest degree by his sermons, Herod became alarmed. Eloquence that had so great an effect on mankind might lead to some form of sedition. . . . Herod decided therefore that it would be much better to strike first and be rid of him before his work led to an uprising.[11]

Because he presses more deeply into the inner logic of John's baptism, Josephus offers a unique window into it beyond what we find in the Bible. Josephus reports that John's baptism was not deemed the instrument that caused the essential cleansing of the person. Josephus expressly says that John's baptism could not be employed instrumentally by participants "to gain pardon for whatever sins they committed" but could be made effective only by a prior cleansing of the soul through right actions.

The water did not serve as the cleansing agent to purify past or present sins during the baptism. An *ex opere operato* interpretation of John's baptism is impossible and is explicitly rejected by Josephus. *Cleansing from past and present sins had already happened before entering the water, so the act of baptism itself (immersion) was not an instrument for cleansing the person.* As Josephus puts it, the *psyche*—traditionally translated as "soul" but better as "the person in his or her essence"—who undertook John's baptism was necessarily "already thoroughly cleansed by right behaviour."

Repentance was the true instrument of cleansing prior to baptism, not the baptism nor the water. This is precisely what we observed at Qumran. For Josephus, regarding John's baptism, the tool that God used to cleanse *the true essential person* (the "soul") was repentance and a righteous life *prior* to baptism.

If a person was not cleansed and sins were not erased through immersion in the water during the baptismal event itself, what was achieved? Josephus states that the physical baptism was purposed toward a "consecration [*hagneia*] of the body [*sōma*]"—that is, to render "pure" or "devoted" (*hagneia*) the outer physical "body" (the *sōma*). For a baptism to be effective, the soul had to be pure from sins prior to baptism, then baptism served to make the outer body pure too.

In sum, for Josephus, if a person had freely undertaken to repent from sins and adopt a new lifestyle so that the soul had *already* been cleansed by repentance and right behavior, then he or she could subsequently undergo John's baptism. John's baptism in water did not remove past or present sins instrumentally from the essential person (the "soul"); only repentance did that. But after repentance, the water did purify the person's physical body, so that it came to match the pure state that their essential self (their "soul") had already attained.

Josephus's description in no way contradicts what we find in Scripture about the initial meaning of John's baptism but supplements and clarifies why Scripture calls it a "baptism *of repentance* for the forgiveness of sins" (Mark 1:4: Luke 3:3). Repentance prior to baptism was the *instrument* that cleansed the "soul" (the essential person), and secondarily the water immersion consecrated the outer body. Of course, once Jesus is revealed to John, the meaning of his baptismal ministry is reoriented to acclaim Jesus as the one who lends repentance and forgiveness ultimate meaning.

The wilderness setting. The geographical proximity between the Men of Holiness at Qumran and John the Baptist helps us further discern baptism's meaning in earliest Christianity. Both emphasize immersion in connection with repentance. Both had deliberately positioned themselves in the Judean desert or wilderness. Yet the connection is more specific. John had gone to the desert to prepare the way for the Lord, to make a straight path for him (Matt. 3:3; Mark 1:3; Luke 3:4). The Qumran community had the same expressed purpose.

The *Yahad* at Qumran had gone out to the desert to separate themselves from the perverse and prepare the way. In their own words, they went "to the wilderness" in order to "prepare the way of truth, as it is written, 'In the wilderness prepare the way of the LORD, make straight in the desert a highway for our God.'"[12] The motivation of the *Yahad* is explained further. They had gone to the wilderness to prepare the way of the Lord by expounding the law of Moses and obeying it in the way revealed for each age by the prophets and God's holy Spirit (1QS 8:16). Thus, the community was living in the Judean wilderness on the edge of the Dead Sea to prepare the way for the Lord.

After the exodus, Israel failed in the wilderness. They wandered there for forty years. After that time of purification and preparation, they were led across the Jordan River by Joshua into the promised land. But they fell away again, eventually being taken into exile. During the exile, God sent prophets to announce a marvelous wilderness action. The words "prepare the way for the LORD" are from Isaiah's description of a future new exodus associated with return from exile.

The sentinels see a highway through the wilderness—the exiles returning with the glory of Yahweh at their head—"prepare the way for the LORD" (Isa. 40:1–5). They shout, "See, the Sovereign LORD comes with power, and he rules with a mighty arm. See, his reward is with him, and his recompense accompanies him" (40:10 NIV). The heralds shout a message of salvation, "Gospel! Your God reigns" (52:7 AT). Isaiah announces, "When the LORD returns to Zion, they will see it with their own eyes" (52:8 NIV). The gospel in Isaiah is that God is reoccupying his temple and reestablishing his sovereign rule over his people through the mysterious suffering servant.

The implied question for the Qumran community and John is the same: What wilderness actions will prepare the way so that the kingdom of God—the gospel of God's definitive rule as described by Isaiah and other prophets—will usher forth? John's wilderness location is symbolic, yes, but it is more: it is a prophetic announcement of a vanguard movement that will usher in the gospel of God's reign.

Why the Jordan? We find confirmation that John's withdrawal to the wilderness is a prophetic speech-act that announces kingdom readiness when we consider the Jordan. John was not alone in making use of the Jordan to advance a symbolic message. Josephus tells us about Theudas, a prophet in Judea who was active in AD 44–46, some fifteen years after John:

> When Fadus was governor of Judea, a charlatan named Theudas persuaded most of the common people to take their possessions and follow him to the Jordan river. He said he was a prophet, and that at his command the river would be divided and allow them an easy crossing. Through such words he deceived many. But Fadus hardly let them consummate such foolishness. He sent out a cavalry unit against them, which killed many in a surprise attack, though they also took many alive. Having captured Theudas himself, they cut off his head and carried it off to Jerusalem.[13]

Theudas summoned the people to come out of Judea, along with all their possessions. He announced that at his command the

Jordan would split so the people could cross on dry ground. When Joshua first led the people of God out of the wilderness, after he gave commands, the Jordan was divided when the priests bearing the ark crossed into the promised land (see Josh. 3).

The whole scenario suggests that Theudas fancied himself to be a new Joshua. He was seeking to create a purified wilderness people and then to reoccupy the promised land. It also implies that Theudas would have viewed those who opted to remain in Judea rather than follow him to the Jordan as illegitimate offspring of Abraham. Regardless of their actual lineage, they had become Canaanites who needed to be reconquered to purify the Holy Land. The governor Fadus dispatched troops to deal with Theudas.

The episode with Theudas helps us weigh the meaning of John's baptism. John's immersive activity at the Jordan was politically subversive. *By calling the inhabitants of Judea to join him in the wilderness and to immerse in the Jordan, John the Baptist was prophetically announcing that those who opted to cleanse their essential selves by repentance and then to receive his baptism were the forgiven, wilderness-purified vanguard that would survive the impending judgment and usher in the gospel of God's rule.*

Is it any surprise that Herod Antipas decided to make a preemptive strike by killing John before the crowds were led into rebellion?[14] Fadus made the same decision with regard to Theudas.

From John to Jesus. Like Theudas, John symbolically announced that Judeans who opted not to join him at the Jordan were not true offspring of Abraham. They were compromisers who did not support God's impending rule. He warned those arriving for voluntary baptism not to consider physical descent from Abraham as giving them status with God. Only repentant behavior could give them that. John spoke emphatically of God's coming wrath, demanding evidence of repentance prior to baptism: "Produce fruit *in keeping with repentance*" (Luke 3:8 NIV). This repentance involved at the very least sharing with the needy, rejecting greed, and ceasing extortion (3:10–14).

John's repentance for baptism for the forgiveness of sins had a meaning that was both personal and communal before Jesus arrived on the scene. It called individuals to reject personal wrong-doings within a framework of national repentance and the reconstitution of God's covenant people.

In sum, when John's baptism is located in its Jewish context, we discover that those who repented were cleansed in their essential selves (the "soul") from past and present sin through that repentance *prior* to baptism, not through the instrumentality of the baptismal action or the water. Since the soul had already been cleansed before baptism, the baptism itself only devoted the outer body subsequently and secondarily. Those who opted to join John in the wilderness were announcing their commitment to serve as a purified remnant—Abraham's true offspring—uniquely fit to enter the Jordan and occupy the promised land. In so doing they believed that they were preparing the way for the return of Yahweh, the gospel that God would decisively reinstitute his temple-based rule over his people.

When Jesus appears, John is told that he is the coming one. Unlike John, he will immerse not with water "but with the Holy Spirit" (Mark 1:8; John 1:33). By undertaking John's water baptism, *Jesus identifies completely with John's voluntary baptismal intentions and with the need of the nation to repent.* The Spirit descends and the Father confirms Jesus's unique sonship, making Jesus the Christ within history.

Is it any wonder, then, that after his baptism Jesus "returned *from the Jordan* and was led by the Spirit in *the wilderness* for *forty* days, being *tested*" (Luke 4:1 AT). All the key themes that inform the meaning of John's baptismal ministry are affirmed and recapitulated, showing that Jesus has accepted their validity. Moreover, he passes the test as the obedient Son in the wilderness at precisely the points where Israel had failed. John recognizes that his job is now to point exclusively to Jesus. Accordingly, Jesus's disciples set up a baptismal ministry in parallel to John's which eclipses it.

Baptism as a Multipart Event

We opened this chapter by examining why it is too simple to say without qualification that *baptism is saving*. We have explored how baptism in John's ministry is described as "*of repentance* for the forgiveness of sins" (Mark 1:4; Luke 3:3). That is, repentance alone was the instrument that cleansed the essential person, not the water. As we will see, the same is true for early Christianity—repentance, not water, cleanses the essential person—although that repentance from sins now must be combined with expressed loyalty to King Jesus.

In early Christianity, only personal repentance that was combined with faith could cleanse the soul. For example, the author of Hebrews states, "Let us draw near to God with a sincere heart in full assurance of faith, having cleansed the heart from an evil conscience and having washed our body in pure water" (Heb. 10:22 AT). Notice the order: a "sincere heart" and initial "faith" are in place first. An individual repents from "an evil conscience," and this is the act by which the heart is cleansed.

In Hebrews 10:22 repentance is what cleanses the heart prior to the washing in water, just like at Qumran and in John's baptism, although faith is added to repentance. The act of washing in water doesn't serve as the instrument for cleansing the heart, the essential person. Meanwhile, the outer body is "washed in pure water" in baptism secondarily, but it is not what cleanses the inner person. That repentance acts to cleanse the essential person *prior to* immersion in the water is confirmed.

In what follows we will explore baptism in the New Testament and other early Christian sources from a different yet ultimately complementary angle.

The Baptismal Process in Earliest Christianity

John's baptism was not fully saving because it did not cause personal union with the Spirit. All four Gospels and Acts stress that this—Spirit immersion—is what makes Jesus's baptism distinct from John's (Matt. 3:11; Mark 1:8; Luke 3:16; John 1:33; Acts 19:2–6).

In the Christ, personal justification or forgiveness is decisively entered for the first time *when a person receives the Holy Spirit.* Since this point is not particularly controversial and can readily be illustrated from Scripture (e.g., Acts 15:8; 1 Cor. 6:11), I will not expand discussion but simply reassert it for the sake of maximal clarity: however it happens within the larger sequence of events that connect with water baptism, immersion in the *Holy Spirit must be achieved*, for that is put forward as *the moment* personal salvation is decisively entered for the first time.

If personal salvation decisively begins at the moment of Spirit union, then we must seek to uncover how Scripture presents its timing with respect to water baptism. What makes this complex is that water baptism is not one uniform event but multipart. Furthermore, water baptism's many parts are not presented as equally essential to salvation.

Pre-baptismal Activities

The New Testament's overall witness makes it clear that prior to baptism into Jesus's name, a person or group had (1) heard the gospel, (2) been summoned to repent from sins, (3) and arrived at initial belief or faith. Although this pattern isn't always fully narrated, we have no descriptions of Christian baptisms that conflict with or contradict this pattern. Furthermore, although there are important exceptions, it is normally presupposed that Spirit union will be achieved during the baptismal process.

Volunteering for Baptism

In every New Testament instance baptism involves free initiative. Individuals or groups *willingly* undergo immersion in water. There are no reports in the New Testament of baptisms that do not involve a conscious human choice and active or permissive voluntary agency.

Infant baptism? For those weighing the question of infant baptism, every single description—in the New Testament and

119

elsewhere—of a Christian baptism *prior to the third century AD* involves an adult making a voluntary choice.

Household baptisms are described (e.g., Acts 16:15, 33; 18:8; 1 Cor. 1:16). These were based on the choice of a household leader—usually the *paterfamilias*—but we have no descriptions of children participating, nor any indication that members of a household ever undertook baptism in anything other than a conscious voluntary capacity. On the contrary, our New Testament authors take pains to highlight the retention of agency by subordinates within the household. For example, "Crispus, the ruler of the synagogue, *had faith in the Lord, together with his entire household*, and many of the Corinthians hearing Paul believed and were baptized" (Acts 18:8–9 AT). After the Philippian jailer's household is baptized, Scripture says, "He was filled with joy because *he had come to faith* in God—*he and his whole household*" (16:34 AT). These texts indicate that the members of the household had come to faith too and had voluntarily undertaken baptism—actions impossible for infants—even though the decision originated with their respective heads.

We have no genuine historical evidence in favor of infant or child baptism in the New Testament and earliest Christianity. Within John the Baptist's ministry—which Jesus and the apostles affirmed and furthered—*voluntary repentance* is what cleansed, not immersion in the water. The same is true at Qumran. Given that voluntarism is relentlessly emphasized in early Christianity too—and more evidence will be presented as this chapter unfolds—it is highly likely that baptism in the apostolic age was restricted to adults or those approaching adulthood. On the question of baptism as a seal of the new covenant—and what this might mean for infants and regeneration—see chapter 6.

Voluntary personalist baptism. It is best to call baptismal decisions of subordinates within a household *personalist* rather than *personal* in order to acknowledge that many subordinates constructed personal identity through their role in the household. Within that structure they preferred to exercise their subordinate agency by deferring to its head. This does not mean that subordinate household members had no agency but acknowledges that their social location encouraged them to exercise agency by deferring to the judgment of another. It is hard for those of us who are products of the fiercely individualistic West to enter into this way of seeing the world, but it was normal in the New Testament time period.[15]

Group baptism doesn't always save the individual. Voluntary personalist faith was required for each individual within a group baptism, or else it was not saving. We know this because we have an example in the New Testament of a group baptism that did not prove effective for one member, Simon the magician, because he did not *personally* repent. Many responded in faith to Philip's good news about the kingdom and Jesus as the Christ in Samaria, including Simon (Acts 8:4–25).

Simon's example teaches us that *voluntary individual repentance was required* as the true cleansing agent for personal salvation as part of the baptismal process—even amid a group baptism. Since infants cannot perform voluntary personal repentance, Simon's example shows that even if infants were baptized as part of household baptisms (contrary to the evidence), such infant baptisms would not have resulted in Spirit union. Even though Simon had personally believed and received baptism along with others (Acts 8:13, 16), these acts proved insufficient to cause Spirit union. When hands were subsequently placed on those who believed, Simon did not personally receive the Holy Spirit so as to decisively enter salvation *because, although Simon had believed and received baptism, he had not personally repented.*

Simon sees others receiving the Spirit when he has not, so he offers to buy it. Peter tells Simon, "*You have neither part nor lot in this matter,* for your *heart* is not right before God. *Repent,* therefore, of this wickedness of yours, and pray to the Lord *that, if possible, the intent of your heart may be forgiven you*" (Acts 8:21–22). The group to which Simon belonged believed the gospel, was baptized, and received the Spirit when hands were placed, but because Simon had not truly *repented personally,* he had no part in the matter, so the baptism did not result in Spirit reception for him.

Simon's example indicates that within group baptism in the New Testament, individual voluntary agency remained intact and its legitimacy was discerned by God, so that the gift of the Holy Spirit was offered accordingly. By extension, we can conclude that within group baptisms any subordinate household member—including any purported infants—who failed to repent and give loyalty to King Jesus *personally* during baptism would also fail to enter saving union with the king by not receiving the Spirit. This speaks strongly against the compatibility of a nonpersonalist, nonvoluntary *ex opere operato* theology of baptism with the New Testament witness.

Personal salvation amid a group. In summary, once we recognize that saving faith is more about a repentant declaration of loyalty to a rescuing king than about trusting in the effectiveness of the atonement, we see why subordinates in a group or a household could voluntarily enter salvation even if they were not fully trusting personally in the efficacy of the atonement.

Subordinates could follow their leader in opting to exercise personalist agency in repenting from previous sinful actions and loyalties while expressing allegiance to King Jesus. If their declared allegiance was sincere, they would receive forgiveness and other benefits of the gospel, even if their trust in or understanding of those benefits was inadequate or partial. If an individual's repentance was not sincere in the midst of a group experience, as in the case of Simon the magician, the Holy Spirit would be given to the rest of the group but withheld from that individual.

Invoking Jesus as a Sovereign (Personal Oath of Allegiance)

Apart from the need to volunteer, baptism in the New Testament consistently includes *the invocation of Jesus as sovereign.* At baptism, a person "called upon the name" of Jesus as a ruler. In "calling upon the name"—language that typically suggests the swearing of an oath—the acknowledgment of Jesus's authority is the nonnegotiable constant. Yet it is apparent from the New Testament that variety was permitted in the exact name invoked during baptism: it is in the name of Jesus the Christ (Acts 2:38; 8:12; 10:48), or Christ Jesus (Rom. 6:3), or Christ (Gal. 3:27), or the Lord Jesus (Acts 8:16; 19:17).

Once, in a passage that emphasizes Jesus's complete authority over everything in heaven and on earth, the disciples are told to baptize "in the name of the Father and of the Son and of the Holy Spirit" (Matt. 28:19). The invocation of the threefold name in baptism is fitting with respect to the New Testament's complete witness, provided that an emphasis on Jesus's sovereignty is maintained. But contrary to standard Catholic, Orthodox, and some Protestant norms, baptism in the threefold name is certainly not required for a "valid" baptism—whatever that might be thought to mechanistically mean.

Yet baptism into the threefold name is wise, because baptism into the name of the Father, Son, and Holy Spirit vouchsafes King Jesus's saving work within the context of a trinitarian narrative: the gospel describes how God the *Father* sent a royal *Son* who secured salvation and was enthroned, so the *Spirit* could then be sent to apply saving benefits to the king's people. Baptism in the threefold name helps to safeguard the gospel, because Jesus's sovereignty is correctly located within a trinitarian narrative. In subsequent church history baptism into the threefold name supplanted the more frequently attested apostolic practice of swearing to Jesus alone as the sovereign.

Self-Baptism

We have indication in the New Testament that *the baptismal candidate—not the person leading the baptism—was to baptize himself or herself while calling upon the name of the Lord Jesus.* For example, after the resurrected Christ appeared to Paul, Paul was told, "Get up, *baptize yourself*, and wash your sins away, *while calling on his name*" (Acts 22:16 AT); contextually, the name to be called upon is that of the Lord Jesus. Self-baptism and self-washing are indicated by the reflexive middle voice in the second-person singular commands: "baptize yourself and wash yourself" (*baptisai kai apolousai*). Although a leader "baptized" by conducting others through the process in earliest Christianity, the person undertaking baptism was to perform a *self-immersive* action in the water—*to baptize himself or herself and wash while calling upon the name of the Lord Jesus.*

Acts 22:16 is particularly important because it casts light on what it meant to call on Jesus's name, an act that is described in other scriptural passages. *Calling upon the name* during baptism in earliest Christianity was not fundamentally about the one who was leading the baptism speaking the divine name for the baptismal candidate in order to effect a spiritual change in the soul of the candidate. Baptism in the New Testament and by the apostles and their immediate heirs was not interpreted as effective by virtue of the sacramental action itself as performed by a priest or other functionary. *Baptism was a self-immersion and self-washing.* Also, there were no Christian priests during this time period, and the *ex opere operato* explanation for how baptism is effective does not even appear in church history until the third century at the absolute earliest.

Rather, the baptismal candidate's own invocation (oath) was essential. *The baptismal candidate was expected to call upon the Lord Jesus personally as part of self-immersion and self-washing during the baptismal process.* This "calling upon the name of the Lord" is the language of oath.[16] Given that baptism in the New Testament consistently fronts Jesus as the Lord or the Christ, this is an oath of fidelity (faith) to a sovereign. *The decisive baptismal utterance—calling upon the name—is best described as an oath of allegiance to King Jesus.*

In fact, one reason why baptism came to be called a *sacrament* over time was that earliest Christianity featured a *voluntary personal oath of loyalty* to Jesus as the Christ during baptism. The Latin word *sacramentum*, from which we get *sacrament*, means "oath." Ironically, however, the belief that baptism *as a sacrament* is effective for an individual by virtue of the act itself (*ex opere operato*) leaves out what the New Testament and earliest Christianity say makes it effective—the *personal and voluntary* dimension of the *sacramentum*, the *oath of allegiance.*

In sum, when we synthesize how the New Testament describes baptism, there are three standard pre-baptismal activities: hearing the gospel, initial belief (enough to form a preliminary loyalty intention), and repentance from sins. Then there are three main activities that constitute the total baptismal event: voluntary decision for immersion, invoking King Jesus by swearing a personal oath of allegiance to him (faith), and self-immersion and self-washing.

It is noteworthy that none of the six can be carried out by an infant or small child, because they all require personal or personalist voluntary agency. It is not possible for infants or young children to hear the gospel, repent from sins, have initial faith, volunteer for baptism, swear an oath of loyalty to King Jesus, or immerse and wash themselves in the water. An infant cannot complete any of the six steps that make up the preliminary and actual process of a baptism in the New Testament and early Christianity.

A Theological Peek inside the Baptismal Process: The Interface of Loyalty, Justification, and Baptism

A baptismal oath of allegiance helps us make sense of the precise relationship between faith and baptism as described by our earliest witness, the apostle Paul. The New Testament in general and Paul's letters in particular regularly put forward *pistis* as the instrument of justification.[17] If Paul understood saving faith as a definitive loyalty oath that causes justification—which was coterminous with union with the Holy Spirit—then all the pieces fit.

Baptism per se is never described as justification's specific instrument in Scripture. This suggests that the apostles *deemed baptism saving because it was the premier or definitive occasion to invoke the name—to express loyalty to King Jesus.* Remember Peter's words, "Baptism saves, not by the removal of filth from the flesh, but by *the pledge [eperōtēma] of a good conscience toward God*" (1 Pet. 3:21 AT). Again, the water is not the tool that provides cleansing; the repentant appeal to God for mercy cleanses as that takes the form of *a pledge of commitment* (see discussion above of Qumran, John the Baptist, and Heb. 10:22). That pledge is owed to God inclusive of Jesus as the Christ. Within the baptismal process, from the standpoint of human initiative, it was the declaration of repentant allegiance to King Jesus that specifically caused God to respond by justifying that person, at which moment that individual was united to the Spirit.

The profession of repentant allegiance retained primacy over baptism per se. It was possible to be justified by loyalty so as to receive Spirit union apart from water baptism into the name of Jesus. This happens for the crucified thief and Cornelius and his guests (see previous discussion). It is also probable for Peter, the eleven other apostles, and the 120 at Pentecost. This also explains why Paul radically prioritized preaching the gospel and the faith response over baptism (1 Cor. 1:17).

We find confirmation that the declaration of loyalty was the specific instrument of justification (and hence Spirit union) within baptism when we inspect Paul's letters with care. Baptism and justification are rarely correlated in the New Testament, but in the few passages where they are juxtaposed—Romans 6:3–7, 1 Corinthians 6:11, Galatians 3:24–27—the correlation suggests that *pistis* is justification's precise instrument.

Galatians 3:24–27 is particularly helpful because in this passage beyond all others Paul provides a window into his deeper theological reasoning with regard to how justification, *pistis*, and baptism interrelate:

> So the law was our guardian until the Christ came, in order that we might be justified by allegiance [*pistis*]. But now that allegiance [*pistis*] has come,[18] we are no longer under a guardian, for in the Christ, Jesus, you are all sons of God through allegiance [*pistis*], for as many of you as were baptized into the Christ have put on the Christ. (Gal. 3:24–27 AT)

When Paul correlates faith, justification, and baptism, he identifies *pistis* (not baptism) as justification's specific instrument. But Paul also indicates that the *pistis* activity coincides with baptism in such a way that it causes a person to put on the Christ, which is a metaphor for union with him.

The most likely explanation is that Paul gives *pistis* primacy as justification's actual instrument—since that is what is affirmed here and consistently elsewhere—but that Paul believed *pistis*'s definitive instrumental expression was *ordinarily* (but not necessarily nor exclusively) a subportion of the larger baptismal process. That is, Paul affirms that loyalty to King Jesus was normally expressed in a decisive way as a subevent within the baptismal process, and that this oath of loyalty was what caused a person to be united with the Christ and hence to enjoy benefits like justification.

Consider how this helps disentangle Catholic and Protestant claims. If the entire event of baptism (or its desire) is considered *necessarily and exclusively* the sole instrument of justification—as it is within Catholicism—it is exceedingly difficult to explain why Scripture never once says that baptism is justification's instrument. Nor is it possible to explain counterexamples in which justification happens apart from baptism and the great number of passages that say that faith is justifying or saving apart from any concern with baptism.

But, on the other hand, if water baptism is *ordinarily* the event during which justification occurs, then, unlike many Protestant traditions, we cannot say that all that matters is personal *mental* trust in Jesus's saving work and that baptism is irrelevant for justification. *Preliminary faith was not justifying until faith as loyalty was bodily expressed by repentantly swearing an oath to King Jesus ("calling on his name").* This voluntary and repentant oath of loyalty ordinarily (although not necessarily or exclusively) was declared for the first time during the baptismal process for the cleansing of the heart, at which time the outer body was also washed as a secondary act that devoted it to God.

When we recognize that the essential feature of the baptismal process in the New Testament and early Christianity—that which precisely and definitively justified—was the voluntary repentant personal oath of loyalty to King Jesus but that this was ordinarily embodied for the first time during the process of water baptism, we may begin to move beyond the salvation wars of the past.

The Baptismal Process after the New Testament

Since the New Testament does not appreciably detail the baptismal process beyond what I've sketched above, our earliest sources beyond the New Testament take on heightened importance. Several of these sources were not available to Catholics or Protestants at the time of the sixteenth-century Reformation, so when claims were made at that time about the theology of the early church, they were not taken into account. Although they are not as authoritative as the New Testament, they describe how baptism was carried out and interpreted just after the New Testament, so they help us weigh how baptism probably was undertaken and understood earlier.

The Didache

Our earliest description of Christian baptism outside the Bible is in the Didache (alternatively titled Teaching of the Twelve Apostles). It was written sometime between AD 100–130 but was mostly lost to history until 1873. In the Didache we find that baptism was to be carried out in the threefold name in running water (7:1). If none was available, immersion in warm water was permitted (7:2). If neither running water nor warm water could be had, it was acceptable to pour water on the head three times (7:3). While immersion was strongly preferred, it was not deemed essential.

Vitally, the one leading the baptism was to "review" basic instructions with the one undergoing baptism (7:1). Then they would fast together for one or two days, along with any others able to join (7:4). There is no hint here that baptism can be anything other than a voluntary and conscious undertaking by a person old enough to understand Christian teaching, review it, and fast as an expression of sincere repentance.

Justin Martyr

After the Didache, the next important witness to the baptismal process is Justin Martyr, who was active in Rome. Justin's *First Apology*, written around AD 160, was not available to the first generation of Protestant Reformers but was rediscovered and then published during the middle of the Council of Trent, a Catholic council that met sporadically over the course of eighteen years. Although Trent began in 1545, Justin's *First Apology* did not impact deliberations until 1551, when the first printed edition became available to select council members.[19] Yet the Catholic "Decree on Justification" and "Decree Concerning the Sacraments" were both promulgated four years earlier (1547). So, unfortunately, the first Protestants and official Catholic decrees made claims and decisions about how salvation functioned in earliest Christianity—decisions that are still considered binding by many today—but did so without access to crucial texts that describe the true history. Fortunately, we are in a better position today.

Justin describes a pre-baptismal dedication, renunciation, and faith decision. These were followed by the baptism proper. Justin reports that before baptism,

> all those who are persuaded and believe [*pisteuōsin*] that these things which we teach and say are true, and who give an undertaking that they are able so to live, are to pray and to ask with fasting for forgiveness from God for their past sins, and we pray and fast with them.[20]

There are several things to note about the pre-baptismal process: the baptismal candidate needed to affirm the intellectual truthfulness of basic Christian claims (to "believe"). Moreover, they had to indicate a willingness to commit to a Christian lifestyle (to be "able so to live"). In other words, they were expected to have formed a preliminary *faith* and *obedience* intention to Jesus *prior* to baptism.

The baptismal candidates were then to fast and pray as an embodied repentant request to receive forgiveness. Context makes it clear that, typically, God's definitive forgiveness was believed to come about not through these preliminaries but rather via some portion of the larger multipart baptismal event. All of this accords with what the New Testament describes for Christian baptism under ordinary circumstances.

After these preliminaries, the baptism proper transpired. The overarching categories that Justin uses to explain what is happening are *rebirth* (*anagennēsis*) and *enlightenment* (*phōtismos*):

> Then they are led by us to where there is water and they are reborn in the kind of rebirth in which we ourselves were also reborn. For at the name of the Father of all and Lord God and of our savior Jesus Christ and of holy Spirit they then wash in water.[21]

Notice that Justin says that baptismal washing is something that the baptismal candidates themselves perform, not something that is performed by a priest on or for them. There is no indication that Christian priests existed, let alone that they performed baptisms at this time—all of which is a formidable obstacle to an *ex opere operato* theology of baptism.

Yet there are developments beyond the New Testament. By Justin's time the invocation of the threefold name appears to be standard. It is unclear whether the candidate or the one leading the baptism was to speak the threefold name, but it is clear that *the baptismal candidates are expected to voluntarily baptize themselves, each one washing his or her own body through self-immersion in the water.* Although there are modest developments, Justin's description of preliminary faith, repentant actions, voluntarism, a spoken loyalty oath, and self-washing all accord with baptism in the New Testament.

After his description, Justin offers a short explanation of *rebirth* along the lines of what we find in John's Gospel, quoting the Christ, "Unless you are reborn you shall not enter the kingdom of heaven" (see John 3:5; cf. Matt. 18:3).[22] This affords Justin opportunity to explain the deeper logic of baptism. Since here Justin explicitly interprets what he believes is happening *theologically* during a baptism, this passage is uniquely important and is worth citing in full:

> And we have learnt from the apostles the following account of this matter. Since with respect to our first birth we have been born in ignorance and by necessity out of moist seed when our parents had intercourse with one another, and we have come to be in wicked customs and evil patterns of nurture, *in order that we should not remain children of either necessity or ignorance but should become children of choice and of knowledge, and should attain the forgiveness of sins,* that is, those committed previously, there is pronounced, in the water, over *the one choosing to be reborn and who repents of sins committed,* the name of the Father of all and the Lord God. . . . This washing is called "enlightenment" [*phōtismos*] because those who learn these things are being enlightened with respect to their mind. And the one being enlightened *washes himself* at the name of Jesus Christ who was crucified under Pontius Pilate and at the name of holy Spirit who proclaimed through the prophets beforehand everything concerning Jesus.[23]

In his description of what the apostles taught, Justin affirms that what is essential to baptism as rebirth is its *voluntary* nature. Above all Justin stresses that being born again is different from our first birth *primarily because each person undertaking baptism willingly takes the initiative in choosing to be born again.*

One *opts* to undergo baptism to be reborn because she or he has seen a more enlightened way and *wants* forgiveness and a new lifestyle. Regeneration or rebirth is what happens *after* we have seen enough of the light that we choose to believe, repent, and be baptized while expressing fidelity. Contrary to standard Reformed (Calvinist) theology, regeneration happens not before a person can express loyalty or choose baptism but only at the moment that loyalty is declared. This is precisely how the New Testament uses regeneration imagery, as we'll see in the next chapter.

Elsewhere Justin stresses that "the bath of salvation" is for those who have repented and have knowledge of God.[24] Justin says that the baptismal purification associated with the Christ is uniquely

131

life-giving, over against Jewish purification rituals that merely feature repentance, because it is made effective "by *pistis* through the blood and death of the Christ, who suffered death for this precise purpose."[25] Justin affirms that it is the Messiah's sacrificial death that makes baptism effective from the divine side. But on the side of human initiative, in addition to the repentance that is the cleansing agent within Jewish baptism, the saving instrument within Christian baptism is *loyalty* (*pistis*).

Far from suggesting that we have inherited a sin *nature* from our parents that leaves us in total bondage, Justin literally says that the problem is "nurture." We are nurtured into a world with "wicked customs" and "evil patterns," so that conformity to these is inevitable within our nonvoluntary first birth.

Yet, for Justin, the human will is not in total bondage despite this evil nurture. When we catch a glimmer of the light of the Christian truth, *each of us can voluntarily choose rebirth for ourselves*. Jesus and Paul say much the same, indicating that *the light of the Christ is able to rouse even unbelievers who are presently in bondage to sin and darkness* (see John 12:36, 46; Eph. 5:11–14). On its own, Christ's light in his first coming is ample grace to awaken those who are trapped in darkness, so they are then sufficiently free to choose to repent and leave the patterns inculcated by evil nurture. For Justin, this is achieved through baptism.

The result, after this has transpired, is that those who have baptized themselves are *enlightened*, because now they have *decisively entered the process of receiving true knowledge in their minds from God*. It is significant that Justin uses *phōtismos* ("enlightenment"), for this word was used in antiquity to describe a radical shift in basic outlook, community, loyalties, and practices that we today call conversion (cf. 2 Cor. 4:4–6; Heb. 6:4; 10:32). God will respond to those who freely seek rebirth in baptism by supplying it through the Spirit—forgiving past sins and providing mental enlightenment that will subsequently help the baptismal candidate undertake good deeds and so make progress toward final salvation.[26]

After their self-immersion, those who had participated in the baptism prayed together and then joined the larger community in greeting one another with a holy kiss. Finally, they proceeded to partake in a eucharistic meal.[27]

Given Justin's description of baptism's preliminaries, its actual process, and its underlying theology of personal voluntarism, it is impossible for small children to meaningfully complete even a single one of baptism's steps or to receive its new life and mental "enlightenment" benefits.

Tertullian

It is not until about AD 210 that we have a complete description of Christian baptism and its interpretation, with Tertullian's treatises *On Baptism* and *The Crown*. Hailing from a slightly later period, after AD 250, is a document known as *On the Apostolic Tradition*. The latter is traditionally attributed to Hippolytus but is more likely the product of numerous authors.

For Tertullian, prior to baptism the candidate had already indicated initial faith and repentance. The candidate entered the water in the nude. While the candidate was in the water, "faith" (*fides*) was publicly professed, the devil was renounced, and the threefold name was invoked. We can surmise that the public *fides* was the loyalty oath. The candidate emerged from the water and drank milk with honey. Then he or she was anointed with oil, hands were placed on the candidate, the presider prayed a benediction, appealing to the Spirit to descend on the individual, and finally a eucharistic meal was taken. The candidate was not to bathe for a full week afterward.[28]

As in the New Testament, an oath of fidelity is featured as part of the baptism. But unlike in the New Testament, where loyalty's definitive expression is regularly described as causing justification or Spirit union, by Tertullian's time Spirit union is believed to come later in the baptismal process, when the presider prays for it. The description in *On the Apostolic Tradition* is similar to what we find in Tertullian's but with a heightened emphasis on exorcism prior to baptism.

Tertullian, writing in the third century, opposes infant baptism. Tertullian is our first source in history to mention the baptism of

young children—proposed earlier references are highly dubious—
and he argues against the practice.[29] This is unsurprising since all
the evidence from the apostolic age and the second century suggests that baptism had to be *personal* and *voluntary* and *required
steps impossible for infants*. Tertullian opposes the baptism of
young children, saying it is best to delay until they have grown to
the age where they "know how to 'ask' for salvation."[30]

Like Justin Martyr and the vast majority of early Christians
prior to Augustine in the fifth century, Tertullian does *not* view
infants as having inherited a sin nature. Rather, children evidence
what Tertullian calls "an innocent period of life," so that it is
pointless to hasten to offer them what they don't yet need, "remis-
sion of sins."[31]

Tertullian says that the baptism of children who are underage
puts those who speak the baptismal oath on behalf of the children
needlessly at risk because they cannot guarantee the fulfillment
of these baptismal promises; also, the child might develop an evil
disposition—all of which would implicate the speaker in guilt.[32]

Both earlier evidence and Tertullian's discussion suggest that
the baptism of children who cannot speak for themselves was an
innovation of the late second century rather than an apostolic
practice.[33] Tertullian says that children should not be baptized
until they have learned how to "come" to Christ on their own.

Meanwhile, the slightly later document *On the Apostolic Tradition* allows infant baptism. It is probably the earliest source to
affirm the practice, but its complex compositional history lends
uncertainty because around the same time Origen begins to speak
in favor of it too.[34] *On the Apostolic Tradition* prefers that each
baptismal candidate be able to speak for themselves but permits a
family member to speak on behalf of a child. This practice gradually surpassed adult baptism in both East and West.

In sum, what do we learn from our New Testament and early
Christian sources about how baptism saves? To enter salvation

personally is not to arrive at its final destination. Since baptism is only part of the initialization process, it is certainly not completely saving for an individual within life's journey. Furthermore, baptism is a multipart event that consists of essential and inessential components, so it is inaccurate to say that baptism is the true starting point rather than an individual's declaration of fidelity without pressing into how these interrelate. When baptisms are described as part of an effective salvation process in the New Testament and the first two centuries of the church, there is variation in the exact baptismal words spoken, the practice of the laying on of hands, and the necessity of full immersion, and hence we should conclude that precision about these is inessential to salvation.

Voluntary repentance and personally expressing fealty to Jesus as sovereign are essential to how baptism is saving in the New Testament and earliest Christianity. This causes Spirit union and cleanses the heart, soul, or essential self. Spirit union *always* comes after an individual hears the gospel, repents, and gives loyalty (faith). Spirit union sometimes happens before, during, or after baptism, showing us that while baptism or the water itself is not the necessary instrument of justification, it is nevertheless the ordinary context for the repentant oath of fealty to Jesus as the Christ, which is justification's precise instrument.

Secondarily, one was to wash oneself with water to devote the outer body. This could be an individual or group washing. This accords with the meaning of baptism within Judaism that Christianity inherited. Repentance and declared fidelity were the instruments by which the essential person (the soul) was cleansed, not water.

Baptismal Practices Today

Let me briefly address today's pastoral situation with regard to baptism. An infant or young child cannot personally hear the gospel, believe, repent, volunteer for baptism, self-immerse and wash, and express an oath of faith to King Jesus. Thus, an infant cannot do what the New Testament and earliest church deem necessary to decisively enter into union with the king and his people by receiving the Holy Spirit. Nothing uniquely saving happens for an infant during an infant baptism.

An infant born into an allegiant household will be influenced by the Spirit's presence in countless beneficial ways. The same is true for a person born into a largely Christian culture. But theologically we have no evidence that Jesus, the apostles, or their immediate heirs believed that an infant within an allegiant household can be regenerated by receiving the Spirit and in so doing enter the true church any more than a person can receive the Spirit simply by being born into a predominantly Christian society.

The Spirit's influence through family and culture is not the same as personal saving immersion in the Spirit via repentant allegiance to King Jesus. For this reason, it is best to wait, as Tertullian suggests, until a child or young adult is of sufficient age to ask. Waiting keeps the personal repentant oath of allegiance, baptism, and Spirit reception together per New Testament and earliest Christian historical norms. Not only is infant baptism not saving, but it is also an unwise pastoral practice.

Again, valid church traditions can develop beyond Scripture if they accord with Scripture, but illegitimate traditions can emerge too. When invalid traditions develop, no matter how long-standing, reform is necessary. Valid traditions, even for Catholics, must accord with Scripture and early Christian history (see chap. 4). The doctrines and practices that allow infant baptism to persist in the church require ongoing reformation.

Reform becomes especially urgent when faulty dogmatic claims emerge within traditions about *how salvation must happen always and for everyone*. But the problem isn't simply infant baptism; it is also the *ex opere operato* sacramental theology that undergirds it. For instance, Catholic, Orthodox, and some Protestant churches claim that baptism is effective by virtue of the sacramental action itself (*ex opere operato*)—moreover, this baptism, which need not involve personal repentance, faith, or choice, is mandatory for initializing salvation. For example, in its authoritative dogma, the Catholic Church claims, "The sacrament of baptism is the sacrament of faith, *without which no man was ever justified.*"[35] An impersonal, involuntary, *ex opere operato* interpretation of baptism as that which is always necessary to initialize each person's salvation contradicts both Scripture and early Christian history and excludes the apostles from salvation, because they didn't hold to or practice it.

All this being said, widespread reforms around *ex opere operato* sacramental theology and infant baptism are unlikely to happen anytime soon. Infant baptism is practiced by the majority of Christians worldwide, although as the evidence from early Christian history has become more widely available over the last five hundred years, the percentage of Christians who practice it has declined steadily. For those who are persuaded by the gospel-allegiance model or other models that do not affirm infant baptism, what should be done?

In the long run, those who are persuaded should advocate against it so that the practice of infant baptism continues to decline and so that pressure is applied to denominational leaders to reform their dogmas, confessions, and practices. In the short term, whether those who are persuaded by gospel-allegiance belong to an infant-baptism tradition or not, the answer is exactly the same: *Do whatever you can to help individuals or groups voluntarily to repent and to undertake a decisive oath of allegiance to King Jesus.*

The New Testament bears witness that when baptism is regenerative, it is the personal voluntary repentant declaration of fidelity to King Jesus that makes it so, for that is what causes Spirit union. But God is not constrained. Down through the ages, the church has had a harmful, misguided obsession with what counts as a "valid" baptism. We should relax because God's saving work is not in the least bit constrained by our modes and forms of baptism. During the apostolic age, Spirit union could and did happen on the basis of repentant allegiance to King Jesus apart from, before, during, and after baptism in the New Testament. We should expect nothing different today.

Therefore, even though nothing decisively saving happens during an infant baptism, God's saving purposes can be fulfilled through infant baptism if it paves the way for a repentant oath of personal allegiance in the future. Although confirmation doesn't always focus upon voluntary declared allegiance to King Jesus, in its best forms it can and it does.

Therefore, my recommendation is simple, although doubtless the particulars require creative reflection: regardless of your tradition or denomination's understanding of baptism, *do whatever you can to help individuals decide to definitively declare allegiance to King Jesus.*

For those who belong to a youth-baptism or adult-baptism tradition, let's stop advocating for mere credobaptism or believer's baptism in our doctrinal statements and practices. Believing in Jesus's saving work is not enough. Instead, let's articulate a doctrinal and practical preference for *allegiant baptism* or a *loyalist's baptism.* Before undertaking baptism, a youth should be of sufficient age to know King Jesus and his ways, to repent, and to swear loyalty personally with the intention that the oath will remain forever binding.

Consider having candidates for baptism write their own oaths under guidance. Of course, as part of that oath, make certain that it is being sworn to the real King Jesus, the one who demands repentance from sins and who is described in the Father-Son-Spirit gospel. I have guided others through this. I know pastors who are doing this too.

If you belong to an infant-baptism tradition, advocate for change when appropriate, but in the meanwhile make every effort to ensure that confirmation or other coming-of-age events at church or in camps feature an opportunity to voluntarily yet decisively repent and undertake an oath of allegiance to King Jesus. For according to the New Testament and our earliest Christian history, this, rather than infant baptism, is what actually causes Spirit union.

Regardless of your church tradition, seek to create opportunities to renew allegiance frequently. Consider working with your local church's leadership to create an oath-renewal ceremony to be carried out periodically—perhaps once a year. Ponder how you can involve the mind and the body in such a ceremony. A sincere personal declaration of loyalty to King Jesus that persists is what is essential to salvation. God will pour out the Holy Spirit in response to it.

6 Why Election and Regeneration Are False Starts

This book contends that loyalty to King Jesus, decisively rendered, is the true starting point for an individual's salvation. Any authentic profession of allegiance to King Jesus is predicated on a sufficient belief in the truthfulness of the King Jesus gospel. Meanwhile, a person need not have 100 percent certainty. It is not necessary to have perfect "faith," however that word is understood. We simply need enough to give ourselves over to King Jesus's rule, despite whatever lingering doubts and setbacks in our attempts to give loyalty we might suffer along life's way.

Some Christian traditions disagree that faith is the actual starting point for personal salvation. Apart from baptism, which I've just discussed, the two most popular alternatives are to suggest that an individual's salvation instead begins at the moment of (1) *personal election* or (2) *pre-faith regeneration*.

To these, I say no. To suggest that personal election or pre-faith regeneration is the true starting point for personal salvation does not respect what Scripture teaches holistically. In what follows I discuss each in turn, showing why it is inaccurate to say that individual election or pre-faith regeneration is the actual starting point for personal salvation.

Personal Election First?

Theoretical objection 1: You say that repentant loyalty to King Jesus starts personal salvation. But doesn't an individual's salvation actually begin before time as part of God's eternal decree, within which he chose certain individuals for eternal life while allowing others to be damned?

The Eternal Decree and Personal Salvation

What is meant by the "eternal decree" is that before creation or time's beginning, God determined to unfold creation according to a certain logical process, taking into account human disobedience and salvation. Although we may wonder how God's sovereignty interfaces with God's gifts of agency and freedom within creation, we cannot doubt that God decreed salvation in the Christ before the foundations of the world.

We can't doubt this, since God's election of the Christ for salvation is straightforwardly taught in Scripture. Yet this doesn't mean that *personal* salvation begins within God's eternal decree. On the contrary, if we are to respect what Scripture teaches about salvation, we actually cannot begin with an eternal decree in seeking to understand an *individual's* salvation. In other words, both those in favor of the Synod of Dort's (1618–19) conclusions (Calvinists) and those against Dort (Arminians) start in dubious places. There are three reasons why.

1. *The decree's meaning is future determined.* If our theology is to remain grounded in Scripture, God's decrees cannot be the ultimate starting place, because they have no meaning on their own. They rely on the subsequent story of humanity and of Israel's place within that story in the Bible for their meaning. Consider the Bible's leading statements regarding God's eternal decrees:

> Blessed be the God and Father of our Lord Jesus Christ, who has blessed us in Christ with every spiritual blessing in the heavenly places, even as he chose us in him before the foundation of the world, that we should be holy and blameless before him. In love he

predestined [*proorisas*] us for adoption to himself as sons through Jesus Christ, according to the purpose of his will. (Eph. 1:3–5)

[God] saved us and called us to a holy calling, not because of our works but because of his own purpose and grace, which he gave us in Christ Jesus before the ages began, and which now has been manifested through the appearing of our Savior Christ Jesus, who abolished death and brought life and immortality to light through the gospel. (2 Tim. 1:9–10)

[You were redeemed] with the precious blood of Christ, like that of a lamb without blemish or spot. He was foreknown before the foundation of the world but was made manifest in the last times for the sake of you. (1 Pet. 1:19–20)

At the foundation of Calvinist and Arminian soteriology is God's eternal choice in favor of "us" prior to the foundation of the world. But notice that in all these passages this choice is only *in the Christ*—that is, in the Messiah. The "Christ" refers to the promised-in-advance Davidic king, the one who would arise to restore Israel and rule over the nations through a historical process.

It is only *in the future* with regard to the decree that God the Son would unite himself to the humanity of a historical person named Jesus of Nazareth, who would through real events *become* the Christ, the messianic king. The phrases "in Christ" and "of Christ" in the passages about God's before-creation decree are not timeless references but rather refer to *the royal office* that would come about only *through future historical processes* with respect to the decree itself. In other words, biblically speaking, it is impossible to make the eternal decree the first move in our story of salvation.

The decree's meaning depends on Israel's future history because "Christ" (as Paul and Peter intend it) is a royal title specific to that history, not a personal name. This *royal* emphasis is largely missing from both sides in the Reformed-Arminian disputes about predestination and election. Both treat "Christ" as if it intends to refer in a nontitular way beyond itself to a person who is eternal or timeless. This imprecision disregards the meaning of *the specific title "Christ" in the decree*, resulting in theological distortion.

"Christ" is not a personal name but rather an honorific title.[1] If we functionally reduce "Christ" in the decree to a personal name in order to locate salvation in an eternal person rather than in a messianic office that will eventually come to be filled by an eternal person who took on human flesh through a historical process, we are running against the grain of Scripture's teaching on salvation. We cannot make the decree accurately refer in the exact *messianic* way Paul and Peter intend without drawing upon time-bound historical processes that occur later in the story. As we will see, the same is true for election more generally.

2. *The decree's meaning depends on the universal story.* The future-determined meaning of the "Christ" is an obstacle to a self-contained eternal decree. The Bible's *universal* foundational story is an equally serious problem for those who wish to begin with a decree that includes the saving election of specific individuals. The Bible's foundational story of creation, Adam, Eve, Noah, the flood, Abraham, and so forth is a *universal* story that is in significant tension with the purported individual-election story.

The foundational story that we find in Scripture is not a story of God's secret and inscrutable choice before time began to extend grace to one portion of humanity while passing by the rest. We must admit that, candidly considered, the story of God's prior-to-creation secret choice of individual humans for eternal life over against others is not found in the Bible *at all*. That alternative foundational story has been concocted by later theologians who patch together various decontextualized references in an attempt to explain how salvation transpires.

The foundational story that we actually find narrated in Scripture is universal. It is about *all* people: the Hebrew word *Adam* means "human." God crafts Eve from Adam's rib, so she is sourced in him. Eve's name is connected to life and is glossed as "mother of the living" (Gen. 3:20). The Bible intentionally puts forward Adam and Eve as universal paradigmatic humans. Their story is foundational because it encompasses the subsequent story of each and every person. Their story is about *all* humanity's universal encounter with God's command, *uniform* choice to transgress, and *united* disobedience. *All humanity* is given hope by the promise of a *future* seed, a human offspring, who will emerge *from within that universal story* to crush the serpent's head (3:15).

The Bible's foundational story is about all humanity, not secretly-chosen-for-salvation-before-creation or secretly-passed-over-for-damnation individuals. When God covenants with Noah, promising never again to undo creation with a flood, it is for "*every* living creature of *all* flesh" (Gen. 9:15–16). Similarly, God covenants with Abraham not so that through his seed one and only one secretly chosen people will be blessed; rather, "*all* nations of the earth will be blessed" (12:3; 18:18; 22:18). When God elects, he chooses individuals like Abraham precisely because he intends to bless *all nations* through that election.

As the story progresses through Moses to the time of David, it becomes clear that this seed that provides hope for all is a future king, a Christ, who will restore Israel and benefit the nations (e.g., 2 Sam. 7:12–16). Even later, Jesus is revealed to the apostles and others as *that Christ*. Because the foundational story is about *united* human disobedience and *united* human hope, *the Christ* is put forward as the *universal* solution for *all* humankind.

In sum, truly the eternal decree is based on election *in the Christ* before the foundation of the world. But "Christ" is not a personal name and does not mean the same thing as "Jesus." *"The Christ" has no meaning until that meaning arrives within subsequent human history (and the story of Israel within it). Moreover, Scripture's foundational story is universal when it defines the Christ's saving significance: it is about united disobedience and hope for all humans rather than about God's secret election for or against certain individuals.*

3. *The decree is collective.* Beyond the decree's future-determined meaning and universality, an even more serious problem prevents us from making the decree the starting point for individual salvation. We know that God collectively chose whomever happens to be "in the Christ" (Eph. 1:4; 2 Tim. 1:10), but this tells us nothing

about whether this predestining choice extended to this or that individual personally. All we know is that God predestined whoever happens to be "in the Christ" *as a group* to be saved. Nothing in the decree passages indicates that God individualized his choice by specifying before the foundation of the world those who do or do not belong to the saved group in any election passage in Scripture.[2] The decree pertains to the *group* that is "in the Christ." On its own it says nothing about the process by which *individuals* enter, remain within, or leave the group.

Two factors show that Paul did not intend to individuate the most foundational text, Ephesians 1:3–14. First, when Paul speaks of "you" and "your" in these predestination passages (and others like them), English readers are tempted to think this means specific individuals. But not so in the New Testament's original Greek text. In the Greek the references are to a plural "you," not to individuals. If you are reading the New Testament in its original language, you see that Paul's use of the word *you* is collective. It explicitly includes more than one *you*.

There is a second reason why it is likely that the decree speaks of the predestination of those who happen to be found in the king in the future rather than of predetermined individual fates. In Reformed discussions of salvation, election ultimately pertains to God's choice to favor certain individuals for salvation, while God chose to pass by others. But election was nearly always *corporate* and *for a vocation* rather than for individualized fate in the New Testament and Second Temple Judaism. We turn to election now.

Corporate Vocational Election

Perhaps everyone can agree that group election is the primary category in Scripture, since it is indisputably far more prominent. But could this be a false dilemma? Surely, to say that one must choose either group election or individual election is to ignore a both/and solution. Aren't groups ("us" and "you" in the plural) simply made up of individuals, so that some specific individuals must be in view in election in order to constitute a group? In light of God's sovereignty and foreknowledge, even if Scripture prefers to speak about group election, why not say that God knows and actively chooses each individual to be saved before the foundation of the world within the saved group?

There are four reasons why it is unlikely that individual election is also intended when Scripture describes the election of a group. First, when Paul or other authors want to emphasize an individual amid a collective group, they can do that. For example, Paul says, "each of us" (e.g., Rom. 14:12; 15:2) or "each of you" (1 Cor. 1:12; 1 Thess. 2:12; 4:4) at various places in his letters. Paul does this when he wants to foreground individuals within a collective, but Paul does not do this in any of the predestination passages.[3] Once we are aware that our biblical authors could have emphasized individual election amid group election but opted not to do so, we are left to wonder why advocates of individual election are eager to emphasize something that Scripture is not interested in highlighting. *It is beyond dispute that if they happened to hold to individual predestination amid group predestination, Paul and Peter could have stressed it, but they did not.*

Second, it is not true that groups are merely a collection of individuals, so that specific predestined individuals must be in view within corporate election to populate the group. Since the Christ is the predestined elect head of the group and the source of the saving benefits, anyone who is incorporated into his body *at any time* is incorporated into his benefits. If a person repentantly swears loyalty to King Jesus, they become predestined and elect because they have entered the group that is united to his status and benefits. If they never do this or cease doing this, they are not part of that group, so they are not predestined and elect.

A person can enter the Christ group *at any time*, because groups and their benefits persist even when individuals enter and leave them. Groups have properties that define them beyond the individual members that constitute the group. Those who lived in the New Testament era knew this. For example, individuals joined voluntary societies to obtain benefits associated with group membership, especially ceremonial meals and burial after death.

145

Voluntary societies were hugely popular in the New Testament world.[4] Ancient individuals who joined such societies for burial necessarily understood that group identity—its membership and benefits—was not reducible merely to its present individual members. Individuals could join or exit such groups (usually by paying or forsaking dues), but they had confidence that if they remained in the group, they would enjoy its benefits. Such groups were valuable precisely because they existed before individual members joined and perdured beyond them. Otherwise, a person would not have valued a benefit that only an enduring group could provide after the individuals who presently populate the group had died, such as burial.

That burial *after death* was valued as a *personal* benefit within voluntary societies in the New Testament world reminds us that group properties and benefits extend beyond the individuals who presently constitute the group—and that this was common knowledge in the New Testament era. The people who are saved in the Christ constitute a group—a corporate body. Predestining election can be corporate in the New Testament, because the Messiah is the predestined and elect kingly head of a body, and he shares that status with whomever enters and remains within his body at any time.

Third, although to propose that both corporate and individual election are in view seems reasonable, we must remember that the biblical cultures are quite different from our own. Many of us are products of the Western theological tradition, with its emphasis on individual salvation. However, the cultures of the Bible emphasized group values and identity more than individual.[5] In short, Christians shaped by the West tend to force Scripture to answer questions about individual salvation that it is not interested in answering.[6] Since group identity was normative within the biblical cultures, it is prima facie improbable that individual election is intended within its descriptions of group election.

Fourth, and most importantly, we can test the degree to which Scripture might intend individual election within the group. The Bible itself is the premier testing ground. Yet, to help us understand the Bible and provide a further probabilistic baseline, we have valuable ancient documents—for example, the Dead Sea Scrolls and portions of the Pseudepigrapha and the Apostolic Fathers—that were either entirely or mostly unavailable to Reformation-era theologians. Using these, we can credibly carry out the search for individual election within group election beyond what was possible during the Reformation. Numerous studies have been done examining Scripture and beyond.[7]

The results? Historically based studies of election agree: out of some hundred possible examples, when it pertains to salvation, election is *exclusively corporate* in the New Testament and related noncanonical literature. *Individual election is not a view Jews or early Christians can be demonstrated to have held regularly, if at all, during this era.*

Chad Thornhill, the author of the most recent and most authoritative historically based study of election in Scripture and beyond, summarizes his survey of the literature as follows:

> We discovered a view of election that was grounded in God's promises to the patriarchs. This overwhelmingly emphasized the collective nature of election as a concept that applied to a bounded community. When individuals were in view, their role, their character or their representation of a group was emphasized, never their being chosen for a particular soteriological standing.[8]

Not only does Thornhill conclusively demonstrate that the literature of the New Testament era (inside and outside Scripture) overwhelmingly presents election for salvation as exclusively corporate, but he also argues that *individual election for ultimate salvation is never exemplified: that is, nobody during the New Testament era (Jew or Christian) evidenced belief that God chose or otherwise predestined specific individuals for eternal life or passed them by for damnation.* There are only a couple of possible exceptions to Thornhill's "never" with regard to individual election for salvation unto eternal life (or the like) in the New Testament era that have been raised by scholars who dispute his results—and even the validity of the status of these as disputed is debatable.[9] So, even if a few exceptions are found to Thornhill's "never" in the future, if we are seeking a theology of salvation grounded in what is overwhelmingly probable, rather than what is remotely possible, we must conclude that Scripture does not teach individual election for eternal life. *Scripture teaches the election of a group in the Christ for final salvation but does not teach that specific individuals have been predestined or otherwise chosen ahead of time to belong to that group or be excluded from it.*

Individual Election in Ephesians 1:3–14?

Given that it is the premier test case, let's see if the passage we looked at previously, Ephesians 1:3–14, shows evidence favoring individual election within corporate. It does not. In fact, there is strong contextual evidence that proves Paul did not intend individual predestination before creation in the decree in Ephesians 1:5.

Ephesians 1:3–12 is one long sentence in Greek that ends with "in the Christ." Paul speaks about how God "chose *us* in him before the foundation of the world" (1:4). The election of *us* is not some first act independent of the Christ but occurs only *in* or through his office as the king. "The Christ" is said to exist prior to the founding of the world (i.e., in his capacity as the eternal divine Son who will eventually fill the office of "the Christ" in the future). But remember: only in the future with respect to the decree will the eternal Son be united to the humanity of a specific man named Jesus who fulfills the office of *the Christ* as that developed within history. So the decree's meaning depends on future historical conditions and developments. Later Paul says that "we" have an inheritance in the king, "having been *predestined* according to the purpose of him who works all things according to the counsel of his will" (1:11).

But then immediately afterward, Paul explains what he means by saying that we were predestined, and he speaks of a *staggered temporal sequence* by which the people of God have come to be constituted:

in order that *we, who were the first to put our hope in the Christ,* might be for the praise of his glory. And *you* [plural] also *were included in the Christ,* having heard the message of truth, the gospel of your salvation. Having performed the *pistis* action [*pisteusantes*], you [plural] were marked in him with a seal, the promised Holy Spirit. (Eph. 1:12–13 AT)

Ephesians 1:11–13 speaks of discrete stages in time by which two different subgroups have entered the larger unified predestined "in the Christ" group. Paul is saying that a group of Jews ("we") entered the Messiah historically first, and subsequently a group of gentiles ("you") did so. This group of gentiles is called "you," which can be singular or plural in English but in the original Greek of the New Testament is explicitly plural—a group—more than one person.

This shows that the predestination of *each specific individual before time* is an impossibly unlikely construal of what Paul means by "in the Christ" throughout Ephesians 1:3–14. For Paul indicates that the first group came to be "in the Christ" when they put their hope in the king. Subsequently a second group—a group called "you" that included the Ephesians—was included "in the Christ" when they heard the gospel and performed the *pistis* action in response to the king.

In other words, in Ephesians the number of those who are predestined "in Christ" as elect or chosen before creation is described as *growing.* We know this to be true because the number of those who are said to be predestined in Christ in Ephesians 1:4–5 is described in 1:11–13 as increasing over time as first one group enters, then another. If individual election before creation happened to be true, then the number of the elect can never shrink or grow, because each and every person was individually chosen before time began, fixing the exact number of the elect. *The expanding number of the elect shows that predestining election does not pertain to God's choice in favor of specific individuals before time began.*

We are weighing the actual point of controversy in Ephesians 1:3–14: Granted that Scripture prefers group election, is individual election likely to also be in view within group election? Let me summarize the result: it is weak constructive theology and poor exegesis to suggest that Paul would use *the same verb for "predestine"* in 1:5 that he uses in 1:11 but with vastly different intentions—first to refer to God's choice of individuals in eternity, but second to groups within time. If the predestination of specific individuals "in the Christ" happened to be in view in 1:5, then the exact number of individuals chosen would be fixed at a precise quantity before the foundation of the world. It could not be expanding. But in 1:11–13 Paul uses the same "predestination" language that he used in 1:5 to say that the number of those who are "in the Christ" is expanding. This conclusion is secure because Paul's language describing the subgroup of gentiles—"you also were included in the Christ, having heard the message of truth"—does not suggest that individuals within this subgroup were in any sense "in the Christ" before hearing the gospel. Paul indicates that it was *at this time* that they were included "in the Christ." They were included once they heard and responded to the gospel—that is, *after meeting a condition*: first they had to perform the loyalty action (*pisteusantes*) with respect to the king. Therefore, Paul does not refer to the unconditional predestination of specific individuals for salvation in either 1:5 or 1:11–13.

So Paul does not affirm that each human is predestined to an eternal fate. What, then, is Paul's positive theological claim about predestination in Ephesians 1:3–14? Here's a summary: God predestined the king individually as a corporate representative. Hence, all who past, present, or future happen to be within the king's group can appropriately be described as predestined too—*but only if they enter and remain in that group by allegiance*. This is why Paul says God chose and predestined "us" but immediately clarifies that this happens only "in him"—that is, in the Christ (Eph. 1:4–5). Paul makes his view explicit subsequently when he uses the same predestination language that he used in Ephesians 1:5 in 1:11–13 to show that a future-oriented *conditional* response *to the king* creates and defines the predestined group's boundary. For Paul, the predestining election of the church as a group is real but only "in the Christ," and that group is populated with members only within history. The Christ is predestined as the elect one, a status he shares as a group benefit with anyone who responds to the gospel as the Christ is revealed within unfolding history. For Paul, God's predestining election is a *future-conditional corporate benefit* for all those who are "in the Christ."

This also matches norms for Jews within the New Testament era. As Chad Thornhill puts it in his survey of election, "The Jewish literature [of this era] was decidedly *conditional*, with various authors defining who was 'in' and who was 'out' by different means and markers."[10] For Paul, because the Christ was predestined in advance and shares his benefits with his body, a declaration of faith in response to the King Jesus gospel is the condition that causes various individuals to enter for the first time into the Messiah's predestined group and to share that status.

God's Vocational Election of Individuals

A similar analysis to the one just carried out for Ephesians 1:3–14 could be undertaken for all purported examples of individual election unto final salvation in Scripture. That is, excluding the Son, there is not a single unambiguous example where God is said to have predestined an individual to eternal life or a bypassing for eternal damnation before they were born. Nary a one.

Jacob? Esau? Pharaoh? Judas? Paul himself? Nope. All of these are chosen in advance by God for specific *vocational* purposes, but none are described as having been chosen before their own births—let alone before creation—for eternal life or condemnation. That is, God elects or chooses specific individuals *for long-term or short-term tasks* that relate to his overarching plans, but Scripture does not describe any person as singularly elect for *final salvation*.

For example, God took the initiative, in and through the resurrected Christ, to reveal himself to Paul, but this didn't inexorably result in Paul's final salvation. More specifically, in speaking about his own election, yes, Paul does say that God "set me apart before I was born and called me by his grace," but he immediately clarifies that this was so that he might *"preach about the Messiah* among the nations" (Gal. 1:15 AT). He is chosen before birth for a task, not for eternal life.

Since scholarship agrees that Paul is drawing on Jeremiah's language of vocation with respect to the nations in his description of his election, Jeremiah serves as further evidence. God chose Jeremiah before he was born for the task of being "a prophet to the nations" (Jer. 1:5), not for eternal life. It is much the same for God's election of Paul to preach about the king.

Moreover, according to Paul's own testimony, he did not regard his own personal salvation as irrevocably established on the basis of this initial calling. He did not consider the prize of resurrection life to be his apart from further striving toward it (Phil. 3:11–14). He disciplined his body, "lest after preaching to others I myself should be disqualified" (1 Cor. 9:27). God's election of Paul was for a specific vocation: to preach the gospel to the nations. This election is not described by Paul as inevitably resulting in his attainment of the ultimate prize of eternal life.

As further evidence of the vocational nature of election, consider how Paul describes the circumstances of the conception and birth of the twins Jacob and Esau:

> When Rebekah had conceived children by one man, our forefather Isaac, though they were not yet born and had done nothing either good or bad—in order that God's purpose of election might continue, not because of works but because of him who calls—she was told, "The older will serve the younger." As it is written, "Jacob I loved, but Esau I hated." (Rom. 9:10–13)

It is true, of course, that Jacob and Esau as individuals were chosen in advance by God before or while in the womb, sometime before either had done good or bad. However, Paul's description of God's "purpose of election" here does not intend election to final salvation—Paul says nothing here about predestined fate, eternal life, or ultimate salvation—but rather the election *pertains to different kinds of service.*[11]

Paul himself states the vocational purpose of their election: the older (Esau) will *serve* the younger (Jacob). God's election in this passage does not aim toward granting Jacob eternal life while allowing Esau to fall into eternal damnation. Rather, God chooses Jacob (the individual) for a task: God uses Jacob to build *an entire people* for himself amid *the nations*. As part of that plan, Esau will serve Jacob so that then Jacob can serve all nations by being a vehicle for the blessing.

In fact, when read in context, Paul's quote from Malachi 1:2–3, "Jacob I loved, but Esau I hated," is a reference to these men not as individuals but as national figureheads, because Paul intends *a collective reference to the nations of Jacob and of Esau respectively*. Look it up: Jacob and Esau are *nations* in the quote from Malachi, and the "loved" and "hated" language refers to the status of the nations that they represent within God's plan at a specific juncture in history over one thousand years after Jacob and Esau have died. Paul's point is absolutely *not* that God predestined Jacob individually for eternal life ("Jacob I loved") and allowed Esau personally to fall into damnation ("Esau I hated"). Rather, Paul's point is that God has worked out his purposes in history in such a way that judgment has presently fallen on Esau as a nation, because God has larger *vocational* intentions in view for the world through his choice to covenant with Jacob as a nation.

As additional proof that vocational election and not eternal fate is in view, consider that Esau as an individual was not eternally passed over for final salvation because God "hated" him before his birth. In fact, even though Jacob steals Esau's blessing, nevertheless God through Isaac does in fact *bless* Esau: although Esau will experience hardship, eventually he will experience freedom from service to Jacob, his younger brother: "You shall break his yoke from your neck" (Gen. 27:40).

As his story unfolds, Esau does in fact acquire tremendous wealth and a huge family—an indication of God's blessing in this era (see Gen. 32–33; 36, esp. 36:6–8). Esau has become so numerous and wealthy that Jacob—a relatively wealthy man himself—is compelled to call himself Esau's servant repeatedly in an attempt to reconcile with him (see 32:4). In the final analysis, despite Esau's immoral choices and his failure to receive the unique blessing that Jacob received (Heb. 12:16–17), *Esau is nevertheless described as "blessed"* (11:20). That would not make sense if God's hatred of Esau intends a damning passing-him-by with regard to eternal life while electing Jacob to eternal life instead.

Predestining individual election for final salvation is simply not in view with regard to Jacob and Esau. It was a vocational choosing. Esau was elected *to serve* Jacob so that through God's election of Jacob (Israel) all nations would be served—preeminently through the elect Messiah, who would serve all. Then Jacob's and Esau's descendants, along with the other nations, would have the opportunity to be blessed as they are saved through allegiance to him. The purpose of individual election is not for eternal fate but rather for service within God's larger saving purposes for the world.

As the passage featuring Jacob and Esau continues, Paul clarifies why God elects various individuals—Jacob, Esau, and Pharaoh. In Romans 9:16–23 even Pharaoh is not *eternally* fated but exemplifies God's vocational choosing. Paul has read Exodus carefully. In Exodus, God foreknows that Pharaoh will ignore Moses's signs, so that God will *eventually* harden his heart (4:21; 7:3). But as the narrative unfolds, Pharaoh (or his heart) first performs the hardening or causes the heaviness (7:13–14, 22; 8:15, 32); God only subsequently solidifies this hardening or heaviness as a form of fitting judgment on Pharaoh (9:12). Then the pattern repeats (9:34–35; 10–14).

When reflecting on Exodus in Romans 9, Paul says nothing about Pharaoh's personal election for eternal life or condemnation, for that is not election's purpose. Instead, Paul indicates that God raised up Pharaoh for a *task* within his overarching plan as it relates to mercy and judgment for the world. Paul unites God's task-oriented vocational election of individuals (such as Pharaoh) with God's historical purposes for entire people groups:

> Now if God, desiring to display his wrath and to make known his power, has carried [*ēnenken*] with much patience vessels

characterized by wrath shaped [*katērtismena*] for destruction, and [has done so] in order to make known the riches of his glory to the vessels characterized by mercy, which he has prepared beforehand for glory—even us whom he has called, not only from the Jews but also from the gentiles . . . (Rom. 9:22–24 AT)

Romans 9:22–24 is not about personal predestination. Paul indicates that God has orchestrated certain instrumentalities pertaining to the salvation of large groups of people within the flow of time.[12] Specifically, two *groups* are mentioned: vessels of mercy and vessels of wrath.

We know that Paul is referring to large groups of people rather than individuals with his vessels imagery, for Paul describes the "vessels of mercy" as those whom God has called among both Jews and gentiles. These are subsequently described as having a righteousness by allegiance to the Christ (Rom. 9:30–10:17). *The vessels of mercy are Israelites in the Christ, inclusive of the gentiles who have been grafted into Israel.*

The vessels of wrath (that is, vessels characterized by wrath or filled with wrath) have been "carried" or "conveyed" (*ēnenken*) by God with much patience. They have been "shaped" or "formed" (*katērtismena*) for destruction, probably by their own willful rebellion against God. It can be inferred that these vessels of wrath were patiently conveyed by God to this moment in history so that God could do something further with them as part of his plan. *The vessels of wrath are Israelites who are presently not allegiant to the Christ.*

The shaping of a vessel for destruction does not mean it is damned or eternally lost. The vessels of wrath are shaped for destruction presently because they stumbled in their race toward righteousness, having failed to submit to the Christ (Rom. 9:33–10:4). In antiquity, when a vessel was destroyed on the wheel, its clay ordinarily was *repurposed*; this *reworking of spoiled clay on the potter's wheel* is precisely how Israel and the nations fit vocationally into God's purposes: "The vessel he [the potter] was making of clay was spoiled in the potter's hand, and he reworked

155

it into another vessel, as it seemed good to the potter to do. Then the word of the LORD came to me: 'O house of Israel, can I not do with you as this potter has done?'" (Jer. 18:4–6).

The vessels of wrath (Israelites apart from the Christ) are presently shaped for destruction, but this is not their irrevocable fate. On the contrary, despite their present obdurate condition, in the future they will be transformed when God uses the vessels of mercy (Israelites in the Christ, inclusive of the gentiles) to help these vessels of wrath attain *life from the dead* through King Jesus (Rom. 11:7–15). Paul thinks that the vessels of mercy have been appointed by God to help save the vessels of wrath—all of which should lead us to praise God for his shocking plan and stunning mercy (11:26–36). Because glory is double-sided, including intrinsic and acknowledged facets, God is most glorified when humans are glorified too—that is, maximally restored in dignity as image bearers.

Here's the larger point: both types of vessels in Romans are instruments for achieving God's redemptive purposes *within salvation history*. Nothing is said about *how long* beforehand these vessels (groups) were chosen by God—certainly nothing about from all eternity within eternal decrees—nor about this pertaining to *preselected individuals* who are destined to final heavenly glory or ultimate damnation within these groups. Again, final salvation is based on the condition of responding to the Christ with loyalty, and the emphasis is on corporate (group) rather than individual predestination.

In short, there is no valid scriptural basis for claiming that individual salvation truly begins with God's predestining election of certain individuals before the foundation of the world rather than when a person responds to the King Jesus gospel with loyalty. According to Scripture, God foreknows, foreordains, and is sovereign over the future—yes—*but God also chooses to exercise his foreknowledge, foreordination, and sovereignty over the future in such a way that he permits personal human choice.* By describing humans as agents capable of choosing to repent, to express faith, and to follow or not (e.g., Mark 8:34–35; Acts 13:38–41, 46; Rom.

10:9–10; 2 Pet. 3:9), the New Testament and early Christianity give ample space to individual human free will in salvation.

Modeling Free Will within God's Sovereignty

How human free will and divine sovereignty interface with respect to personal salvation is not systematically explained in the New Testament or in earliest Christianity. Scripture presents individual humans as ordinarily having sufficient free choice to respond to the gospel with faith, repentance, and baptism. Scripture does this while acknowledging that God desires to rescue everyone: God's saving love extends to the whole world (John 3:16), God is now drawing all to Jesus (12:32), God desires all to repent (2 Pet. 3:9), God wants to save all humans (2 Tim. 2:4). But at the same time Scripture indicates that individuals are not completely free due to sin, the flesh, and evil spiritual forces. Once the grace of the gospel is given, within the boundaries of God's sovereignty over the process of group and personal salvation, individuals are consistently portrayed as having sufficient but not perfect freedom to repent and express saving loyalty to King Jesus.

Much later in church history, speculative models were developed in an attempt to explain how human freedom coordinates with divine sovereignty. These models impacted how salvation was subsequently systematized by Catholics and Protestants. They still impact how the Bible is interpreted today.

Monergistic compatibilism. One innovative model is that of monergistic compatibilism, developed by Augustine. It originated in the fifth century and does not appear to have any significant precedent in Scripture or church history. Monergistic compatibilism contends that God alone graciously supplies all the initiative or lack of initiative in personal salvation—from predestination to final salvation—because God orchestrates all the circumstances of our desires. It is closely associated with Augustine's ideas about an inherited sin nature and the captivity of the human will (see the section "On the Bondage of the Will" below).

It is called *monergism* because God contributes all the required saving energy, and the individual adds nothing. If an individual chooses to respond to the gospel, it is only because God worked according to his predetermined plan to arrange affairs to make the individual *want* to respond favorably. Within monergistic compatibilism, a person always does what he or she truly wants to do with respect to salvation, because God in his sovereignty has arranged that outcome ahead of time. So, when a person makes a choice for or against the gospel, God has provided or withheld all the saving energy by shaping that person's past and present will toward God's predetermined future outcome. Because God alone energizes personal salvation within monergistic compatibilism, God's predetermined choice to save or bypass aligns with that person's ability and desire to respond to the gospel.

Augustine's monergistic compatibilism was the first serious attempt in Christian history to explain how God's predestining sovereignty could be reconciled with human free will in salvation.[13] Despite its novelty it was accepted in the West, impacting how Catholics and the first Protestants systematized salvation—but with important qualifications. After Augustine, many concluded that individuals could not strictly merit salvation (condign merit), but individuals could show a desire for salvation that God would reward by strengthening and assisting that desire (congruent merit). Protestants would reject condign and congruent merit, whereas Catholicism at the Council of Trent would reject condign merit but leave room for congruent.

Although neither Catholics nor Protestants of the sixteenth century embraced Augustine's monergistic compatibilism entirely, it nevertheless was the presupposed framework for explaining salvation. Augustine's monergistic compatibilism especially impacted the soteriology of Luther, Calvin, and other early Reformers.[14] It is still defended by many Reformed (Calvinist) systematic theologians today.

It is not simply monergistic compatibilism's novelty and its foreignness to the apostolic age that concern its detractors. Critics also worry that its limited version of free will doesn't harmonize with Scripture's depiction of individuals as *genuinely* free to decide: If God dictates all my circumstances and desires, such that

I can choose to respond to the gospel only if God energizes my desire to do that, then am I a puppet hanging from a divine string? An even more serious concern arises: critics also wonder whether monergistic compatibilism can avoid implicating God in temptation, sin, and guilt. If God controls all my affairs and desires, then what happens when I sin? If God alone orchestrates my circumstances and energizes my wants (monergism), so that any choice I make merely endorses what he has brought about (compatibilism), then it would appear that God has caused my temptation, sin, and failure to respond to the gospel in a way that contradicts Scripture (e.g., 1 Cor. 10:13; James 1:13). After the Reformation disrupted the Augustinian consensus, these and other possible weaknesses in monergistic compatibilism prompted theologians to search for a new model.

Molinism. In the wake of the initial Reformation and the Catholic response at Trent, a different model, Molinism (named after the Jesuit theologian Luis de Molina), developed in the late sixteenth century. It has subsequently impacted both Catholic and Protestant soteriology. Molinism emphasizes that God foreknows and foreordains reality in an indeterministic way through what is called his counterfactual or "middle knowledge." God knows what each will choose within a range of possibilities, but he does not causally determine each person's choice. God can know what is going to happen in advance without causing specific predetermined outcomes.

Within Molinism, God does not dictate personal desires or circumstances in such a way that the individual's choice to respond to the gospel is orchestrated by God's work alone. Instead, because God has already given the grace of the gospel (which no human deserves), and because he values noncoerced love, he opts to exercise his sovereignty by intentionally leaving the fullest possible arena for humans to exercise their own agency via libertarian free will. Within Molinism, individuals are constrained by sin but sufficiently free to initiate outcomes that God has not predetermined but that God does foreknow. This includes the individual's choice for or against the gospel, with eternal consequences.[15]

Appraising models of free will amid God's sovereignty. It is important to remember that Jesus and the apostles held to neither monergistic compatibilism (fifth century) nor Molinism (late sixteenth century). We shouldn't regard belief in them as essential for salvation, for the apostles did not hold to them and yet the apostles were saved. These models, along with newer approaches like open theism, are much later attempts to explain the Bible's theology.

Yet Scripture does provide boundaries that these models must respect. The New Testament attests that however God exercises sovereignty while retaining knowledge of the future, individuals have sufficient but not perfect freedom to exercise their own initializing agency when the gospel is proclaimed by enacting repentance, fidelity, and baptism. Moreover, God's *causal* predestining election of specific individuals to eternal life or his passing them over is nowhere taught by Scripture—even though God may know the future destiny of individuals. The Bible teaches only group election within the Christ's elect status. Moreover, history-based scholarship has now shown that it is highly unlikely that the predestining election of individuals is presumed as part of group election in the Bible or its world. Because monergistic compatibilism requires individual predestination as part of God's saving work, it lacks scriptural warrant. This doesn't definitively disprove monergistic compatibilism, but it does show that its scriptural foundation is faulty, making it an improbable theory.

Regardless of how we reconcile what Scripture teaches with our models for God's sovereignty, those who take the Bible seriously in constructing theology can't settle for what they wish to be true about Scripture. It is irresponsible to say that the Bible teaches that personal salvation begins when God elected specific individuals before creation for eternal life. Excluding the special case of the Son, it never explicitly teaches this even once, and it is doubtful that it ever teaches it at all.

Regeneration First?

Theoretical objection 2: You say that repentant loyalty to King Jesus starts personal salvation. But isn't it necessary first for God to regenerate that person—to liberate that person's will—so that person is free to respond to the gospel?

What Is Personal Regeneration?

"Personal regeneration" refers to an individual's birth into eschatological new life. In this discussion about whether regeneration might be better considered the true starting point in salvation, I am referring to a specific understanding of *pre-faith regeneration* among theologians: an act of God that imparts new life prior to the individual decisively expressing faith (*pistis*) in response to the gospel.[16]

It is important to clarify what I mean because, as we will see, Scripture uses diverse metaphors that might loosely be labeled "regeneration." The Bible does use imagery related to regeneration to describe personal salvation. That is not what is under dispute. Rather, what is contested is the claim that personal regeneration must happen to erase the will's bondage before a person can decisively express "faith" toward Jesus or the gospel. Scripture does not describe regeneration in that way.

Regeneration is never used in Scripture to describe a personal erasure of hard-heartedness or of the will's bondage so that justifying faith can happen. Although the term *regeneration* imprecisely summarizes a host of biblical metaphors—born again, new birth, new creation, the implantation of a seed—that describe the quality of new life effected at the moment a person is united to the king or his community, regeneration's *reification* as a distinct stage in an individual's order of salvation and its *separation from* and especially its *location prior to* "faith" and baptism in the order of salvation is not exegetically sound. Regeneration is not in view as a distinct pre-faith step in the thought structure of even a single New Testament book or author. Thus, it is dangerous to make dogmatic claims about it within an individualized soteriology.

The False Claim of Regeneration First

Yet dogmatic claims about pre-faith regeneration have all too often been made. "Regeneration" has been found to be theologically essential within some systems, so all statements that might pertain to "regeneration" are squeezed into this regeneration-as-a-distinct-prior-stage rubric as evidence "proving" that the doctrine is biblical. But the desire to separate out regeneration as a specific early step in the *ordo salutis* (order of salvation) is driven by perceived theological necessities—that God acts *alone* in initializing individual salvation (monergism), grace alone rather than merit, the bondage of the will, damage to human thought structures (noetic impairment)—as determined by later systematic theologians rather than by biblical evidence demonstrating that regeneration metaphors are used in this way.

For example, Wayne Grudem's *Systematic Theology* is the most widely used textbook for teaching salvation systematically in the English-speaking world. Grudem is typical of those who desire to prove that regeneration must come before "faith" in the *ordo salutis*. Although Grudem indicates that regeneration and faith often appear simultaneous from our human vantage point, nevertheless he claims that regeneration comes first to break the will and draw a person to God so that they can then repent and respond with faith.

Let's inspect his evidence. Grudem asserts that several passages teach that regeneration "does in fact come before we respond to God in saving faith."[17] For his first piece of testimony, he cites John 3:5: "Unless one is born of water and the Spirit, he cannot enter the kingdom of God." But this passage does not support Grudem's point. This verse does not mention faith at all, so it doesn't tell us whether "faith" comes before or after the "one is born." (Nor is it clear that entering the kingdom refers, as Grudem seems to think, exclusively to initial salvation as opposed to salvation's culmination [on which, see Matt. 7:21 and Luke 18:25].)

As additional evidence that regeneration happens before faith, Grudem cites John 6:44: "No one can come to me unless the Father who sent me draws him" and John 6:65: "No one can come to me unless it is granted him by the Father." Again, these passages say nothing definitive about how personal "faith" coordinates with *the timing* of God's activity—whether the drawing and granting are prior to faith or simultaneous with it.

Regardless, we can't read John 6:44 and 6:65 apart from how the Gospel of John itself qualifies these verses as it pertains to salvation history's progress. Yes, no one can come unless *drawn* by the Father, but now that the Son has been "lifted up" on the cross and exalted to the right hand of the Father, Jesus says, "I will *draw all people* to myself" (12:32). After the gospel has been given within history, Jesus says that *all* are drawn to God—each and every person—not merely certain individuals or all types of people. Not only do John 6:44 and 6:65 fail to describe how regeneration or faith fits into the process of personal salvation, when "drawing" is subsequently explained by Jesus, but we are also told that *all* are in fact drawn after the crucifixion and ascension.

Grudem also appeals to Lydia's conversion in Acts 16:14: "The Lord opened her heart to heed what was said by Paul."[18] Again, this does not demonstrate that regeneration precedes "faith," since the precise moment of Lydia's "faith" within the process of her personal salvation is not mentioned. Lydia's faith could have been present before, at the same time, or after the moment when the Lord opened her heart to heed Paul's message. Lydia's example merely shows that God can take the initiative *by revealing himself* as part of the process of personal salvation. However, no one disputes, as far as I'm aware, that God can take the initiative in salvation *by revealing himself in such a way that the heart is opened*—as he does, for instance, with the apostle Paul.

What is disputed is whether beyond revealing himself, God *necessarily* and *always* takes the initiative by supernatural regeneration prior to faith. If it is the case that God must erase hardheartedness or the complete bondage of the will and regenerate before a person can repent and express faith—and if God *always* must do this—it is strange that *not a single passage of Scripture* describes an individual's salvation in this way, whereas a great many passages emphasize ordinary human agency in initializing the "faith" activity.

Scripture and early Christianity consistently describe humans as having sufficient free agency to respond to the gospel. As Alistair McGrath puts it, "The pre-Augustinian theological tradition is

163

practically of one voice in asserting the freedom of the human will."[19] Libertarian free will was everywhere presupposed in the early church prior to Augustine's development of monergistic compatibilism in the fifth century AD.[20]

I've focused on Grudem's problematic claim that Scripture proves that faith comes before or is simultaneous with regeneration because his textbook is influential and because it manifests common errors. The Bible does not support the claim that regeneration should be considered a distinct pre-"faith" stage in a personalized order of salvation. Instead, it describes God as gifting everyone with the grace of the gospel itself in conjunction with imperfect but sufficient freedom to declare faith when it is proclaimed.

Regeneration Metaphors in the New Testament

What, then, does Scripture teach about regeneration? When we inspect the leading "regeneration" passages, we see that they resist being pigeon-holed into discrete locations in a personalized order of salvation.

Made alive in Colossians. In Colossians 2:11–13 Paul declares that the Colossians were "made alive together with the Christ" (cf. Eph. 2:5). Contextually, Paul frames this as happening in conjunction with a process "in the Christ," suggesting that regeneration occurs concurrent with or after the achievement of decisive union between the Christ and the individual.

> In him also you were circumcised with a circumcision made without hands, by putting off the body of the flesh, by the circumcision of Christ, having been buried with him in baptism, in which you were also raised with him *through faith* [*pistis*] in the powerful working of God, who raised him from the dead. And you, who were dead in your trespasses and the uncircumcision of your flesh, God *made alive* together with him, having forgiven us all our trespasses. (Col. 2:11–13)

Here regeneration involves a nonfleshly circumcision of the Christ, burial with him in baptism, and resurrection with him through *pistis*. Specifically, the "made alive" is associated with forgiveness (Col. 2:13) and the canceling of the record of debt as it was nailed to the cross (2:14). As Paul describes it, regeneration doesn't cause saving faith. On the contrary, faith is already present prior to the "making alive" of regeneration.

Infants, covenants, and baptismal regeneration? Chapter 5 has already given evidence that infant baptism is not saving. Yet, following Calvin, some use the regeneration imagery in Colossians 2:11–13 to contend that water baptism validates entry into the new covenant on the basis of an alleged parallel with fleshly circumcision as what ratifies entrance into the old covenant.[21] The idea is this: just as male infants received circumcision on the penis on the eighth day to validate their inclusion in the old covenant, so also anyone, infants included, can be baptized in water to ratify their inclusion in the new covenant. Since fleshly circumcision and water baptism both involve a physical activity attended by what is perceived to be a spiritual promise—this is felt to reinforce the correspondence. Various understandings of whether baptism is necessarily regenerative attend this logic.[22]

But here is the major problem: a false parallel between *physical* circumcision of the penis and water baptism has been created. In Colossians 2:11–13 Paul is speaking about *nonfleshly circumcision* as that which vivifies our dead uncircumcised flesh—"a circumcision *made without hands*" (Col. 2:11). Elsewhere we discover that this vivifying nonfleshly "circumcision of the heart" is the Spirit's work and has **absolutely nothing** to do with the physical *rite of the circumcision of an infant's penis on the eighth day* (Rom. 2:29; cf. Phil. 3:3–5; cf. Gal. 5:6; 1 Cor. 7:18–19). Those who compare *physical* circumcision and water baptism have created a false parallel that ignores Paul's actual topic in Colossians 2:11–13—*nonphysical* circumcision—and what Paul says elsewhere in his letters about the actual theological value of physical circumcision.

A second problem is the covenantal comparison. Although Scripture does not compare water baptism and fleshly circumcision within a covenantal framework *at all*, some theologians have found it convenient to juxtapose them artificially within that framework. First, granted that circumcision is given as a covenantal sign in the Old Testament and that this was well-known to our New Testament authors (e.g., Gen. 17:10–14; cf. Acts 7:8), Paul never stresses that circumcision is a covenantal sign, here or elsewhere. Colossians 2:11–13 does not say that circumcision of the penis was the seal of a singular Abrahamic "old covenant" or that physical circumcision was the old covenant's ratification or its entry point. Second, neither Paul's letters nor the remainder of the New Testament says anything whatsoever about sealing or entering into covenants with respect to baptism. So the covenantal comparison between circumcision and baptism is doubly artificial.

The idea that circumcision seals the old covenant and baptism the new covenant stems primarily from an unwarranted extrapolation of covenant theology in the Bible as that is combined with a poor exegesis of Colossians 2:11–13 and Romans 4:11. In Romans 4:11 Paul says that Abraham "received the sign of circumcision as a seal [*sphragis*] of the righteousness that he had by faith while he was still uncircumcised." But when Paul explains what this means, he does *not* suggest that Abraham's receipt of circumcision was the "seal" (certification, ratification) of an old covenant—let alone *the* old covenant (however defined)—while baptism is the seal of the new. Paul says nothing about covenants or baptism when describing physical circumcision as the seal.

Instead, Paul explains why fleshly circumcision was a seal for Abraham: "The purpose was to make him *the father* of all who believe *without being circumcised*, so that righteousness would be counted to them as well" (Rom. 4:11). He goes on to speak of how it also seals those who are physically circumcised but share Abraham's precircumcision faith. That is, Paul says that Abraham's fleshly circumcision sealed his *fatherhood* over *all physically circumcised and uncircumcised people* who perform the faith action so they could be counted righteous.

So *fleshly circumcision's seal* correlates not with water baptism at all but instead with *justification by faith irrespective of fleshly circumcision*! In Paul's account, Abraham's physical circumcision is described as sealing not an old covenant but instead something that we identify as climaxing in the New Testament era, *justification by faith: God's inclusion of the allegiant gentile nations into Abraham's righteous family.*

In sum, Paul's words "made alive together" in Colossians 2:13 describe saving union with the king holistically, not a pre-*pistis* activity of God. If regeneration often transpires during the process of baptism—and it does when baptism includes personal declared loyalty to King Jesus (see chap. 5)—it is not because Scripture says that water baptism seals the new covenant. Scripture says no such thing. Moreover, the parallel between fleshly circumcision and water baptism is false—whether for infants or adults—because that comparison is never made in Scripture and it contradicts Paul's explanation of what fleshly circumcision means theologically. For that reason it is incorrect to suggest that baptism is the seal of the new covenant in Scripture and that baptism is regenerative or appropriate for infants.

Born again in 1 Peter. When Peter speaks of being "born again, not of perishable seed but of imperishable, through the living and abiding word of God" (1 Pet. 1:23), does he announce that a person must be personally regenerated before faith? It is implausible that Peter is trying to assert that regeneration happens prior to confession of allegiance.

In context, Peter first speaks of the Christ as the one who ransomed the audience from futility through his blood (1 Pet. 1:18–19). He adds that the Christ is the instrument through whom the audience's *fidelity* (*pistos*) toward God is made effective, so that their "faith [*pistis*] and hope are in God" (1:21). We are then told that these Christians have purified themselves "by obeying the truth," so that they have "sincere love" (1:22 NIV), and Peter exhorts them to love one another even more deeply. Only after this does he say they have been "born again" (*anagennaō*).

Peter mentions human faithfulness (*pistos*) and faith (*pistis*) as having already occurred *before* he applies the language of regeneration. Although God's grace in choosing and sending the Christ to be revealed as the Lamb of God comes prior, Peter's "born again" language describes the quality of life that has emerged from human *pistis*, which Peter further describes as "obeying the truth." He describes regeneration as a benefit that comes from faith and obedience to the truth, not as the pre-"faith" work of God that eradicates the bondage of the will.

Born again in John. The same can be said about "born" or "born again" language in the Gospel of John: those who receive King Jesus—that is, "those who have faith in his name"—have "the authority to become children of God" (John 1:12 AT). Notice that *human agency is repeatedly emphasized with regard to initializing new birth*: humans decide to receive the king, have faith in him, and themselves hold *the authority* with regard to becoming God's children.

Thus, *the faith-possessing human agent authorizes the choice to become a child of God by being born from God* (John 1:12). On the basis of this faith-in-the-king human choice, apart from any other natural human effort normally associated with procreation, he or she is then described as having been born from God (1:13). Even though this new birth from God came *after* initial human faith, such individuals are described as "having been born" from God alone, not by the human will that attends ordinary human procreation (1:13). Later in John we learn why: the "born again" process that attends or follows faith's definitive expression can be accomplished only by the Spirit rather than by the flesh (3:3–8). An individual must first authorize the choice to be "born again" through repentant faith, but then God *alone* via the Spirit accomplishes the actual rebirth.

Other regeneration texts. Other "regeneration" passages give much the same result. Paul's "washing of regeneration and renewal of the Holy Spirit" (Titus 3:5) or "new creation" (Gal. 6:15; 2 Cor. 5:17) language does not involve a pre-*pistis*, God-acting-alone activity.

In the end, none of the biblical passages that invoke the regeneration metaphor indicate that it involves God acting alone to erase a pre-faith hard-heartedness or a depraved mind or will so that the individual is then able to render *pistis*.[23] If this is not a biblical idea, where does it come from? It is a speculative extrapolation drawn primarily from biblical evidence of damage to our free will.

On the Bondage of the Will

Does Scripture suggest a genuine bondage of the will—that humankind has a damaged ability to turn to God apart from God's assistance?

Yes. Numerous passages suggest that humans are bankrupt, depraved, hostile to God, and unable to seek God fully (e.g., John 5:42; 6:44; Rom. 1:21, 28, 32; 3:10–12; 7:18; 8:7). Biblical evidence in favor of the bondage of the will—and there is plenty of it—is what causes many to go beyond what Scripture teaches to argue that God must act alone in giving pre-faith assistance via regeneration.[24] However, this is quite simply not how Scripture describes the matter.

In the Bible, sin's deceitfulness has ensnared individuals who hear the good news, but the Bible consistently describes them as sufficiently free to respond to the gospel by repenting from sin and rendering allegiance (e.g., Matt. 21:32; Acts 13:46; 28:24; Rom. 1:16; Heb. 4:2).[25] Even *unbelievers who are trapped in darkness* are described as free to choose the saving light (e.g., John 12:36, 46; Eph. 5:11–14). These and other passages indicate that however damaged the will might be, once the gospel has occurred within history, a degree of libertarian human agency ordinarily remains: the grace of the gospel events, when announced and heard, are sufficiently freeing in and of themselves to elicit a response among those who choose to heed the call to repentance and allegiance.

In fact, we can be certain that Jesus and the apostles believed that some degree of libertarian free will remained intact, because we know of *no early Christian writer* who believed in monergism, total depravity, or the complete bondage of the will. Such ideas did not arise within the church until Augustine in the fifth century AD.

Early Protestant Reformers like Luther and Calvin mobilized some of Augustine's ideas to bolster their systems, thereby interjecting them into the DNA of certain streams of Protestantism. But

169

Augustine's ideas were novel in his day and age and subsequently were never universally accepted by Catholics, Orthodox, or most Protestants. Luther's intense monergism was tempered within subsequent Lutheranism by Melanchthon and the Formula of Concord. Meanwhile, the Anabaptists, Anglicans, Remonstrants, Methodists, free churches, select Baptist groups, Pentecostals, and more would embrace the Reformation's basic principles while leaving ample space for libertarian free will.

In other words, in speaking of saving initiative, when universal bondage of the will is considered apart from the grace of the gospel, we are permitted to make it a theological axiom, for it is taught by Scripture. *But there is no evidence that Jesus or the apostles believed that the will remained in total bondage with regard to the individual's ability to respond to the gospel when proclaimed.* Such ideas (theologically and philosophically) arise only much later in church history and do not accord with how the Bible and early church describe the process of personal salvation. On the contrary, there is abundant evidence that Jesus and the apostles believed that, once the events of the gospel had occurred as God's act of grace toward all humanity, the individual's will was endangered by sin but not in total bondage so as to preclude the choice to repentantly pledge loyalty in response to the King Jesus gospel.

The point that I want to stress is that regardless of the precise degree to which the human will is in bondage, our biblical authors never deploy regeneration metaphors to first describe the liberation of a pre-faith damaged will so that afterward (and only afterward) individuals can respond in faith to the Christ. Consequently, we should not speak as if regeneration, rather than *pistis*, is the true entry point for personal salvation in response to the gospel.

Personal salvation starts when a person declares loyalty to the Christ decisively so as to enter the Spirit-filled community. In the New Testament this ordinarily (but neither necessarily nor exclusively) takes place when a person voluntarily undertakes baptism. Two alternative proposals are that individualized salvation begins with God's predestining election or with God's pre-faith regenerating action. Both of these proposals fail in light of Scripture's testimony.

With regard to election, the New Testament teaches that God predestined for salvation a group of people *in the Christ* before the foundations of the cosmos. But we have no indication that God individualized that election by appointing specific individuals to eternal life within that group. In fact, we have strong evidence against this view. For Paul, *the number of the predestined elect is increasing over time*, as more and more people join the church, because *predestination is based on a future condition*: confessing allegiance to the king. When it does appear in the New Testament, individual election is vocational, to serve a task-oriented purpose within God's plan, not a definitive appointment to an eternal fate.

Regeneration is a biblical metaphor, but it never describes the erasure of the bondage of the will or pre-faith hard-heartedness toward God. Humans indeed are wicked, undeserving, and in bondage. But once the grace of the gospel has been given in time and is proclaimed, it is contrary to Scripture and early Christian history to deny that individuals have an essential but imperfect libertarian agency to choose for or against King Jesus. We are on more secure biblical ground if we treat "regeneration" language as a general metaphor explaining the new quality of life that emerges once allegiance is given.

7

Once Saved, Always Saved?

Christians have nearly always affirmed that it is necessary for an individual who has become a Christian to persist in faith over the remainder of that person's life in order to attain final salvation. It is not enough to have had "faith," however we might define *pistis*, but then to cease.

For faith to be considered *saving*, it must remain living and active throughout life's journey, and it will be evidenced by good deeds. Catholics and the Orthodox believe this, yes, but all the major Protestant groups do too.[1] Some Protestants misunderstand their own story on this point.

Yet the question of eternal security has been highly contentious. In the wake of the Protestant Reformation there have been fierce disputes regarding whether a person who initially expresses true "faith" will *inevitably* find it enduring unto final salvation. In other words, granted that all agree that perseverance in a faith that produces good works is necessary, does genuine faith, once given and expressed, invariably continue so that the believer is eternally secure?

Eternal Security—Advocates and Detractors

For some Protestant theologians, especially Calvinists and Lutherans, to suggest that true initial faith might not persevere is to doubt the sufficiency of Christ's atoning work.[2] Upon my initial profession of genuine faith, so it is asserted, many decisive and irreversible things happen: Jesus's blood covers *all* my sins—past, present, and future—so that Christ's righteousness is imputed to me and I am justified ("declared righteous") in God's eyes; sin is defeated as my personal master; I am sealed as a member of God's family by personal reception of the Spirit; I am regenerated, so that I am a new creature; God's resurrection power begins to work an irreversible sanctifying process in me. For these traditions, from the moment when an individual first receives these saving benefits, they cannot be altered or revoked, so heavenly glory has already been granted: genuine initial faith is necessarily persevering faith.

All Christians agree that a confession of faith may be insincere. Advocates of the "once saved, always saved" slogan generally acknowledge that the reality of a person's saving faith and regeneration can be measured only by inner assurance and "fruit" evidenced after the fact—and even then only tentatively.[3] Why? Because we can deceive ourselves (James 1:22–26).

Inner assurance can be false. Thus, we are encouraged to examine ourselves precisely so we can gain increased assurance or take warning. Moreover, those who confess Jesus may indeed excel in righteous deeds (1 John 2:29; 3:7) but are not without sin (1:8). At the end of the day, believers and unbelievers both perform good and evil deeds, making it difficult to regard fruit as a definitive criterion.

However, the majority of Christian theologians—Catholic, Orthodox, and many Protestant groups—have tended toward the opposite conclusion: perseverance in salvation for individuals is not inevitable.[4] Opponents of "once saved, always saved" note that when future conditions are made the measuring stick, the slogan has subtly morphed into a different claim altogether. When fruit-in-the-future is made a condition, the *once* and the *currently* stated and implied in the *once saved* has been replaced by contingent future occurrences.

That is to say, when future fruit becomes the measure of whether "once saved, always saved" is valid, the slogan ceases to make a meaningful statement about an individual's past or the present status as saved. In other words, if the strike of an individual's faith arrow on the final-salvation target in the future is the *only* way to measure whether the arrow has truly been launched, then we have ceased saying anything meaningful about its past or present status. We are merely playing word games. "Once saved, always saved" cannot be made contingent on future conditions, such as fruit-bearing or still-trusting-at-the-time-of-death, and still remain a meaningful claim about the past and the present.

Eternal Security within Gospel Allegiance?

The gospel-allegiance model adds an additional wrinkle to this conversation. It asserts that saving faith (*pistis*) is best regarded as *allegiance* to King Jesus, not merely as *belief* or *trust* in God's promises that we are forgiven and righteous through Jesus's sacrifice. Reframed, the question becomes: Is a person who decisively swears allegiance to Jesus the king, so as to receive the benefits of forgiveness, saved at once and for all time, or can a person subsequently lose salvation by failing *to maintain* allegiance?

Eternal Security Evidenced?

Those who favor "once saved, always saved" can point to texts that seem to support it.[5] Supporters usually are comfortable individualizing statements of security made to the collective ancient audience, seeing these as immediately applicable to all sincere individual Christians today.

For example, supporters note that Paul speaks as if eternal life and salvation are already a *past reality* and a *present possession* for those who have given *pistis*:

But God, being rich in mercy, because of the great love with which
he loved us, even when we were dead in our trespasses, made us alive
together with Christ—by grace you have been saved. . . . For it is
by grace you have been saved through faith [*pistis*]. (Eph. 2:4–5, 8)

Moreover, Paul might be judged to suggest that those whom God
has chosen are following a predetermined sequence toward glory.
For if God is "for us," the saving process seems inevitable:

For those whom he foreknew he also predestined to be conformed
to the image of his Son, in order that he might be the firstborn
among many brothers. And those whom he predestined he also
called, and those whom he called he also justified, and those whom
he justified he also glorified. (Rom. 8:29–30)

In light of this text, we should all agree that the predetermined
sequence by which God constitutes his people includes foreknowing, predestination, calling, justification, and glorification—all
of which is bound up with entrance into the Son's family and
conformity to his image (for further discussion, see chap. 8). However, we must be cautious about individualizing texts that describe
group outcomes.

Elsewhere Paul also speaks as if salvation is inevitable for God's
people as a group: "He who began a good work in you [plural]
will bring it to completion at the day of Jesus Christ" (Phil. 1:6).
Paul also says, "God raised the Lord and will also raise us up by
his power" (1 Cor. 6:14), indicating that the resurrection power
that is already at work in the church is the same power that will
inescapably effect the church's final salvation.

Moreover, in speaking of salvation as a present reality for the
one who has given *pistis*, John is even clearer than Paul:

Truly, truly, I say to you, whoever hears my word and believes
[*pisteuōn*] him who sent me has eternal life. He does not come
into judgment, but has passed from death to life. (John 5:24)

Unlike the other passages, this one is clearly not just about the
group but individualized, "whoever." Not only is eternal life a

present possession for these individuals (cf. John 6:37), the sheep that have come to Jesus, but it would also seem that they are eternally secure:

> My sheep listen to my voice; I know them, and they follow me. I give them eternal life, and they shall never perish; no one can snatch them out of my hand. My Father, who has given them to me, is greater than all; no one can snatch them out of my Father's hand. (John 10:27–29 NIV)

No one can snatch them away. On the surface there appears to be considerable support for "once saved, always saved."

Perseverance and Threat of Detachment

Not only must considerable caution be exercised in applying promises spoken to groups to individuals, but Scripture is also full of warning, even to those who have decisively received the good news, that falling away is a real, present danger.

Failed Plants

Jesus speaks of a sower. Some of his seed falls on shallow soil in the midst of rocks. There the plants spring up quickly only to be scorched by the sun's heat. When Jesus interprets, we discover that the sower is actually scattering "the word"—that is, the good news of the kingdom of God. The plants that sprout quickly only to be withered can be compared to a class of people who,

> when they hear the word, immediately receive it with joy. And they have no root in themselves, but endure for a while; then, when tribulation or persecution arises on account of the word, immediately they fall away. (Mark 4:16–17)

Jesus's famous parable shows that it is possible for people to listen to God's word ("hear"), happily take it into their lives ("receive it with joy"), and persist in obedience for a season ("endure for a while") but fail to continue ("fall away"). When this happens, the plant withers.

Paul says something similar when he reminds Timothy that the "newly planted" (*neophytos*)—those who have recently yet truly entered the church—can fall away and come under the same condemnation as the devil (1 Tim. 3:6). Both individually and collectively in these examples, the planting is real, so the gospel has genuinely been received. Yet because of the falling away, no crop is produced. Withering or condemnation results.

Consider a related agricultural metaphor in which Jesus gives an equally stern warning about the absolute necessity of remaining united to him for life to persist:

> I am the true vine, and my Father is the vinedresser. Every branch *of mine* that does not bear fruit he takes away, and every branch that does bear fruit he prunes, that it may bear more fruit. Already you are clean because of the word that I have spoken to you. Abide in me, and I in you. . . . I am the vine, you are the branches. Whoever abides in me and I in that person bears much fruit. Apart from me you can do nothing. *If anyone does not abide in me, he is thrown away like a branch and withers; and the branches are gathered, thrown into the fire, and burned.* (John 15:1–6 AT)

Notice that Jesus says, "Every branch *of mine* that does not bear fruit he takes away" (15:2). There are branches that truly *belong to Jesus* as the vine, branches that are genuinely organically connected to him, that the Father will remove if they fail to bear fruit.

Indeed, it is stated that some "branches," Jesus's closest disciples, have already received cleansing from Jesus—"you are clean because of the word that I have spoken to you" (John 15:3)—but meanwhile at least one who was previously cleansed, Judas Iscariot, has now become unclean (cf. 13:10–11). So, despite this material connection to the Son and this cleansing, some of the branches/disciples are not bearing fruit or will not. They will be removed by the Father.

This removal of a branch that previously had been connected to Jesus results in nothing less than its utter condemnation. Such an individual branch is "thrown away" and "withers" (John 15:6). Then this dead branch is gathered together with other dead branches and "thrown into the fire, and burned" (15:6). The message is clear: even those who have been or are currently connected to Jesus the vine—those described as "a branch *of mine*" (15:2)—can fail to bear fruit by not remaining in him. They will be personally removed, thrown away, and burned in the fire.

Although Jesus will never cast away any who approach him (John 6:37), and no *external power* can snatch God's people away from Jesus or the Father (10:28–29), personal failure to remain in Jesus (i.e., an unrepentant departure) will result in destruction. We are not permitted to suggest that this removal of one of Jesus's branches is a hypothetical yet actually unreal possibility, for contextually, in John's Farewell Discourse (John 14–17), Judas is in view as a branch that has failed to remain (13:27–30). As one of the Twelve, Judas was united to Jesus the vine, fully sharing in the apostolic ministry (Acts 1:17), but he departed from Jesus by failing to bear fruit (Luke 22:3–6; 47–48), so the Father removed him and he came under condemnation (Matt. 26:24; Mark 14:21; Acts 1:25).

Hold Fast or Nothing Is Left

Not only Jesus but also Paul speaks of the danger of failing to persevere. Paul tells the Corinthians that the process of salvation is conditional. They are "being saved" (*sōzesthe*)[6] only if they "hold fast" (*katechete*):

Now I would remind you, brothers, of the gospel I preached to you, which you received, in which you stand, and by which you are being saved, *if you hold fast* [*katechete*] *to the word I preached to you*—unless you rendered allegiance [*episteusate*] in vain. (1 Cor. 15:1–2 AT)

Not only is perseverance necessary, but initial *pistis* also does not invariably result in enduring *pistis*. According to Paul, it is possible to have "rendered allegiance in vain." How so? The verse itself yields the most compelling answer: initial *pistis* ("allegiance") ends in bankruptcy when it fails to "hold fast" (*katechete*) to the proclaimed gospel about the Christ. Saving *pistis* with regard to the gospel can be relinquished, resulting in futility.

Paul says elsewhere that initially resilient faith can end in bankruptcy. He recounts his fears to the Thessalonians: "I sent to learn about your faith [*pistis*], for fear that somehow the tempter had tempted you and our labor would be in vain" (1 Thess. 3:5). According to Paul, it is possible to have genuine allegiance but, by capitulating to temptation, for that faith to become worthless.

Similarly in Galatians, Paul declares that some who previously were recipients of grace in the Christ in such a way that they were attached to him have now become separated: "You are severed from Christ, you who would be justified by the law; you have fallen away from grace" (Gal. 5:4). Paul gives other like-minded dire warnings to the Galatians (e.g., 1:6; 5:19–21; 6:8). John Barclay, in his authoritative book on grace, summarizes aptly, "Since these warnings are directed to the believing community, it is clearly possible to lose all the benefits of the Christ-gift."[7]

In other words, God's grace is extended to undeserving humans, but Paul indicates that grace is not invariably efficacious on the basis of divine agency alone. For Paul, God's agency must be met with a collaborating human agency in response or else grace can be rendered null. Our ongoing Spirit union with the Christ does not annihilate but instead enhances our libertarian human agency.

Perseverance and Conditionals

There are also numerous conditional statements ("if . . . then" type statements) that are relevant to the "once saved, always saved" question. These conditionals indicate that persistence will be rewarded, but falling away will result in the loss of the gospel's saving benefits. For example, Paul exhorts the Colossians to remain allegiant to Jesus, asserting that their estrangement with God has ended and their reconciliation has been effected, but only conditionally: "*if* indeed you *continue in the faith* [*pistis*], stable and steadfast, not shifting from the hope of the gospel that you heard" (Col. 1:23). Paul's warning has power only if there is real risk that their faith might cease, causing them to lose the gospel benefit of reconciliation.

Are Conditionals Only Theoretical?

Now I need to head off a wrongheaded approach to future conditionals. Thomas Schreiner and Ardel Caneday have argued that with regard to perseverance and the "once saved, always saved" question, such conditionals are merely theoretical—designed instead to exhort the audience toward an *inevitable* outcome. They conclude that the conditionals pertaining to eternal life or eternal reprobation in the New Testament are *the means by which* genuine initial "faith" is bolstered so that it perseveres until the end.[8] In short, they think that God uses unreal possible warnings to stimulate those who have faith to perseverance.

We should begin by acknowledging that Schreiner and Caneday are correct when they claim that the mere presence of a conditional says nothing about whether a given condition will invariably be met in the future. But Schreiner and Caneday's mistake is this: when doing *historically informed theology*, we are not permitted to undertake a *merely theoretical* analysis. Their solution falters for diverse sets of *real* historical authors and audiences. The theoretical approach treats conditionals as if they are timeless abstracts, but since our New Testament authors were real people speaking to genuine audiences, we must undertake *a historically informed analysis of probable meaning*.

An analogy might help show why Schreiner and Caneday's proposal fails when historically considered. A *certain* real parent might tell a *specific* child, "If you get an A, then I'll buy you an ice cream, but if you get a C, then you are grounded," merely because it is all but certain that the child will get an A and the parent recognizes that these conditions will help the child persevere. But *historically considered*, it would be highly unusual for a parent to be absolutely certain the child will get an A but at the same time to threaten grounding for a C, for if the matter is absolutely certain, then the threat would lack purpose. If we can scarcely imagine even one real parent imposing totally unreal conditions to motivate, how much less can we imagine all real parents in the world doing this? Indeed, as a matter of history, it is *impossible* to affirm that *all* conditional rewards and warnings spoken by *all* real parents within history are *always* merely a means toward an inevitable outcome for *all* their *diverse* children.

Likewise for the New Testament. As a matter of history, it is *impossible* that *all* the pertinent conditionals given by *all* the various real New Testament authors are *always* merely a means toward an inevitable outcome for *all* their *diverse* audiences. Although it may be tempting to say that such a use of future conditionals for inevitable outcomes may be impossible for humans but not for an omniscient God in Scripture, that move is not valid. To make future conditional language appropriate for God apart from human concerns as part of inspiration evacuates Scripture of its humanity. God inspired Scripture by using real humans to address the pastoral needs of actual audiences within history using ordinary language patterns, so its meaning needs to be construed accordingly.

New Testament authors frequently invoke athletic metaphors, urging the necessity of perseverance to reach final salvation (1 Cor. 9:22–27; Gal. 5:3–7; Phil. 3:7–14; 2 Tim. 4:6–8; Heb. 12:1–3). They express concern that until the saving goal is reached at the end of life, they themselves as well as their audiences could quit the race or give allegiance to another. They speak of rewards for persevering unto final salvation and the total loss of these saving benefits for quitting.

Would such language be used to motivate if it were *absolutely guaranteed* that all those who have begun the race will invariably finish? Is it not much more likely that the conditions would be motivating precisely because real, uncertain outcomes are at stake? Historically considered, the New Testament authors were far more likely to pose a condition when trying to encourage a certain behavior when the outcome was *genuinely uncertain* than to pose one merely to help the audience reach an inevitable outcome.

Perseverance Threatened

In addition to those conditionals already mentioned, a great many passages in the New Testament warn those already within the Christian community that they will not receive salvation if they unrepentantly fall away from Jesus or if they fail to persevere by walking in the truth—so many that a comprehensive discussion here is impossible.[9] However, to give a final example, the book of Hebrews is especially frank about this danger, issuing numerous stern warnings (Heb. 2:1–4; 3:1–4:13; 5:11–6:12; 10:19–39; 12:1–29) about the very real danger of falling away:[10]

> Take care, brothers, lest there be in any of you an evil, unbelieving heart, leading you to fall away from the living God. But exhort one another every day, as long as it is called "today," that none of you may be hardened by the deceitfulness of sin. *For we share in Christ, if indeed we hold our original confidence firm to the end.* (Heb. 3:12–14)

Sin's deceitfulness can cause the heart to harden against God, so that it can become "unbelieving" or, better, "disloyal" (*apistia*). Even though the author of Hebrews is addressing fellow Christians, "holy brothers . . . who *share* in the heavenly calling" (Heb. 3:1), he nevertheless recognizes that "we share in [the] Christ" only if "we hold our original confidence firm to the end" (3:14). Or, to translate that last phrase more precisely, "only if we grasp securely the beginning of the underlying reality until the end" (*eanper tēn archēn tēs hypostaseōs mechri telous bebaian kataschōmen*).

This "beginning of the underlying reality" connects intimately with the famous description of *pistis* that will subsequently be offered by the author of Hebrews: "Now faith [*pistis*] is the underlying reality [*hypostasis*] toward which hope is directed, the demonstration of affairs not seen" (Heb. 11:1 AT).

The point of Hebrews 3:14 is that our participation in the Christ (and his saving benefits) is contingent on remaining loyal to the Christ—persevering to the end in our conviction that God's saving realities (e.g., Jesus's high priestly offering of his own blood) are deeper and more fundamental than any apparent realities.

Holy Spirit as Guarantee?

For those who favor the idea that the true Christian is eternally secure, the Bible's statements about the Holy Spirit's role as guarantee serve as vital evidence. Paul's testimony to the Spirit as guarantee is forceful: "And it is God who establishes us with you in Christ, and has anointed us, and who has also put his seal on us and given us his Spirit in our hearts as a guarantee" (2 Cor. 1:21–22). The Spirit serves as the "seal," the certification of authenticity. Later in the same letter Paul compares final salvation to the act of clothing, adding, "He who has prepared us for this very thing is God, who has given us the Spirit as a guarantee" (5:5). Paul is even more emphatic in Ephesians:

> In him you also, when you heard the word of truth, the gospel of your salvation, and gave *pistis* to him [*en hō kai pisteusantes*], were sealed with the promised Holy Spirit, who is the guarantee of our inheritance until we acquire possession of it, to the praise of his glory. (Eph. 1:13–14 AT)

Here Paul seems to see the receptive hearing, the *pistis* action, and the sealing with the Spirit as interlocked aspects of a single event. That is, Paul is now telling the Ephesian community, whom he calls "holy ones" and "loyal [*pistois*] in the Christ, Jesus" at the outset of the letter (Eph. 1:1 AT), that they should regard the Holy Spirit as the present-tense installment, to be enjoyed now, that certifies that they really are part of God's family—a guarantee of the full future inheritance.

So, does the Spirit's seal make final salvation certain? Yes! But notice that the words about the Spirit as guarantee are spoken to "you" in the plural, to the entire community. *The Spirit is a communal seal, not a personal seal.* This is true across the New Testament as a whole.

When Paul says, "Do you not know that you are God's temple and that God's Spirit dwells in you?" (1 Cor. 3:16), the "you" is plural in the Greek text, and Paul is speaking about how the Corinthian house churches collectively form a temple where God has taken up residence in Corinth. In fact, even when we would most expect Paul to speak of the Holy Spirit as indwelling the individual, he politely demurs. For example, in 2 Timothy where Paul is writing predominantly to an individual, Timothy, we might have expected Paul to say, "By the Holy Spirit who dwells within *you*, guard the good deposit entrusted to you," but instead he says, "By the Holy Spirit who dwells within *us*, guard the good deposit entrusted to you" (2 Tim. 1:14).

This is not to say, of course, that Paul and our other New Testament authors did not also believe that the Spirit personally infuses discrete individuals. For example, the logic of Paul's application of the temple metaphor demands that he regarded the Spirit as individuated to specific members of the community (1 Cor. 6:18–20). Furthermore, Peter individualizes the Spirit's reception when interpreting Joel's prophesy (Acts 2:17–28), and he personalizes repentance for the Spirit's reception in Acts 2:38 ("every one of you"). The question is not whether the Holy Spirit resides in discrete individuals—the Spirit emphatically does.

The Spirit's Directional Flow

A better question pertains to what we might term the *directional flow* of the Spirit's indwelling. Is it individual first? Is the Spirit sent to indwell the allegiance-giving *individual* first, and then the Spirit's personal presence permits, facilitates, and maintains community membership? Or, conversely, is it community first? Do the Father and the Son send the Spirit to the allegiance-giving *community* first, and individuals receive it when they "tap into" the Spirit as communally present by pledging allegiance?

In John's Gospel, Jesus *breathes* on the community, the disciples who have gathered to him after the resurrection, saying to them, "Receive the Holy Spirit" (John 20:22). Meanwhile, in Acts, on the feast day known as Pentecost "all were together in one place"

(Acts 2:1). This "all" intends at least the Twelve but probably also the 120 mentioned in Acts 1:15. Suddenly the sound of a violent rushing wind/Spirit (*pneuma*) "filled the entire house" (2:2), and "all were filled with the Holy wind/Spirit [*pneuma*]" (2:4 AT). The parallel between the *filling* of the *whole house* with *pneuma* and the *filling* of *all those gathered* with *pneuma* strongly suggests the primacy of a collective indwelling. But, just as we might expect, we find that sandwiched within this collective framing, the corporate indwelling is nevertheless individually experienced: "divided tongues as of fire appeared to them and rested *on each one* of them" (2:3). The Spirit is given to the community first, but nevertheless is individually experienced.

In the New Testament, the Spirit is given to the *community* first. Not only does the New Testament's nearly uniform language of plurality in speaking of indwelling give strong prima facie evidence in favor of a community-first model over an individual-first model, but so also does the basic shape of the scriptural story. God does not first send the Holy Spirit to isolated individuals who then somehow find one another to form a Christian community. On the contrary, God first establishes a Spirit-filled community, and then groups and individuals subsequently join it when they receive the good news.

We are invited by the Scriptures to conceptualize the Holy Spirit using a variety of *personal* metaphors: counselor (John 14:26; 16:7), testifier (15:26), judge (16:8–11), teacher (16:13), convincer (1 Thess. 1:5), inspiring agent (Matt. 22:43; Luke 2:26), assistant (2 Tim. 1:14), and indeed even as a speaking divine *person* (Heb. 1:8–12). So, it is highly appropriate to consider the Spirit a divine *person*.[11]

But we are also encouraged to think of the Spirit as a *fluid*. Language about filling (Luke 4:1; Acts 2:4; 4:8; Eph. 5:18), dipping/baptism (Matt. 3:11; John 1:33; Acts 1:5), pouring (Acts 2:17–18; 10:45; Rom. 5:5; Titus 3:6), and drinking (1 Cor. 12:13) features liquid metaphors. Beyond *person*, Scripture also invites us to think of the Holy Spirit as an *invisible liquid or infusing substance*.

Following this analogy, consider as a gift of common grace the Spirit as a personal liquid gathered *around* and *upon* the mind-heart of every individual who has ever entered the world; it is this same Spirit who also empowers proclamation of the gospel and facilitates receptivity to it. At Pentecost, for the first time, the Holy Spirit was allowed to reside *within* the human community (and specific individuals) as an abiding indwelling presence. At Pentecost, think of the Spirit as an invisible reservoir of fluid that *proceeds from* the Father and the Son *to the Christian community*, indwelling and interconnecting them all, uniting heaven and earth.[12]

Before an individual confesses allegiance, the mind-heart of the individual is already *externally* connected to the reservoir of the Holy Spirit. The Spirit can rest *on* or *upon* or *temporarily indwell* people who have not yet been abidingly indwelt, influencing them (e.g., Judg. 15:14; Luke 1:41; 2:25). Yet when an individual responds to the gospel by proclaiming allegiance to Jesus the king, then the valve in the mind-heart that allows the Spirit to flow *inside* that individual is opened, and the Holy Spirit as an abiding presence fills or infuses that person. The reception flows from the Father and the Son in such a way that they extend the Spirit-filled community, so that this individual is engulfed by the Spirit's abiding communal presence.

Why the Guarantee Is Not Individualized

Once we understand the community-first direction of the Spirit's flow to the individual, we are prepared to understand why personal receipt of the Spirit does not guarantee final salvation. The Holy Spirit seals and guarantees the salvation of the authentic church; individual security depends on staying within it. The true church on earth is nothing more and nothing less than the community constituted by professing allegiance to Jesus the king in response to the gospel, so that the Holy Spirit is dwelling in its midst. Alternative definitions of the church's essence falter.

The following can be advanced as a *corollary* to the true church as the allegiance-confessing and Spirit-filled community: (1) *The Holy Spirit **always** abides in individuals when they are members of the allegiance-declaring community*, (2) *but the Holy Spirit* *never abides in an individual who never has given or has entirely stopped giving allegiance.* In support of the corollary's two principles, consider Paul's exact language in speaking to the Roman house churches:

> You [plural] are not in the flesh but in the Spirit, *if* in fact the Spirit of God dwells in you [plural]. But if any person [singular] does not have the Spirit of the Christ, this person [singular] does not belong to him. But *if* Christ is in you [plural], although the body is dead because of sin, the Spirit is life because of righteousness. (Rom. 8:9–10 AT)

We see both principles in this text: (1) *if* you (the churches in Rome) truly have the Spirit dwelling in your midst, then you have been decisively delivered, for you are "not in the flesh"—that is, you are no longer in the sphere where sin invariably dominates; (2) but *if* any singular individual in the midst of the churches of Rome does not have the Spirit, that person does not belong to the Christ.

Both parts of Paul's statement are crucial. Together they compel us to recognize that Paul normally assumed he was writing to churches and individuals therein who remained loyal to Jesus as Lord and hence were part of the Spirit-filled community. But Paul was fully aware that this assumption was a risky overgeneralization, hence his qualifications: "*if* in fact the Spirit of God dwells in you" and "*if* any person does not have the Spirit of the Christ, this person does not belong to him." So, Paul tempers God's marvelous promises to the churches in Rome by affirming that promises about the Spirit as a life-giving guarantee are valid only for groups and individuals that do in fact have the Spirit of God as an abiding presence.

We might call this the *overgeneralizations must be qualified* interpretive principle. Our New Testament authors frequently make blanket statements about the absolute benefits enjoyed by their churches in the Christ, but they were aware that these were overgeneralizations, since some in the audience might not truly be allegiant to the Christ and therefore the Christ or the Spirit might not be in them. Paul explicitly says as much to the Corinthians:

Examine yourselves [plural], to see whether you are in the faith
[*pistis*]. Test yourselves. Or do you not realize this about yourselves,
*that Jesus, the Christ, is in you?—unless indeed you fail to meet
the test!* (2 Cor. 13:5)

We see that Paul (and other New Testament authors) were totally aware that some groups or ostensible members of the church
might prove upon testing to be outside the *pistis* boundary. That
is, they might fail to have Jesus the Christ in them via the Spirit
and so be found to be outside the true church.

For the sake of style, our biblical authors mention such beware-
because-the-promises-may-not-apply warnings only at suitable
times rather than constantly. They are nevertheless always operat-
ing in the background. Thus, when we read about the marvelous
promises that we might otherwise presume are necessarily given
to *all* members of the Corinthian church—

And we all, with unveiled face, beholding the glory of the Lord, are
being transformed into the same image from one degree of glory
to another. (2 Cor. 3:18)

or

He who has prepared us for this very thing is God, who has given
us the Spirit as a guarantee. (2 Cor. 5:5)

—then we are *required* to apply the "overgeneralizations must be
qualified" interpretative principle.

Paul says "and we *all*" in 2 Corinthians 3:18, speaking as if he
and his *entire* audience are "in the Christ" and will invariably be
conformed to Christ's image even though he knows better. Likewise Paul speaks about God's resurrection purposes and says that
the Spirit guarantees salvation for his whole audience (5:5). But
at the end of the letter, in 13:5, Paul clarifies that these promises
apply only to those who can *presently* pass the "in the *pistis*" and
"Jesus the Christ is in you" tests. He is aware that some purported

members of the church, present and future, may not pass the test, in which case the promises don't apply to those individuals.

Here is why this matters: statements in Scripture that seem to promise the inevitable movement of the entire audience from God's foreordained choice to final glory, like Romans 8:29–30, must be tempered, for it can be proven that such promises were regarded as valid by Paul only for those who remain united by confessing Jesus as the Christ so as to share in the Spirit (e.g., Rom. 8:9–10; 1 Cor. 12:3). Such passages speak of the inevitable results for those who do in fact remain united but say nothing about the certainty of specific individuals remaining united.

The passages reviewed in this section make it absolutely certain that Paul (and other New Testament authors) believed that the local community that is indwelt by the Holy Spirit truly and unshakably enjoys the first installation of a guaranteed fully salvific inheritance, but we cannot apply words about the Holy Spirit as "guarantee" immediately to the individual who confesses Jesus as king without reflecting on how the Spirit relates to the group and to the individual. On the contrary, as the next subsection will continue to argue, an individual who initially gives allegiance to Jesus as Lord but who without repentance ceases to give it can lose their personal status as "saved."

Loss of the Holy Spirit?

We have already explored some scriptural evidence that shows that a person's initial saving allegiance can fail to persevere to final salvation. The last subsection defined the church and suggested a corollary. We can summarize as follows: *The Holy Spirit as the community-first, unifying, indwelling presence is precisely coterminous with the community that gives allegiance to Jesus as Lord. Any individual who gives allegiance immediately comes to share in the Spirit, who is already present in the invisible church; any individual who entirely ceases to give allegiance is no longer indwelt by the Spirit.* Now I would like to give additional evidence showing that this summary explains what the

New Testament teaches about salvation. I will offer three additional lines of evidence.

1. Individual Loss of the Spirit

There are several passages in the Bible that state that an individual can cease to be indwelt by the Spirit. The most famous is in Hebrews:

> For it is impossible to restore again to repentance those who once having been enlightened, who have tasted the heavenly gift, and who have become partners of the Holy Spirit, and have tasted the goodness of the word of God and the powers of the age to come, if they then fall away, since they are crucifying once again the Son of God to their own harm and holding him up to contempt. (Heb. 6:4–6 AT; cf. 10:26–27)

Those favoring the doctrine of eternal security for the individual engage in a variety of exegetical and hermeneutical gymnastics in an attempt to avoid what the text states: those who "have become partners of the Holy Spirit" (*metochous genēthentas pneumatos hagiou*) can fall away to such a degree that restoration unto repentance is impossible.

Some commentators contend that the author of Hebrews is putting forth a hypothetical but unfulfillable condition: "If X were to happen, then Y would result; but in reality, we all know that X cannot really happen, but I am warning you about X and Y anyway so as to keep you on the right path." As discussed above, historically considered, this unfulfillable-condition solution is extraordinarily improbable.

Others argue that the surrounding description, "*tasted* the heavenly gift" and "*tasted* the goodness of the word of God and the powers of the age to come," suggests that the individuals in question were mere dilettantes—temporary dabblers in the things of God—but they weren't regenerated or indwelt by the Spirit.[13] This is wrongheaded because in antiquity "tasting" (*geuomai*) is only rarely a metaphor for dabbling.[14] "Tasting" usually indicates a sensual, participatory experience associated with the process of eating or drinking in general.

Moreover, in the crucial phrase "who have become *partners* of the Holy Spirit," the Greek word in question, *metochoi*— "partners, sharers, participants"—leaves no real doubt that genuine *sharing* in the Holy Spirit is envisioned. Nobody asserts that the author of Hebrews intends anything less than a full and real participation when he uses the exact same word elsewhere: "Holy brothers, who *share* [*metochoi*] in the heavenly calling, consider Jesus" (Heb. 3:1). Elsewhere the word *metochoi* is used for the disciples' *partners* in their fishing business (Luke 5:7) and for universal *participation* in human forms of discipline (Heb. 12:8). Full partnership is intended in all these passages, so it is tendentious to contend otherwise with regard to the Spirit for Hebrews 6:4.

Finally, against the less-than-full-partners (or the dabblers) view is the phrase in Hebrews 6:4 that precedes the metaphors of tasting and of sharing in the Spirit: "having been enlightened" (*phōtisthentas*). This "having been enlightened" language in the New Testament and related literature frequently pertains to the receipt of inner light so as to awaken a knowledge of transcendent matters and is consonant with what we today would call conversion.[15]

Moreover, that this "conversion" meaning is intended in Hebrews 6:4 is confirmed by the use of the same word, *phōtisthentes*, in 10:32 to describe a clear, community-defining break with a past non-Christian way of life—a break that was so firm that afterward the community was able to persevere together through a "hard struggle" characterized by "sufferings."

Both sharing in the Holy Spirit and conversion to the life of Christian discipleship are in view in Hebrews 6:4. Yet, even while giving dire and real warnings, the author of Hebrews indicates that he is persuaded of a better result for his collective audience than the burning that awaits worthless farmland; indeed, he anticipates "things that accompany salvation" (6:9 AT).

In sum, Hebrews 6:4–6 shows that saved individuals can fall away to such a degree that it is impossible for them to be brought

back to repentance. They were once saved because they were partners of the Holy Spirit and had experienced conversion (enlightenment) but are no longer saved.

Notice that the text says not that God disallows any such individual *the opportunity* to repent and find reconciliation with God
should he or she so choose but rather that repentance is in fact
impossible. Free will is free but not of its own momentum-building
consequences. Our choices launch us toward or away from God,
and as these choices compound, the spiritual reward or risk connected with the momentum is real.[16]

It is best to see the impossibility of repentance as a human limitation, not a divine restriction. As Dallas Willard puts it, "Whether
or not God's will is infinitely flexible, the human will is not. There
are limits beyond which it cannot bend back, cannot turn or repent."[17] We might surmise that the author of Hebrews believes
that an individual can become so hardened to God's ways as to
find himself or herself unable to choose repentance and renewed
loyalty, even though God would welcome it if the choice could be
made. The author of Hebrews believes that those who formerly
had a genuine *partnership* with the Holy Spirit can reach a definitive terminal point in "falling away," so that it becomes impossible
for them to initiate a reversal of course.

This interpretation aligns with several other passages that teach
something similar. For example, the author of Hebrews warns his
audience further:

> For if we go on sinning deliberately after receiving the knowledge of
> the truth, there no longer remains a sacrifice for sins, but a fearful
> expectation of judgment, and a fury of fire that will consume the
> adversaries. (Heb. 10:26–27)

Spiritually hardened by sin's deceitfulness, those who deliberately keep on sinning after receiving knowledge of the truth are at
incalculable spiritual risk (cf. Heb. 3:13). Previously, God's provi-
sion of "sacrifice for sins" was effective for such people (10:26),

but it is no longer, since all that can be expected is judgment and a furious consuming fire.

This passage is speaking about those who previously were cleansed by the blood of Jesus. We know this because their action is further described as "trampling the Son of God underfoot" and "treating as an unholy thing the blood of the covenant that sanctifies" and "outraging the Spirit of grace" (Heb. 10:29 AT). The language "outraging the Spirit of grace" probably implies that such people previously had a full share in the Holy Spirit as communally and personally experienced but that this share has been relinquished (cf. 6:4). Regardless, this passage certainly is describing those who have abandoned their loyalty to King Jesus, so they are now liable for their sins, are no longer forgiven, and now are subject to God's judgment. Personal salvation had been decisively entered, but now it has been lost.

In a thematically related passage Peter speaks sternly about the grim fate of false teachers (and those deceived by false teachers) who have been corrupted away from the truth that at one time had cleansed them:

> For if, after they [false teachers and those deceived by them] have escaped the defilements of the world through the knowledge of our Lord and Savior Jesus Christ, they are again entangled in them and overcome, the last state has become worse for them than the first. For it would have been better for them never to have known the way of righteousness than after knowing it to turn back from the holy commandment delivered to them. (2 Pet. 2:20–21)

These false teachers are described as having previously "escaped the defilements of the world through the knowledge of our Lord and Savior Jesus Christ."

It is very difficult to argue that these false teachers had not genuinely entered salvation, given this description. They knew Jesus the king as "Lord and Savior" so as to escape the defilements of the world—all of which suggests they had made an authentic confession of faith as part of the baptismal process that had genuinely cleansed them (cf. 1 Pet. 3:21). But now they have reentered defilement by deliberately turning away from the gospel. They are now in a worse state than before their initial saving experience. This suggests that Peter thinks that a reentrance into salvation via repentance for these individuals is possible but that their momentum away from God makes this unlikely.

John speaks about those who have committed a sin that leads to death—a sin so serious that it is inappropriate for a sister or brother even to intercede before God (presumably apart from that sinner's repentance first), requesting that sinner's forgiveness:

> If anyone sees his brother committing a sin not leading to death, he shall ask, and God will give him life—to those who commit sins that do not lead to death. There is sin that leads to death; I do not say that one should pray for that. (1 John 5:16)

One can surmise, on the basis of comparison with the other letters of John, that the "sin that leads to death" is apostasy, emphatically turning away from Jesus—an action ordinarily associated with departure from the Christian community (see, e.g., 1 John 2:18–19).[18] In the end, this failure to remain in the teaching of the Christ quite simply means a total lack of God:

> Everyone who goes on ahead and does not abide in the teaching of the Christ, does not have God. Whoever abides in the teaching has both the Father and the Son. (2 John 9)

Those who do not remain do not have God, and vice versa. That is, those who previously were part of the Spirit-filled community by abiding and hence are personally Spirit filled (cf. 1 John 4:13) but who fail to abide in the teachings of Jesus by leaving that community no longer have the Father or the Son. It would be beyond daring (and would misunderstand the Trinity) to suggest that an individual who no longer has the Father or the Son nonetheless still can have the Spirit. The implication, then, with respect to 2 John 9 is straightforward: *the failure of an individual to abide*

*(as a settled condition) in the teaching of King Jesus results in loss
of the Father and the Son, and hence also the personal loss of the
Holy Spirit as a permanent indwelling presence.*

2. Lack of Contravening Evidence

We have explored passages that indicate an individual can cease
to be personally indwelt by the Holy Spirit. In light of the full
counsel of Scripture, is there contravening data that would suggest
a Spirit-filled *individual* rather than a group is eternally secure?
No. There are zero passages that unambiguously support this idea.

The only passage that can be marshaled by serious exegesis
in support of the permanent security of the indwelling of the
Holy Spirit not merely in a group but in the individual is 1 John
3:9: "Each one born [*pas ho gegennēmenos*] from God does not
practice sin, *because his seed remains in him*, and he is not able
to keep practicing sin, because he is born [*gegennētai*] from God"
(AT). But, note well, even if one reasonably grants that "his seed"
refers to the Holy Spirit here (cf. 1 John 3:24; 4:13), nevertheless
this passage does not suggest that the removal of the Holy Spirit
as the seed within an individual is impossible.

What is impossible is continuing to practice sin *if one has the
present status of being born from God, because in that case the
seed remains.* The text is speaking only about a person having
been born from God *and who still possesses that status.* This is
indicated by the perfect passive participle and the perfect passive
verb in the Greek text. In Greek the perfect passive emphasizes
how past action contributes to *present status.* All we know from
this text is that the individual who *presently* is born from God
also presently has the Holy Spirit as a seed, and for that reason
this individual will not keep on habitually sinning.

The question of eternal security for this text, then, is parried
to a related question: What does it mean for security to have the
present status "born from God"? Can a person who presently has
the status "born from God" die spiritually, so that they experience condemnation? Regeneration metaphors were discussed in
the previous chapter. Regeneration does not happen pre-faith but

happens only when allegiance is decisively given, usually but not always at baptism. New birth is certainly an attainable present-tense spiritual reality, so that right now those who have been born again genuinely possesses the quality of life that is characteristic of the age to come (John 3). Moreover, it is true that no one who is presently born of God keeps sinning, such that he or she cannot be overcome by *external threats* from the evil one (1 John 5:18) or the world (5:4).

But this does not preclude willful apostasy. Confession of the Son must remain intact and a person must allow it to continue for the individual to persist in eternal life (e.g., 1 John 2:23–25; cf. 2 John 9). This also explains passages like John 5:24 that feature *presently maintained faith* when mentioning an individual's certainty of eternal life. That willful apostasy is a live threat in John's community cannot be seriously doubted (e.g., John 13:27–30; 1 John 2:18–19; 4:1; 2 John 7–11). The uniform witness of the New Testament and earliest Christianity is that even if a person has been regenerated so that they are "born from God"—and ordinarily this coincided with baptism—they can fail to attain to final salvation by ceasing to give loyalty to King Jesus. While a person who is presently born of God has the Holy Spirit, we have no evidence that someone who is presently "born of God" or who presently possesses "eternal life" cannot die spiritually if they renounce King Jesus. Rather, John says that *if* the seed remains, the person born of God can't keep on sinning. John's letters as a whole show that this *if* implies that *if not* is a real possibility.

Ultimately, in John's letters the maintenance of "born from God" status and eternal life is contingent upon maintained *pistis*, so that the individual remains in Jesus: "Everyone who is believing [*pas ho pisteuōn*] that Jesus is the Christ is born of God [*gegennētai*]" (1 John 5:1 AT; cf. 5:4, 10–13).

In summary, there are numerous statements affirming that *the church* (the allegiance-confessing *community*, often addressed as the plural "you" in the New Testament) will not fall away, not be separated from God's love, or cease to be indwelt by the Holy Spirit, but there are no such statements pertaining to the individual. The passages that suggest eternal security can best be explained as *corporate affirmations*, generalized statements to the present-tense community that are not intended to refer to individuals who decisively leave the allegiance-affirming community.

We cannot distribute promises made to a group to its individual members without reflecting on the porous nature of group membership and attendant benefits. There are no passages in the Bible that prove that the individual is eternally secure or that the Holy Spirit cannot cease to dwell inside an individual. This absence of evidence speaks a potent word when combined with the passages examined in this chapter that indicate the Spirit can be lost by an individual.

3. Loss of the Spirit and Church Discipline

Thus far it has been claimed that Scripture affirms that individuals can cease to be indwelt by the Spirit and that there are no passages that contradict this. One way of further testing this matter is to weigh whether the claim can cast fresh light on a related area of inquiry such as church discipline.

Paul describes a distressing case of sexual immorality in Corinth. A man is having sex with his father's wife (his stepmother). Paul commands the Corinthians to expel the man from the community. We should weigh carefully what Paul reveals about how the Spirit relates to individual and community as he renders his judgment:

> For though absent in body, I am present in spirit; and as if present, I have already pronounced judgment on the one who did such a thing. When you are assembled in the name of the Lord Jesus and my spirit is present, with the power of our Lord Jesus, you are to deliver this man to Satan for the destruction of the flesh, so that his spirit may be saved in the day of the Lord. (1 Cor. 5:3–5)

Paul has already described the Corinthian community as the authentic temple of the Holy Spirit in Corinth (1 Cor. 3:16–17). Thus, when Paul speaks of the Corinthians as assembled in the name of the Lord Jesus, and of his own Jesus-empowered human spirit being present with the Corinthians even in Paul's physical (geographic) absence, he speaks in terms congenial to the notion of a worldwide, invisible, Spirit-filled church.

Paul's imagery implies that his own human spirit is permeated with the powerful, personal presence of the Lord Jesus—a presence of the Christ that he elsewhere describes as the Holy Spirit (see Rom. 8:9–11; 2 Cor. 3:17; Phil. 1:19). Paul has not abolished the distinction between his personal human spirit and the Holy Spirit, but he has suggested that his own physical body has been imbued by the Holy Spirit to such a degree that the Spirit is truly and emphatically present in an authoritative capacity alongside his human spirit in the midst of the Spirit-filled Corinthian congregation. All this even though Paul's outer body is hundreds of miles away!

Not only is the Holy Spirit present with Paul's human spirit and in the Corinthian congregation, but the logic of Paul's command to remove the sexually immoral man strongly suggests that Paul affirmed that his removal would entail the man's loss of his share in the Holy Spirit apart from repentance. Paul instructs the Corinthians to "deliver this man to Satan for the destruction of the flesh, so that his spirit may be saved in the day of the Lord" (1 Cor. 5:5; cf. 1 Tim. 1:20). As Gordon Fee explains, this handing over to Satan is a quasi-technical term for expulsion from the Spirit-filled community into the realm where Satan is currently allowed to dominate.[19] The man is being placed outside God's true temple in Corinth (1 Cor. 3:16–17), outside the place where the Spirit of God and of Jesus is specially localized.

In line with the teaching of Paul and the New Testament elsewhere, the desired effect for the man is more remedial than punitive. His removal is purposed toward the destruction of his flesh for the salvation of his spirit. Paul expects that this man, by being allowed to pursue his carnal appetites to their logical end, will be buffeted by Satan (and self) to such a degree that his flesh—the physical location where sin is most freely at work in him—will be destroyed. That is, Paul remains optimistic that sin's fleshly appetite will exhaust itself so that repentance will be stimulated.

Paul holds out hope that this man, having experienced the indwelling Spirit in the past but now lacking it, will choose to return to the realm dominated by the Spirit, to the Corinthian church, so that "his spirit may be saved in the day of the Lord." As with Hymenaeus and Alexander, who are described as "having shipwrecked their *pistis*" and "having been handed over to Satan" so as to be taught not to blaspheme (1 Tim. 1:19–20 AT), Paul does not describe this man's salvation as guaranteed on account of his prior experience of the indwelling presence of the Holy Spirit. Instead, Paul speaks of the saving intention of the disciplinary measure.

Sometimes disciplinary expulsion in the early church did result in repentance and reassimilation into the Spirit-filled community (2 Cor. 2:3–11). At other times we have no indication that the individual or subgroup returned to the church. Then only fearsome judgment can be expected for the apostasy (Heb. 10:26–27; 1 John 2:19).

In sum, the logic behind this case of church discipline reinforces both the community-first direction of the Spirit's work discussed earlier in this chapter and the notion that an individual can cease to be indwelt by the Holy Spirit. The Spirit is invisibly present in the midst of the allegiance-yielding church both locally and globally. The incestuous man was a member of the Spirit-filled community in Corinth. It would be historically dubious to suggest that he was not regarded by Paul as personally Spirit filled prior to the incest. But his settled refusal to repent—he and some in Corinth are in fact proud of the sin!—was a cessation of allegiance to Jesus as the Lord. His expulsion would remove him from the Spirit-filled community and hence from his personal share in the Holy Spirit.

The New Testament teaches that it is necessary to persevere in faith in order to attain final salvation. This is not controversial. Nearly all Christians at all times and in all places have held to this view. Thus, this chapter focused on the hotly disputed "once saved, always saved" slogan.

A small but vocal minority of Protestants hold to "once saved, always saved," but it should be totally abandoned. There is no decisive evidence in favor of it and a mountain against it. A person can authentically enter salvation by swearing allegiance to King Jesus, be united to the Holy Spirit, and then fall away into apostasy. This happens not when a person simply doubts or sins but when allegiance to King Jesus and his ways are unrepentantly abandoned, so that the person no longer is embedded in the Holy Spirit's community (i.e., the true church) and hence is no longer personally indwelt by the Holy Spirit. When an individual ceases to make repentant allegiance to King Jesus their life's intention, that previously "saved" person is now "unsaved." They also cease to have any of the Holy Spirit's special saving benefits and now stand condemned.

God's grace is unfailingly offered, but a person who commits apostasy by rejecting Jesus's saving kingship chooses not to receive it. Scripture warns that the deceitfulness of sin can make it hard or even impossible for apostates to reverse course as they are hardened by it. But God will *always* accept any individual who opts to repent and renew allegiance.

Despite its weak biblical foundation, "once saved, always saved" has had staying power in the church for three reasons: (1) it was taught by the first wave of the Protestant Reformers (although many early Protestants disputed it subsequently); (2) reassurance is emotionally and pastorally attractive; (3) "once saved, always saved" was packaged with a faulty way of systematizing personal salvation within the *ordo salutis*. In particular, the "once saved" was coordinated with justification, while the "always saved" was aligned with sanctification and perseverance unto glory. In the next chapter we will seek to remodel the justification-sanctification discussion in light of the gospel-allegiance proposal.

8
Disrupting the
Order of Salvation

During the sixteenth century there was an attempt to correct perceived gospel abandonment within Western Christianity. Even where reform was embraced, it was only partly successful. Confusion persisted because the theological center of the gospel was misidentified by the Protestant Reformers and their Catholic opponents alike. While we should celebrate the rediscovery of justification by faith alone, the Reformers made the questionable claim that it was the central tenet of the gospel, the doctrine by which the church stands or falls—as Luther famously put it.[1] The Catholic response at the Council of Trent reinforced the false perception that justification was indeed the centerpiece of the gospel.

As we discussed in chapter 4, the Reformers were wrong on this point. Justification by faith is true and an important doctrine, but if Scripture is the standard, a person's justification by faith is not even part of the gospel, let alone its center. Beyond that, the way in which justification by "faith" (*pistis*) is a true doctrine was misarticulated by both the Reformers and their Catholic opponents, because they subtly misconstrued faith, works, and grace as these relate to the gospel and final salvation.

Since the boundary of valid fellowship in the gospel among Catholics and Protestants is of central concern both to this book's topics and to ecumenism, space has been devoted to justification by faith in previous chapters. Yet pressing questions remain: How does justification relate to other categories that have classically been deemed vital, such as sanctification or perseverance unto glory? How does right-standing come about for each individual who has responded to the gospel? Is it imputed (the traditional Protestant view)? Is it infused/imparted (the Catholic perspective)? Our task in the next two chapters is to answer such questions.

This discussion can be confusing, so first a word about terminology. Disagreements about *justification* are at the same time disputes about *righteousness*. Two word families are used in English to emphasize different aspects of the single *dikaio-* word group in the original Greek of the New Testament.

Translators must make a choice. They typically select *righteousness* terminology when they sense that the moral or behavior aspect of the *dikaio-* word group is foregrounded. *Justification* language prevails when the context is judicial, especially God's activity as judge. But a single word family is in view in earliest Christianity when we talk about a person being right, just, righteous, justified, or about righteousness or justification.

As this chapter unfolds, we will analyze central Catholic and Protestant differences with regard to models of justification or righteousness. First, however, we must deal with a preliminary boundary issue that has plagued the conversation. After Luther a sharp distinction was drawn between justification and sanctification. This distinction soon became crucial to classic Protestant articulations of the gospel and the order of salvation, wedging Catholics and Protestants even farther apart.

If we're going to move beyond salvation wars of the past, it's high time we reappraised the justification-sanctification boundary with regard to the order of salvation.

Dislodging Justification from the Order of Salvation

An order of salvation (*ordo salutis*) seeks to give the sequential steps, from initial to final, for the personalization of salvation.

Because these steps are rooted in God's eternal self-life, they are not deemed purely chronological but are believed to reflect a *logical* ordering by which God determined to unfold his saving purposes.

Everyone agrees that the Father, Son, and Spirit have acted in history to save humanity through specific events such as the Christ's death for our sins. But how do God's saving events within history connect to you or me today personally? The theological goal for the order of salvation (*ordo salutis*) is to describe correctly the logical sequence that each and every "saved" individual must and will move through as part of the salvation process.

On Justification and Sanctification as Ordered

Due to its significance for Catholic-Protestant disputes, the proposed boundary between *justification* and *sanctification* requires special attention. Let's start with the basic distinctions.

The *process of justification* traditionally has been considered the change in an individual's status from guilty to innocent. When the change is complete, a person can be described as justified, righteous, or having the status of righteousness in God's eyes.

Protestants typically have described the movement associated with God's justifying activity as *declarative*: justification happens when God *declares* that a person is no longer guilty for sins but is innocent in his eyes. For Protestants, sanctification traditionally describes a justified person's growth in holiness of life.

Catholics describe God's justifying activity as *making* a person righteous through the impartation of moral virtues: justification happens when a person who was previously not righteous is made righteous, so that they are deemed righteous in God's eyes because they truly have become precisely that. For Catholics, sanctification does not tend to describe a distinct portion of the process of personal salvation but is a fitting description of the holiness of life that all individuals should seek.

203

The order of salvation derives from a certain interpretation of Romans 8:29–30 that was combined with philosophical reasoning. This passage does not mention sanctification at all but does use other key soteriological terms:

> For those God *foreknew* he also *predestined* to be conformed to the image of his Son, in order that he might be the firstborn among many brothers. Now, those he *predestined*, he also *called*; those he *called*, he also *justified*; those he *justified*, he also *glorified*. (Rom. 8:29–30 AT)

Although theologians who articulate an order of salvation acknowledge that Paul may not have listed all of the steps, they find that his outline gives many of the necessary links in the sequential chain: *foreknew, predestined, called, justified, glorified.*[2] The task of delineating this sequence correctly has become so central to systematic theology that the whole sequence is frequently called "the golden chain."[3]

It should be obvious by now that the gospel-allegiance model disagrees with such an ordering of terms, because these are group categories not intended for individualization. In chapter 6 we explored how Scripture teaches that neither election for predestination (or foreknowing) nor pre-faith regeneration is a valid category for describing how an individual first enters the process of salvation.

Since *effectual calling* depends upon these categories, it is excluded also. Effectual calling claims that those who are personally elect are irresistibly drawn to God so that God can then regenerate each one before that person comes to saving faith. In seeking to describe the true order, individual election and pre-faith regeneration are false starts, so effectual calling is also. Repentant allegiance in response to the gospel is the true starting point for personal salvation.

Even though it is not straightforwardly biblical, a *notional* distinction between justification and sanctification became central to classic Protestantism in its infancy for reasons we will look at.

Through a combination of theological and philosophical reasoning, it became standard to insert sanctification after justification within the order.

The Heart of the Order

Neither Paul nor any other New Testament author makes this move, but nevertheless theologians who propose an order of salvation invariably insert sanctification into the order between justified and glorified, so the heart of the sequence becomes *justification → sanctification → perseverance unto glorification.*

Why have so many Protestant theologians concluded that an individual's sanctification must immediately follow justification, even though Scripture does not say this? The logic is as follows:

1. good works cannot in any way be the basis for a person's justification without violating grace; yet
2. an individual's good works will invariably come *after* justification as evidence of its genuineness;
3. therefore, *God must justify a person—that is, declare his or her innocence—as the first logical step and then, second, begin to sanctify or make that person holy.*

In short, it is felt that justification must logically precede sanctification because otherwise good works would infringe, violating grace.[4] If it is not a straightforward teaching from the Bible, where did this idea arise?

Creating the Justification-Sanctification Distinction

Although Luther's associate Philip Melanchthon first articulated the distinction between justification and sanctification, John Calvin defended and popularized it. Calvin first emphasizes their inseparability: "These fruits of grace [justification and sanctification] are connected together, as it were, by an indissoluble tie, so that he who attempts to sever them does in a manner tear Christ in pieces."[5] For Calvin, justification and sanctification must go hand in hand: "Christ justifies no one whom he does not at the same time sanctify."[6] Meanwhile, Calvin is careful to say that justification doesn't produce sanctification. Christ is the source of both:

> But, since the question concerns only righteousness [i.e., justification] and sanctification, let us dwell upon these. Although we may distinguish them, Christ contains both of them inseparably in himself. . . . Since, therefore, it is solely by expending himself that the Lord gives us these benefits to enjoy, he bestows both of them at the same time, the one never without the other.[7]

Thus, for Calvin, justification and sanctification both emerge from union with Christ. Justification is *logically* not chronologically prior to sanctification, while Christ remains the source of both.

Famously, Calvin considered justification and sanctification to be like light's brightness and heat. Just as light and heat must go together inseparably when the sun shines, but they can and must be philosophically distinguished, so also justification and sanctification. He says, "Reason itself forbids us to transfer the peculiar qualities of one to the other."[8] Calvin considers justification and sanctification to be philosophically and qualitatively distinct yet inseparable gifts that flow from Christ through union with him.

Today, Calvin's notional distinction between justification and sanctification features regularly in Protestant teaching on salvation—even among Protestants in denominations that do not generally look to Calvin as a primary theological resource. For instance, the distinction is common for Methodists, following John Wesley. But the justification-sanctification distinction is misguided.

Problems with the Justification-Sanctification Distinction

There are three reasons why the justification-sanctification distinction is invalid: (1) the distinction lacks basic biblical warrant;

(2) justification is not merely declarative but transformative and liberating; (3) Romans 8:29–30 describes benefits (such as justification and glorification) that belong to the church in the Christ collectively in such a way that individuals enjoy those benefits only conditionally. Let's look at each of these.

Lack of Basic Biblical Support

Calvin's inseparable-yet-distinct analysis of justification and sanctification certainly sounds impressive, but it cannot be demonstrated to be true from Scripture. The only biblical proof that Calvin can muster is 1 Corinthians 1:30, where justification/righteousness (*dikaiosynē*) and sanctification (*hagiosmos*) happen to be listed separately: "You are in the Christ, Jesus, who became to us wisdom from God—that is, righteousness and sanctification and redemption" (AT). A list of qualities like this is flimsy evidence at best. If my wife were to give me too much credit by saying, "You are tall and handsome and thoughtful," nobody would think these attributes are inseparable yet distinct. It is not the case that stature in height, handsomeness, and thoughtfulness are really indissolubly bound if we could just learn to see them from the proper angle—as if no tall person could be ugly and unthoughtful.

Calvin's analysis makes this mistake when he suggests that it can be proven that justification and sanctification are inseparable yet distinct on the basis of 1 Corinthians 1:30. Paul's list there comes nowhere near proving that he thought that justification and sanctification were two philosophical distinctions of a single inseparable gospel benefit. Nor does it even begin to show that Paul intended justification and sanctification to connect logically as holistic steps within an order of salvation. Calvin's biblical evidence is woefully inadequate.

Moreover, if you search the New Testament in the Greek attempting to prove that justification (*dikaio-* terms) and sanctification (*hagia/o-* terms) really are two logically ordered sides of a single gospel benefit, you'll discover that they are never explicitly treated in this way in Scripture. In the entire New Testament, 1 Corinthians 6:11 and Romans 6:19 are the only plausible square pegs that one can attempt to force through that round hole. But to force them to affirm that justification and sanctification are distinct yet inseparable benefits within an individual's "order of salvation" is contrary to their intent and imposes an alien system. Unfortunately, this has been a common imposition.

In 1 Corinthians 6:11 Paul speaks about the transformed status of the Corinthians. Previously they were unrighteous sinners, "But you were washed, you were sanctified [*hēgiasthēte*], you were justified [*edikaiōthēte*] in the name of the Lord Jesus Christ and by the Spirit of our God." Paul is not articulating a notional distinction between washing, justification, and sanctification as part of an order, chain, or stages by which an individual comes to be saved. First Corinthians 6:11 is about the experience of the whole Christian community, not individuals at all (the "you" is plural in the Greek).

Moreover, if Paul did intend the logical order of classic Protestantism in 1 Corinthians 6:11, then we would expect justification to come prior to sanctification. Instead, sanctification is listed prior. Why? Because Paul is not articulating an order at all. Paul is simply employing three diverse metaphors—washed, sanctified, justified—to describe *the single transformed reality* that *all* the members of the Corinthian churches *corporately* enjoy. Paul doesn't speak about an individual's order of salvation in this passage in any fashion.

Romans 6:19, while mentioning righteousness (justification) and holiness (sanctification), likewise fails to show that they should be considered a single gospel benefit that is ordered yet patient of philosophical distinction. Paul is not making normative soteriological claims about individualized processes of justification and sanctification that God initializes and orchestrates.

Instead, Paul is giving a moral exhortation, telling the Roman Christians how they should behave and what the result will be. Paul tells them to present the members of their bodies as "slaves to *righteousness* [*dikaiosynē*] leading to *holiness* [*hagiosmos*]" (Rom. 6:19). Paul is speaking pastorally about how the Romans should behave with their body parts under their new master, trying to lead them to a good outcome: if the Romans submit to *God's righteous lifestyle*, the result will be *lives characterized by holiness*. Although Paul uses "justification" or righteousness language here, this passage is not about *God's action* of "declaring humans righteous" (justification) at all but about liberated humans *taking the initiative* in the Christ to submit to a righteous (justified) lifestyle. Paul personifies righteousness (justification), portraying it as a master to which we can willingly submit in the king, leading to a life of holiness.

In short, even in the few passages—1 Corinthians 1:30, 6:11, and Romans 6:19—where justification and sanctification are mentioned together, *Scripture never even approximately claims that justification is a holistic status in an individual's order of salvation that logically precedes sanctification while remaining inseparable from it.*

I think we can all agree about this: it is easy to make a consistent system if we make biblical words mean things that they don't actually mean and instead fill their content with whatever "closely related" concepts we fancy. The vast majority of popular Protestant pastors and scholars who write on the topic of salvation—for example, John MacArthur and Thomas Schreiner—do this when they follow Calvin's inseparable-yet-distinct analysis of justification and sanctification in an individualized order of salvation.[9] But if we are trying to create a systematic theology that derives its authority and legitimacy from Scripture, we must begin with clear and definite examples that give proof. In the case of the justification-sanctification distinction for an individualized *ordo salutis*, there are none.

We are not permitted to unmoor the biblical language from its foundations in this thoroughgoing way. The bald but accurate truth is this: *Scripture does not support a notional distinction between justification and sanctification in a personalized order of salvation.* Since the classic Protestant distinction has no scriptural authority, a revision is urgently required.

Liberating Justification from Mere Declaration

Classic Protestantism was pressured in its polemic against Catholicism to carve out a space for justification that was entirely untainted by works. The primary strategy was to create a category after justification within the *ordo salutis* called sanctification and to reify it. The early Protestant Reformers deployed a parallel strategy that complemented the justification-sanctification distinction and likewise was designed to keep justification free of the threat of works: the claim that justification is purely declarative. This view was also developed especially by Luther's associate Philip Melanchthon, but Luther, Calvin, and others mostly came to embrace it.[10] A candid assessment of God's justifying activity in Scripture shows that justification is declarative, yes, but it is more than declarative.

Justification is not just declarative. In Scripture justification goes beyond mere declaration of innocence to include transformation. That is, justification includes much of what traditionally has been reserved for the category of sanctification. Much of the pressure from within Protestantism to distinguish justification and sanctification comes from the desire to exclude works from justification. This falls foul of what Paul, James, and the rest of the New Testament say about *doing* and *deeds* as part of the basis for justification or final salvation (e.g., Rom. 2:6–8, 13; James 2:21–24; cf. Matt. 16:27; John 5:28–29; Rom. 8:12–13; 14:9–12; 2 Cor. 5:10; 2 Tim. 4:14; Rev. 20:12–15).[11] It also is difficult to square with what Paul says about justification's new-life dimensions.

Justification is primarily declarative and judicial in orientation, but as far as Scripture is concerned, it also includes *deliverance* and *new-life transformation* in ways that go beyond a self-contained declaration. For example, in speaking about a person in the Christ, Paul says, "The one who has died *has been justified* from Sin" (Rom. 6:7 AT). Since in context "Sin" is an enslaving power, this involves ontological change for an individual that impacts present behavior. For this reason, it is usually translated, "The one who has died *has been set free* from sin."

Such a translation is accurate. Unfortunately, the substitution of "set free" for "justified" prevents the English-only reader from seeing that in the Greek text God's *justifying* activity is in view, and that *justification goes beyond mere declaration to ontological*

changes that include present bodily liberation. Because justification includes new-life liberation that extends to the body, it is not
merely a not-guilty verdict.[12] As Peter Leithart whimsically and
helpfully states, justification is a "deliverdict."[13]

Justification as deliverdict. Justification is a *deliverdict* because
God's declarative speech-act "Justified!" creates a new-life reality
for the Christ and his body (i.e., for the king and any members who
are sourced "in him"). This is why Paul can add, "No longer let Sin
reign in your mortal *body* so that you *obey* its evil desires" (Rom.
6:12 AT)—and he can mean it. If united to the kingly head and
the rest of the king's body (the church), the individual's personal
body has changed in a fundamental (ontological) way because
it participates in the new-creation power of the Spirit. It is now
liberated.

Moreover, justification extends into areas traditionally reserved
for sanctification because it goes beyond what happened at the
cross. Our justification depends not just on Jesus's crucifixion but
also on *the new-life power associated with the resurrected king.*
This is why in his justification language Paul points not only to
the cross but also to the resurrection: the Christ was "*raised* for
our justification" (Rom. 4:25). The new-creation resurrection life
of the enthroned Messiah spills over metaphysically to us for our
justification.

It is necessary that the enthroned king share his resurrection
life with us in our justification. Why? *Justification is a declaration not merely of innocence but also that the resurrection life
of God's new creation is at work in our bodies.* Since it involves
bodily transformation associated with the king's resurrection life,
justification is not mere declaration. Other passages are similar
in extending justification language into the liberation and transformation associated with resurrection life.[14]

In sum, because justification includes bodily transformation
in Scripture, it transgresses the classic Protestant justification-
sanctification divide and in so doing shows that the divide itself
lacks warrant. In Scripture, justification includes much of what
has been termed sanctification by systematic theologians, since

justification involves participation in the transformative new life of the resurrected king.

Removing Justification from the Individualized Order

There is a final reason why the classic Protestant justification-sanctification ordering is invalid: Romans 8:29–30 is referring to group benefits. Paul has a fondness for corporate categories, and he speaks to all the Roman house churches as a *group*. Paul is detailing the holistic *applied benefits* that God has already accomplished for his *entire people* in the Messiah.

There is a loose sequence in Romans 8:29–30, but it refers to benefits God intended for his people as a group *in the past*—all of which have now been historically realized in *the present and* will endure into *the future*, but only in the Christ. We can view this from a community-first *eternal* and *historical* perspective.

Considered first from an *eternal* perspective, those who are *in the Christ*, no matter which individuals make up that nonindividuated *corporate group*, are *foreknown, predestined, called, justified,* and *glorified*, because these are all benefits that timelessly describe the status of anyone who becomes a member of the Christ's collective body. This is true because all these attributes belong to the kingly head and hence also to any member of his body.

Considered, second, from a *historical* perspective, a people (community) that is fully foreknown, predestined, called, justified, and glorified was established at Pentecost when the first followers of Jesus received the benefits of the gospel via Spirit union. Let me spell out the historical perspective more fully. Once an individual professes, "Jesus is Lord," she or he immediately becomes part of the community that possesses all the benefits listed in Romans 8:29–30. If we opt to profess Jesus as king, as individuals, then we come to possess the benefits that attend incorporation at that moment, so we are foreknown, predestined, called, justified, and glorified. If we choose not to profess, then none of those terms apply, because they apply only *conditionally* to those who are in the Son. Meanwhile, as individuals, we remain in that group if we persevere in profession, but if we desist, those attributes no longer apply. (See chap. 3 on collective versus individual language, and chap. 7 on perseverance.) From an eternal or historical perspective, then, individual salvation depends on belonging to the "Jesus is Lord" confessing community.

As evidence that Romans 8:29–30 describes conditional group benefits and not an individualized sequence of salvation, consider that Paul does not speak of *future* glory in 8:30. If Paul intended an individualized order of salvation, we would expect justification (and sanctification, which tellingly Paul doesn't even mention) to be described to the Romans as past or present events, but for glory to be purely for the future. Yet this is not the case. Paul is clear that the church's "justified" identification with the king's death and suffering through the gospel involves a sharing in his royal glory *right now*: "those he justified he also glorified" (Rom. 8:30; cf. 6:4; 8:17; 2 Thess. 2:14).

But if Paul is using nonindividuated group categories in Romans 8:29–30, it makes sense that glory is already attained rather than purely future. Paul frequently speaks not only of the church's future glory but also about its *present* glory in the Messiah, because in the Christ glory has already been restored (2 Cor. 3:7–11, 18; 4:6; 8:23; cf. Rom. 6:4). The church's glory has *past*, *present*, and *future* dimensions. The same is true for justification because these are corporate benefits that can be conditionally experienced by individuals who opt to become incorporated into the king's body (e.g., Rom. 3:24; 5:1; 1 Cor. 6:11; Gal. 2:16). In Romans 8:29–30 Paul is not speaking about an order of salvation pertinent to individuals that culminates in future glory.

All told, justification is best regarded not as God's initial declaration of an individual's innocence but as a gospel benefit that always defines the vindicated-unto-new-life people of God—past, present, and future—in such a way that individuals can swear allegiance and enter it. Sanctification always defines the people of God as holy. Glory always defines the restoration of untarnished image-bearing for the people of God. Elect always defines the people of God as chosen. Each of these is always past, present, and future for God's entire people, but such language cannot be applied to individuals apart from a conditional if-you-are-giving-allegiance-to-the-king qualification.

Since Paul is speaking about the church's collective status as a whole, not commenting on how individuals enter or leave the church, Romans 8:29–30 does not support the view that presently "justified" individuals are predestined or chosen for salvation before creation. Nor does it suggest that an individual who is presently confessing Jesus as king will necessarily persevere unto final salvation, for this both inaccurately individuates the passage and misconstrues the meaning of glory (*doxa*), treating it as if glory pertains exclusively to final salvation (e.g., in heaven). These results mesh with the conclusions about justification's actual relationship to the gospel articulated elsewhere in this book. Personal justification is not part of the gospel but rather a benefit of the gospel.

In sum, at least three problems exist with regard to the traditional Protestant distinction between justification and sanctification in an individual's order of salvation. First, it is not biblical, since there is radically insufficient evidence in Scripture that these are inseparable but qualitatively distinct benefits attained in the Messiah.

Second, in Scripture personal justification cannot be restricted to a judicial declaration of innocence but rather involves liberating ontological change that extends into resurrection life and behavior, including bodily actions. In fact, Paul says that actual behavior, *deeds*, will form part of *the basis* of an individual's final justification.

Third, Paul nowhere intends to describe an individualized *order of salvation* in the first place with regard to justification, but he does describe the collective church's vindicated position in the king as a whole. Justification is a corporate benefit that belongs to the church; individuals come to experience this benefit only conditionally if and when they become united to the king.

The nonbiblical justification-sanctification distinction has hindered advancement toward unity in the truth among Catholics and Protestants. More specifically, classic Protestantism has wrongly used the artificial separation of justification and sanctification to exclude *any and every work or deed* from justification, hindering us from seeing what truly distressed Paul. Paul was not distraught by good deeds or moral effort. Trying to do good and succeeding is consistently praiseworthy in Scripture. Paul was distressed by claims that something more specific, *works of law*, has any role to play with regard to justification. *Paul's real aim was to denounce systems of salvation that advocate mandatory rule-performance rather than Spirit-led allegiance* (see chap. 4).

Catholic and Protestant Models for Justification

The previous section was largely a ground-clearing exercise. Indeed, much within this book and its prequel, *Gospel Allegiance*, is aimed in that direction. It is impossible to discern what ails the classic Protestant and Catholic models of justification if words such as *gospel, grace, faith, works, regeneration, justification,* and *sanctification* are defined in sub-biblical ways and then deployed systematically.

Now we are in a stronger position to assess the classic Protestant model for justification: imputed righteousness. The faulty justification-sanctification scheme has been paired by classic Protestantism with another idea that lacks biblical support: imputed righteousness. This has resulted in overly restrictive ideas among Protestants about how righteousness belongs to an individual. Meanwhile, as we will see, the Catholic view is even more problematic. Inspecting both may offer hints that help us in our quest to speak as truly as we can about such matters. Now that the faulty justification-sanctification division has been discussed, we are in a better position to understand the basic models for justification (or righteousness).

Protestant Righteousness

The dominant Protestant model for personal justification is called *imputed righteousness*. The basic idea is that Jesus's right-standing is credited to a person by faith alone. A person is declared righteous in God's presence by faith in Jesus because when faith is present for a person, God looks upon Jesus's perfect righteousness rather than that person's unrighteousness. Imputed righteousness stands at the fountainhead of the Protestant Reformation, because according to Luther's own account, this new understanding of righteousness is what changed everything for him.

Luther had been taught that the righteousness of God in Paul's Letter to the Romans refers to "formal or active righteousness," meaning that "God is righteous and punishes the unrighteous sinner." That is, the righteousness of God in Romans 1:17, 3:21–26, and so forth refers to God's own character quality that demands he uphold a standard of justice by punishing wrongdoing. This greatly troubled Luther:

> Though I lived as a monk without reproach, I felt that I was a sinner before God with an extremely troubled conscience. I could not believe that he was placated by my satisfaction [i.e., performance of the sacrament of penance]. I did not love, yes, I hated the righteous God who punishes sinners.

But as he was reading the New Testament in Greek rather than Latin, he came to the conclusion that the righteousness of God means not God's punishing righteousness in Romans 1:17 but rather "that by which the righteous lives by a gift of God, namely by faith." That is, it is a righteous status that God declares over an individual as a gracious gift. He called this a passive righteousness. Upon this discovery, Luther exclaims, "I felt that I was altogether born again and had entered paradise itself through open gates." He further describes it as "imputed righteousness" and "the righteousness with which God clothes us."[15]

Protestant imputed righteousness. Protestants agree with Catholics that personal justification is based on Jesus's merit. In disagreement with Catholicism, for classic Protestantism, Jesus's right-standing is credited to humans by one and only one instrumental cause: faith alone. Faith is the only tool or means that God uses to bring about justification. In contrast, Catholics believe that baptism as the sacrament of faith is the only tool.

For Protestants, imputation means that by faith alone a person is declared righteous in God's sight, because God looks upon Jesus's perfect righteousness rather than the person's unrighteousness. Such an individual has not actually been *made righteous* by God in such a way that moral character has improved but rather has been *declared righteous* despite an ongoing sinful condition. Christ's righteousness is reckoned or credited to the individual's account. Each person remains simultaneously righteous and sinful but is considered righteous by God on account of Christ's righteousness.

To better understand what is meant by *imputed righteousness* within classic Protestantism, let's use Luther's clothing analogy. Think of Jesus's righteousness as a spotless white garment that covers your filthy, unrighteous sin. In terms of judgment, even though you remain dirty, God no longer sees your dirt nor cares about your sinful filth. By faith alone you have been covered with the perfect cleanliness of Jesus's righteousness as a garment through your union with him. Meanwhile, God is in the process of changing you so that your personal dirtiness is alleviated. You are being sanctified, and this sanctification is inevitable if your justifying faith is genuine. But your personal transformation through sanctification is not the judicial basis upon which you are declared righteous in God's sight. The judicial basis is Jesus's righteousness (his garment) being credited or imputed to you by faith alone.

Beyond Luther, the basic model of *imputed righteousness* was further developed and refined within Protestantism. For instance, the Reformed (Calvinist) tradition would develop a philosophically informed "exchange" model of *double imputation*: by faith all our human unrighteousness is considered Christ's (so it could be dealt with on the cross), while all Christ's righteousness (his active obedience) is considered ours. Nevertheless, Luther's sketch was the foundation for these further refinements.

The irony is, as we will see in the next chapter, that despite Protestant *sola scriptura* ("by Scripture alone") ideals, imputed righteousness is not taught by Scripture in a straightforward fashion. The gospel-allegiance model points to a model for human righteousness that aligns more closely with Scripture.

Catholic Justification

Since the two models were defined over against each other, to grasp Protestant justification is also to begin to understand the Catholic model. We have already begun to discuss these matters.

In chapter 4, I sought to demonstrate that, broadly speaking, neither Protestants nor Catholics have compromised the actual gospel, so both are fully Christian. This is not, however, to say that classic Protestantism and Catholicism are without error in all that they teach about salvation. In particular, the classic Protestant interpretation of Galatians accuses Catholicism of compromising the gospel—but it misconstrues the biblical gospel. Contrary to the classic Protestant tendency to center the gospel on justification by faith, in actuality the gospel is that Jesus is the Christ, and this gospel results in certain benefits. Personal *justification* is a *benefit* of the gospel and repentant *faith* (fidelity) is the saving *response* to the gospel, but neither is properly part of the gospel itself. Catholicism also has errors in its teachings about justification. In the spirit of truth and love, I outlined four ways that Scripture should pressure the Catholic Church to reconsider its doctrine of justification. Here we'll go deeper with regard to Catholic teaching on justification.

To understand Catholic justification more thoroughly, the best place to begin is the Catholic Council of Trent. In its sixth session (1547), Trent's bishops issued their "Decree on Justification." Justification has never been treated in any significant way subsequently by councils or popes, so Trent's decree remains uniquely authoritative for Catholics today.

218

Although Trent is definitive, this is not to say that Catholics have been silent about justification. It is simply to say there has been no truly authoritative teaching beyond Trent. This is true except for one small but vital piece of data: Catholicism now recognizes that other Christian communions genuinely share the Holy Spirit.[16] This softens the standard Catholic claim that its sacraments are absolutely mandatory for everyone for salvation. Yet it is unclear how to reconcile this recognition with Trent's more explicit and thorough treatment of salvation and its sacramental absolutes.

In recent years the Joint Declaration on Justification (1999) was issued by the Pontifical Council for Promoting Church Unity and the Lutheran World Federation, but the Pontifical Council is advisory rather than dogmatic. It does not carry the full authoritative weight of the Catholic teaching office. In any case, although the Joint Declaration on Justification is a hopeful sign, it doesn't contradict or appreciably clarify Trent's or Vatican II's decrees.

Professional Catholic theologians have also written on justification (e.g., Hans Küng, Joseph Fitzmyer, Thomas Stegman), but their views are simply private opinion—no different than yours or mine—unless subsequently affirmed by the teaching office. Only what is issued by the teaching office—for example, a dogmatic decree issued by the pope or by an ecumenical council—can serve as *primary data* in terms of an analysis of truthfulness or error of Catholicism. This is why I restrict my conversation here to Trent's dogmas.

The Council of Trent draws on different types of causes as they were understood within medieval Catholic theology. Understanding these different types of causes is key for unlocking Protestant-Catholic differences regarding justification. Drawing from traditional understandings of causation as articulated by Aristotle and refined by scholastic theologians, Trent articulates five different causes of justification: *the efficient, the meritorious, the instrumental, the final,* and *the formal.* To fully understand, we need to explore where Protestants and Catholics agree, but we must give special attention to matters about which they remain in sharp dispute.

The Efficient Cause

The *efficient cause* is what we most readily identify as a cause today: it is that agent (or source) ultimately responsible for bringing about an effect. If I hit a billiard ball toward a pocket, I caused it to move, bringing about motion as an effect.

For Catholics, God causes a saving movement within a human, so that justification is brought about by God as an effect. "The efficient cause" of justification, for the Council of Trent, "is the merciful God who *washes and sanctifies* [1 Cor. 6:11] gratuitously, signing and anointing *with the holy Spirit of promise, who is the pledge of our inheritance* [Eph. 1:13–14]" (§7).

Classically, Protestants have agreed fully with Catholics about the efficient cause. For example, Calvin describes the efficient cause of justification as "the mercy of the heavenly Father and his freely given love for us."[17] There is agreement that God is the one who causes a person to be justified in the sense that God brings about justification or righteousness as an effect.

The Meritorious Cause

The Council of Trent declares that Jesus himself is the *meritorious cause* of justification. The meritorious cause refers to the restoration of the value or worth that we lacked but that God's justice required. Trent says, "The meritorious cause is His most beloved only begotten, our Lord Jesus Christ, who [loved us even when we were his enemies and] . . . merited for us justification by his most holy passion on the wood of the cross and made satisfaction for us to God the Father" (§7). It is the Son's work on the cross that supplies the merit required for humans to attain justification.

The working assumption for Trent's decree is that justification can be modeled in terms of a ledger or balance sheet. An individual's personal account before God has a merit deficit caused by sin that the individual cannot possibly repay on his or her own. Satisfaction must be made. The gracious gift of Jesus's death and resurrection supplies the merit that we personally need in order to render satisfaction but that we in no fashion deserved. Jesus's merit can be savingly applied to a person's account, bringing restoration.

During the Protestant Reformation, Protestants and Catholics largely agreed about the meritorious or material cause and its gracious character. For example, Calvin says, "The material cause is Christ with his obedience, through which he acquired righteousness for us."[18] Calvin focuses on Christ's holistic active obedience (his righteous life unto death) rather than more narrowly on Christ's work on the cross, but nevertheless there is broad agreement. Both Catholics and Protestants were content at that time largely to follow Anselm's satisfaction theology of the atonement in articulating the meritorious cause.

Today we can and should be more exacting about the degree to which the meritorious cause is an acceptable grammar for individual salvation. This is necessary because the acceptance by both sides within the early phases of the Protestant-Catholic debate of a questionable merit-satisfaction systematic framework has made it difficult subsequently for theologians to track the Bible's actual theology of personal salvation. This impacted Protestant ideas about imputed righteousness and Catholic conceptions of imparted righteousness. This will be discussed more fully in the next chapter.

Beyond the efficient and meritorious causes, Trent configures grace in several ways that most Protestants find unacceptable.

THE INSTRUMENTAL CAUSE

For Catholics, more is necessary for justification than the initial merit supplied by Jesus. As we move beyond the meritorious cause, we begin to see why Protestants disagree with Catholicism. For Catholicism, justification is imparted by one and only one instrumental cause: the sacrament of baptism, which is regarded as the sacrament of faith.

What is an instrumental cause? An *instrumental cause* is akin to a physical tool that an artist uses to craft a statue. You can't carve a statue without using some sort of tool, even if that tool is your fingernails. Similarly, for Catholicism, God can't justify a person without a tool. And baptism turns out to be the one and only tool he has ordained for this purpose: if a person has not been baptized, then God has no tool to justify that person. Therefore, that person cannot possibly be justified. This is why Trent decrees, "The sacrament of baptism is the sacrament of faith, without which no man was ever justified" (§7).

In light of Scripture, for the reasons discussed in chapter 5, most Protestants dispute that baptism per se is in any sense God's precise tool for justification—let alone his only tool. God justifies the thief on the cross and those at Cornelius's house entirely apart from baptism—and probably Peter, the other eleven apostles, and the 120 too. Calvin identifies the instrumental cause simply as "faith."[19]

Since the sacrament of baptism is called the sacrament of faith by Trent, at first glance there would seem to be room for Protestant-Catholic agreement on the instrumental cause. That is, if it could be shown that baptism uniquely and exclusively expresses saving faith, then perhaps Protestants and Catholics could agree.

However, most Protestants, correctly, do not find that the Bible supports such an idea. For instance, Scripture testifies that saving faith and Holy Spirit union can be present *prior* to baptism (see chap. 5). This makes it impossible for most Protestants to accept the Catholic *ex opere operato* sacramental view.

Moreover, many Protestants are rightly troubled by *how* baptism is construed as the sacrament of faith within Catholicism. Since *for Catholicism, the faith in view during baptism is not that of the baptismal candidate but rather that of the church as a whole as embodied via the candidate and the sponsors (e.g., the godparents)*, saving faith has been redefined in ways that depart from what the New Testament intends. Contrary to what we find in the New Testament, for Catholicism the personal or personalist faith of the baptismal candidate is largely irrelevant. When Catholics call baptism the sacrament of faith, they mean the faith of the whole church, not the personal faith of the baptismal candidate, for the baptismal candidate ordinarily is an infant. This impersonal nonvoluntary understanding of faith directly contradicts the early Christian witness regarding how baptism is saving (see chap. 5).

Even though baptism is the sacrament of faith within Catholicism, the instrumentality is quite different for Catholics when compared with that of most Protestants. For Catholicism, the instrumental cause of justification is the baptismal action as an expression of the faith of the collective church. For Protestants, generally, it is the faith of the individual, while that faith can be tied or untied from a specific sacrament depending on the Protestant tradition in question.

THE FINAL CAUSE

The final cause of justification is that toward which justification is ultimately aimed or purposed. What is God's end goal for it? Catholicism (Trent) identifies the *final cause* of human justification as "the glory of God and of Christ and life everlasting" (§7). That is, our justification's ultimate aim is bidirectional, with an intended benefit for God and for us. On the one hand, it brings God (and Christ) glory. On the other hand, it is purposed toward human attainment of eternal life.

John Calvin identified the final cause of justification similarly. It is "both in the proof of divine justice and in the praise of God's goodness." He cites Romans 3:26 as defining the final cause of justification: "in order that he himself may be righteous and the justifier of him who has faith in Christ."[20] That is, Calvin describes the final cause as God's own righteous behavior, which, of course, secondarily redounds to God's glory when justified humans praise God for their justification. The final cause, God's glory, has not been a major source of controversy between Protestants and Catholics.

THE FORMAL CAUSE

There is an additional cause of justification for Catholics: the formal cause. The Catholic formal cause is what made Protestants howl in protest in the early days of the Reformation. A *formal cause* is that which constrains a thing to be what it is.

The formal cause is what causes a potentiality to take a specific, defined form or shape within reality. Water as possible ice has the potential to become actual ice if circumstances allow. Consider the formal cause to be like an ice-cube tray in a freezer: the *shape* of the tray dictates the *form* that water (possible ice) must and will take when it is frozen into a sphere or cube (actual ice).

In a similar way, the formal cause of justification indicates that possible justification has the potential to become actual justification within the circumstances that God ordains for that purpose. For Catholicism, the formal cause of justification dictates the shape that possible justification must and will take as it is brought into reality as actual justification by God.

The formal cause of justification, that which compels potential justification to be justification as we really find it, is declared by official Catholic teaching to be God's *making* us righteous:

> The single *formal cause* is *the justice of God, not that by which He Himself is just, but that by which He **makes** us just*, that, namely, with which we being endowed by Him, are renewed in the spirit of our mind, and not only are we reputed but we are truly called and are just, *receiving justice within us, each one according to his own measure*, which the Holy Ghost distributes to everyone as He wills, and *according to each one's disposition and cooperation*. (§7 [emphasis added])

For Catholicism, possible justification becomes actual when God *makes* humans righteous.

There are four things to note about the formal cause of justification for Catholicism. First, *humans are made righteous or just*. The notion that a person could be declared (or merely reputed) righteous without receiving an actual improved behavioral uprightness is forthrightly rejected. A person who is justified is not simply regarded as just (righteous) by God but actually has the moral quality of justness (righteousness). This is a deliberate and explicit rejection of Protestant imputed righteousness (on which, see below) by Catholicism at Trent.

Second, *the righteousness or justice received is not a participation in God's own righteousness.* As Trent puts it, the righteousness that a person enjoys as part of justification is "not that by which He Himself is just." This is critical. For Catholicism, human justification is not a direct sharing in God's or Christ's own righteousness in such a way that God or Christ remains the perpetual extrinsic source of human righteousness. For Catholicism, the righteousness that the justified person comes to have is not the righteousness that God possesses but instead her or his own.

Third, *not everyone receives the same amount of justification.* The amount of justification a person has after baptism is described as "each according to his own measure." The Holy Spirit gives different amounts of justification to each, depending on the "disposition and cooperation" of the one who is receiving justification. The amount of personal justification likewise varies after absolution and penance. Since everyone starts with different amounts of justification at baptism, it also follows that not everyone has the same amount of justification after it is lost through mortal sin and then subsequently restored through the sacrament of reconciliation. For Catholics, the precise quantity of right-standing before God that a person has varies considerably.

Fourth, the amount of righteousness received at baptism depends upon a person's previously formed disposition and present cooperation, so *the quantity of initial justification received depends upon an individual's prior and present merit.* In this case the quantity is directly proportional to the quality, because for Catholicism, at the end of a person's life, the quantity of righteousness that a person has accrued determines whether he or she will be saved or damned. Hence, the quantity is a measure of the quality. For Catholics, a person who is less deserving of initial justification receives a lesser quantity of it, for the Holy Spirit grants it on the basis of a person's prior merit—his or her "disposition and cooperation."

Traditionally, Protestants have found all these points about the formal cause highly objectionable. The formal cause merits extended discussion.

225

How Does Possible Justification Become Actual for Catholics?

As the "Decree on Justification" continues, we learn that for Catholics this *making righteous* transpires when the merits of Jesus's passion are communicated to us. Trent uses several metaphors to describe how this *making righteous* occurs: the "charity of God is *poured forth* by the Holy Ghost"; we are "*ingrafted*" into Jesus Christ; faith, hope, and charity are "*infused*" at the same time as justification and "*added to it*" (§7, emphasis added).

When justified, a person not only is declared righteous but also has faith, hope, and love added to his or her righteousness. The result is that a person has actually been made righteous by the addition of these morally superior qualities or budding virtues. These virtues are truly present, but in varying degrees, because the quantity of received righteousness depends on the merit, disposition, and cooperation of each person—the majority of whom are infants.

For Catholicism, after a person has been made righteous (to a certain degree) at baptism, it is then required that she or he make progress in justification by becoming even more righteous over time by multiplying good works:

> Having, therefore, been thus justified . . . they, through the obser-
> vance of the commandments of God and of the Church, faith co-
> operating with good works, increase in that justice received through
> the grace of Christ and are further justified. (§10)

Remember, within Catholicism the quantity of initial justification received depends on personal merit, disposition, and cooperation. After that, initial baptismal justification must be increased by the performance of good deeds (with the assistance of God's grace) in the hope that the "crown of justice" can be received when the final curtain drops on this present life (§16). If the initial justification received at baptism has not increased sufficiently at the time of death to meet the bar of God's ultimate standard of final justification through the multiplication of good deeds, then condemnation to hell is expected. What this ultimate standard might be is left unspecified by the Council of Trent.

Meanwhile, a person who commits a mortal sin after baptism has "forfeited the received grace of justification" (§14) and is "cut off from the grace of Christ" (§15). Mortal sins are serious and intentional sins. After a mortal sin, saving grace can be restored only by completing the sacrament of penance or, if such is impossible due to circumstances, earnestly desiring to complete it (§14).

In sum, in the Catholic view, the formal cause of justification, that which constrains possible justification to be what it in reality actually is, does not communicate a *perfect righteousness*. It does not do this because an individual's righteousness is not a perpetual sharing in God's own righteousness or in the Christ's own but rather depends on a person's capacity and disposition to receive initial and ongoing righteousness. Human justification is expressly "not that by which He Himself is just" (§7). In fact, canon 10 of Trent says that if any person says that humans "by that justice [of Christ] are formally just, let him be anathema." Justification as an ongoing participation in a righteousness that is alien or extrinsic to the individual—that is perpetually sourced in God's own or Christ's own external righteousness—is expressly rejected by Catholicism.

Formal justification as a continual sharing in God's or Christ's own righteousness is explicitly rejected by official Catholic theology. Rather, the amount of righteousness received at baptism and subsequently depends on human disposition and cooperation. Righteousness has become an individual's *own* initial imperfect righteousness, so it must be safeguarded and increased in hope that sufficient good works will result in final justification.

Catholic Imparted Righteousness

It is preferable, following the metaphors of pouring and adding, to say that the dominant Catholic description of righteousness is that it has been *imparted*. Imparted righteousness suggests *momentary contact* followed by *separation* between Christ and the justified person with regard to how justification is fundamentally possessed.

Let's explore the Council of Trent's metaphor of "pouring" to explain imparted justification. For Catholics, at baptism some of God's righteousness, made available through Christ's merit, has been *poured* from Christ's pitcher into *yours* as a gracious gift of initial justifying merit. This baptismal pouring is the *momentary contact*. During this momentary contact with Christ's righteousness, specific virtues—faith, hope, and love—have marked your soul. In the initial baptismal act of justification you've been *made* righteous, inclusive of moral behavior, to the degree your disposition permits it.

But after baptism the pitchers are separated. It is now *your righteousness*. Even if God will graciously cooperate with you to help you keep increasing it, *after baptism your righteousness is no longer continually sourced in God or Jesus the Christ as its extrinsic source*. Your righteousness may be based on Christ's *merit*, but the righteousness that you possess is yours alone, not Christ's or God's. At baptism you were given your own righteousness at that moment of contact, and it remains your own separate possession, not a perpetual sharing in God's own or Christ's own righteousness.

However, for Catholicism, although granted incipient righteousness at baptism, you are almost certainly not righteous enough to meet the ultimate (yet unspecified) standard needed for final justification without performing additional good works after your baptism. Although you received an initial injection of righteousness and pertinent moral virtues that marked your soul, you don't yet have enough faith, hope, love, or righteousness, so you'd best get busy trying, with God's help, to increase these. If you falter along the way by committing a mortal sin, you've forfeited your initial baptismal righteousness. You must seek absolution from a priest and then make satisfaction by performing penance to be restored.

In its articulation of the instrumental and formal causes of justification, official Catholic theology violates what Scripture teaches about how humans are justified. The reasons for this have already been discussed, especially in chapters 4 and 5. Personally declared "faith" (*pistis*) toward King Jesus, not baptism as a sacrament of the church's faith as a whole, is the precise instrument of personal justification—although voluntary baptism remains the premier occasion to declare it. Meanwhile, regulations that demand performance for salvation are part of the Catholic sacramental system, yet, according to the New Testament, such saving regulations are not possible within the new-covenant era.

So, for Catholicism, justification can be summarized thus: God *makes* a person righteous through an *impartation* of righteousness through momentary contact during baptism, but with regard to that righteousness subsequently there is a separation so that it is the individual's own possession. On the basis of Christ's merit that person has been made righteous in the moment of baptismal contact but only to the degree that the baptismal candidate merits, is disposed toward, and cooperates with that gift. Subsequently, it is that individual's *own righteousness*. After baptism, personal voluntary cooperation is required for justification's completion. An individual is responsible for maintaining and increasing his or her own righteousness, realizing that this can be done only via God's gracious assistance.

Yet beyond impartation, secondarily, justification can be described as *ingrafted* or *infused*, which suggests ongoing union with Christ. Because the canons of Trent explicitly deny that an individual's formal righteousness is via Christ's own righteousness (i.e., Christ is not the perpetual extrinsic source of a person's righteousness), we are required to conclude that presently Catholicism rejects ingrafted or infused righteousness as a stand-alone official explanation of justification in favor of impartation.

Protestants often reject the entire Catholic package. If Scripture is the measure, then they must reject the primary metaphor of impartation, while it may be possible to accept the secondary metaphors of ingrafting/infusion. Meanwhile, there are problems with the classic Protestant model of imputed righteousness too, since it does not accurately track what Scripture teaches. Combining Protestant insights with the secondary Catholic metaphors might allow the church to make progress toward a better overall model. The gospel-allegiance model might help us see why slightly different language—*incorporated righteousness*—is the best way forward for the church.

9 Justification Remodeled

The previous chapter showed why the classic Protestant ordering of personal salvation—justification, sanctification, glorification—must be revised. The idea that an individual is logically justified by God first, then sanctified, and finally glorified has no genuine scriptural warrant.

That chapter also sketched the basic models for justification. Protestants traditionally have modeled individual justification as *imputed righteousness*. This means that Christ's righteousness is credited to the individual's account. Meanwhile, Catholics favor *imparted righteousness* as the main descriptive category, emphasizing momentary contact with God's righteousness-creating power through the sacrament of baptism, followed by separation. Before and after baptism, the quantity of justification within Catholicism depends on personal merit, disposition, and cooperation. After baptism a person has been made righteous, so that the righteousness is the person's own genuine moral righteousness, not God's righteousness, and it is each person's responsibility to increase in justification continually with God's help. Secondarily, Catholicism speaks of *infused righteousness* or *ingrafted righteousness*, which suggests organic continuity between Christ's righteousness and our own. The primary and the secondary metaphors within Catholicism are difficult to reconcile with each other, so they are in tension.

This current chapter will further appraise the value for today's church of the classic Protestant and Catholic models previously discussed. It will also address an important recent challenge to the classic Protestant model that has been offered from within Protestantism by N. T. Wright: "the righteousness of God" is not shared with humans directly as part of justification. I will argue that Wright has helped recover a valuable insight into the context of justification but that his proposal—along with the Catholic model—does not fully account for the scriptural witness. We do share in the righteousness of God. Ultimately, a new category, *incorporated righteousness*, can more accurately summarize the biblical witness and can successfully capture the truths present in Protestant and Catholic models while dispensing of their errors.

Let me reiterate that my argument is not that traditions beyond Scripture are automatically unacceptable. What is unacceptable, according to both Protestant and Catholic standards, is doctrine that contradicts Scripture and does not accurately account for earliest Christian history.

To exclude the apostles from the church or justification is impossible for all concerned. Not only Protestants but also Catholics must appeal to Scripture when modeling justification: *Any claim about what is **always true** about how justification happens must be able to take into account what Scripture says about how the apostles and earliest Christians were justified, or else the apostles have been excluded from the church.* Catholics are required to make their case from Scripture too. This is why the Council of Trent did not appeal primarily to tradition in its "Decree on Justification" but sought to make its case extensively from Scripture.

Today we can better appreciate that the initial closure brought by classic Protestantism and Catholicism (Trent) on justification was politically expedient but premature. Classic Protestantism and Catholicism both expressed key truths and made crucial mistakes when attempting to articulate a theology of justification capable of including what the apostles did and taught. The gift of time—nearly five hundred years to reflect—and the recovery of ancient documents that inject new information can help us remodel justification.

Appraising Catholic and Protestant Models

On the basis of the previous chapters, perhaps the reader can already see that the basic Catholic and classic Protestant models preserve vital truths but are problematic in light of the gospel-allegiance model advanced in this book. In preparation for further refining discussion, let's summarize why the gospel-allegiance model offers an improvement over Catholicism and classic Protestantism.

Toward a Truer Soteriology: The Gospel-Allegiance Model

1. *Saving faith as allegiance to a king.* Saving faith (*pistis*) in the New Testament is embodied, enacted relationally, and already includes good works within its purview.[1] Neither the Catholic nor the Protestant model tends to speak about saving faith as inclusive of *active fidelity toward a king* in this way. Both tend to aim faith at proper belief or proper trust with regard to Jesus the atoning savior rather than at the full gospel of *the Christ*, inclusive of the enthronement. Reconfiguring saving faith as an allegiant response to Jesus *the king*, which is the gospel's climax, helps move the discussion forward.

2. *Works are part of justification.* Scripture teaches that allegiance-based good works performed with the assistance of the Spirit are part of the basis of our final justification.[2] The traditional Protestant model that seeks to exclude good works from justification entirely cannot be successfully defended from Scripture. Protestants have sometimes recognized this. Some scholastic Reformed

233

theologians treated faith as the primary cause of justification and works as a secondary instrumental or efficient cause, but such a view has remained a minority report (see chap. 4). The Catholic insistence on the necessity of good works for final justification is correct, but its further insistence that saving good works can be universally mandated within sacramental performance is false.

3. *Grace preserved*. Saving allegiance does not violate grace.[3] Good works as a partial basis for salvation within allegiance (*pistis*) does not compromise grace, for God has graced us with the gospel—what I've summarized as ten Christ events—for our salvation entirely apart from human merit. Once this unmerited grace of the gospel is given and proclaimed, all are freely invited to respond to the gospel's climax, "Jesus is king," by giving allegiance. In the Bible, because grace is effective and demands reciprocation (Rom. 5:2, 21; 2 Cor. 8:1–5; Eph. 3:7–9), grace can still be grace and require embodied allegiance expressed through good works ("the obedience of *pistis*") as a return gift (Rom. 1:5; 16:26). Responding to the gospel-grace with allegiance does not deny grace but rather shows that God's gift has been accepted, allowing the gracious benefits associated with the king's reign to flow via the Spirit.

4. *Resurrection life is part of justification*. The typical Protestant distinction between justification and sanctification within a person's order of salvation cannot be successfully defended from Scripture. Justification itself goes beyond declaration to include new-life liberation—that is, into territory that Protestants have traditionally reserved for sanctification. *Jesus's resurrection was necessary for justification too, because resurrection life is intrinsic to the new-creation transformation that attends justification.* Scripture encourages us to speak of justification as collectively past, present, and future for the Jesus-is-king professing people considered as a whole. It is appropriate to describe individuals who are presently part of that collective as justified too—past, present, and awaiting its future ratification. Present justification includes the possession of the new-creation reality that is best termed resurrection life.

5. *Not made righteous through impartation.* The Catholic view that we are *made righteous* (morally better) upon initial justification lacks any scriptural support and flies in the face of the evidence. The Council of Trent asserts that we are made righteous upon initial justification through the impartation of morally superior virtues such as faith, hope, and love but does not interpret Scripture accurately when making this claim. There is no valid biblical evidence that moral virtues are specially imparted at the moment of baptism by virtue of the baptismal act itself so that an infant or adult is given these as an implanted seed.

6. *Final justification includes growth in virtues, including actual human righteousness.* The Catholic tradition is correct that growth in virtue is part of "justification." Contrary to Catholic teaching, humans are not made righteous through impartation within justification, but according to Scripture they do genuinely become morally righteous in the Messiah. Contrary to popular Protestant teaching, Scripture does not have a separate "sanctification" category as justification's mirror image or next logical step in a sequence where we can slot human moral righteousness. If we are seeking to develop a theology grounded in the distinctions that the Bible actually makes, it is best to use only one category when speaking about God's righteousness-establishing activity—justification—but to speak of its past, present, and future dimensions. An individual's justification includes a person's Spirit-inspired growth in actual moral righteousness and allegiant good works as part of its present expression and future goal.

7. *Allegiance, not baptism, is the sole instrument of justification.* Protestants are correct to insist on the repentant declaration of *pistis* (and *pistis* alone if properly defined as inclusive of bodily activities) as the sole instrumental cause of justification. The Catholic claim that justification is always impossible apart from baptism or its desire, because baptism is the sole instrumental cause, can be demonstrated to be false from Scripture. Such a view excludes the apostolic witness and earliest church: God can and did justify some of the earliest Christians apart from baptism or its desire entirely. Meanwhile, baptism is ordinarily the moment

when initial justification occurs, but it does not lead to Spirit infilling unless it definitively embodies a repentant *personal* allegiance to the Messiah the apostles preached.

How we model justification has consequences. As is discussed immediately below, both the classic Protestant and the Catholic models seek to synthesize what Scripture teaches about justification. I have already discussed why Catholic imparted righteousness cannot be accepted (see chap. 8). In what follows I will show why Protestant imputed righteousness and Catholic infused/ingrafted righteousness point in the right direction but fit better within a different model. Also, N. T. Wright has made an important proposal that seeks to reconfigure the classic Protestant model. The gospel-allegiance model draws from all these but tries to nuance and correct. Ultimately the gospel-allegiance model contends that Scripture points to a more robust way to explain justification: *incorporated righteousness.*

Protestant Imputed Righteousness

The classic Protestant model of justification is that of imputed righteousness. Its development was briefly sketched in the previous chapter. The language of imputation (*logizomai* in Greek) intends reckoning or crediting. Admittedly, imputed righteousness has the correct sensibility to the degree it stresses union with the Christ's righteousness. So, why not just retain the traditional Protestant terminology of imputed righteousness? Despite the overwhelming popularity of *imputed righteousness* among Scripture-loving Protestants, imputed righteousness is not a biblical metaphor at all.[4]

There is no mention of imputed righteousness in Scripture. This is important, so let me make sure the point is clear: while the Bible speaks of "faith" as "imputed" for righteousness (e.g., Rom. 4:5, 9–11, 22), it never speaks of God's or Christ's "righteousness" as "imputed" for human righteousness. *Pistis* ("faith") is said to be reckoned or credited or imputed for righteousness, but righteousness is not reckoned for righteousness. *Despite the popularity of such ideas within Protestantism, Scripture nary a once says that the Christ's righteousness is "imputed" or "reckoned" or "credited" to an individual's account.* Christ's righteousness is not described as a merit in Scripture that can be applied to a person's salvation balance sheet.

The idea that Christ's righteousness is imputed to count for a person's own righteousness assumes a merit-satisfaction framework. The idea is widely accepted today because Catholics and Protestants alike generally accepted that framework as part of *the meritorious or material cause* of justification during the Reformation. The merit-satisfaction framework assumes that personal justification happens when Christ's merits get applied to an individual's sinfully bankrupt ledger, making satisfaction by restoring equity.

Catholics and Protestants disagreed over the formal and instrumental causes of justification, but they agreed about the meritorious (see chap. 8). Catholicism contended that justifying merit is credited (or imputed) via impartation at baptism, while Protestants argued that it is credited (or imputed) by faith alone. But the merit-satisfaction framework is imprecise and largely alien with respect to Scripture's preferred categories for describing how salvation works. Both Catholics and classic Protestants accepted that Christ's righteousness is a merit that can be personally credited when in fact that idea isn't biblical. This is why it is urgent that we remodel justification.

Why a Personal Merit Framework Misleads

What does Scripture say about Jesus's merit? It certainly affirms that Jesus's death is effective for cleansing and conquering sins. Jesus suffered as a substitute to atone for or cleanse our collective sins and to ensure that thereafter each person who is part of his Spirit-filled body can meet God's righteous standard by fulfilling his law (Rom. 8:3–4; 1 Pet. 2:24). The king's one act of righteousness on the cross permits all to experience righteousness and life (Rom. 5:18). Substitutionary atonement is affirmed, and Jesus's climactic righteous deed in dying for sins is effective.

The Christ's life and offering are of inestimable value for cleansing and liberating individuals. That is not under dispute here. What is under dispute is whether this cleansing and liberation can be modeled under the umbrella of the *personal* crediting of righteousness. Scripture doesn't describe the Christ's merit or his righteousness being credited to individual accounts. Since the imputation of personal merit is not emphasized in Scripture, let's explore some relevant images in Scripture to discover what is stressed instead.

What about ransom? Jesus was our ransom payment. "For the Son of Man did not come to be served, but to serve, and to give his life as a *ransom* for many" (Mark 10:45 NIV; cf. Matt. 20:28). Jesus describes the offering of his life unto death in monetary terms, and this worthwhile gift somehow liberates *many* held in bondage.

Doesn't ransom entail personal imputation? Probably not. It may be implied by Jesus that those held captive are in *personal financial debt bondage* because they have accrued a sin debt on their ledger that they can't repay. If so, then Jesus's merit—although not specifically his righteousness—is reckoned or imputed in such a way that it removes each person's indebtedness.

But it is quite unlikely that the metaphor of personal financial debt bondage is intended within Jesus's ransom metaphor in Scripture. Why? First, Jesus says that he has come to ransom a large group of people, "to give his life as a ransom for *many*." A large group is in view, not individuals. Second, bondage due to personal financial debt is not the ordinary reason for a ransom payment in Jesus's day. There are numerous forms of *non-debt bondage* associated with ransom and release.

Group Non-Debt Ransom

It was common in the Roman world for large people groups or entire nations to be subjected to captivity and enslaved. In such cases *the ransom payment did not get credited to each captive person's account but instead paid for the whole group's release all at once as a collective lump sum.* A ransom frequently was required to liberate a group not that had fallen into debt but that had been taken captive by a foreign power, and Jews conceptualized ransom in this way.[5]

This is even true when the captivity was due to God's punishment of the nation for sin. Consider how the deaths of the Maccabean martyrs, who lived about two hundred years before Jesus's death, were interpreted as a ransom for sin by a Jew writing during Jesus's day: "The tyrant was punished, and the homeland purified—they having become, as it were, a ransom for the sin of our nation" (4 Macc. 17:21 NRSV; cf. 6:29). When the martyrs died, their deaths were construed as offering a ransom payment for sin *to release the whole nation collectively* from the foreign occupation that God had permitted in order to punish the nation.

It is most probable that Jesus and our New Testament writers viewed Jesus as offering a similar ransom payment to liberate *a large group.* Luke describes Zechariah, Anna, and the travelers on the road to Emmaus as anticipating the ransoming of *the nation* (Luke 1:68; 2:38; 24:21). Paul says to the Corinthians *collectively*, "You [plural] were bought with a price" (1 Cor. 6:20; 7:23). A ransom more frequently liberated a *group* of captive people (Titus 2:14; Heb. 9:15). Moreover, Paul states in several places elsewhere that *all* humans have been taken captive (Rom. 3:9–20; 6:6; Eph. 2:1–3).

Granted that all humans are captive, it is unsurprising that Paul says Jesus was a "ransom *for all*" humans without limitation (1 Tim. 2:6), and likewise Hebrews describes Jesus's sacrificial and high priestly work as "once for all" (Heb. 9:12, 26; 10:10–14).[6] Jesus is a ransom *for all* because a ransom ordinarily was not paid to release an individual from personal financial indebtedness by imputing (crediting or reckoning) money to that individual's account. Since all humans are captive, King Jesus's ransom payment is a lump sum for all humanity.

Although the ransom has been paid for all, it has not been actualized by all. Individuals indeed have been legally released as part of the group ransom, but the mechanism for that conditional liberation is not personal imputation to individual deficient bank ledgers. After the gift of the ransom payment "for all," the mechanism for actualizing personal liberation is to give loyalty to the victorious king and so to enter his kingdom. This is why the twenty-four elders and four living creatures sing, "You are worthy to take the scroll and to open its seals, because you were slain, and *with your blood you purchased for God persons from every tribe and language and people and nation.* You have made them to be a kingdom and priests to serve our God, and they will reign on the earth" (Rev. 5:9–10 NIV; cf. 1:5–6). Although the ransom has been paid for all, the purchase is effective only for select persons among every tribe and nation, those who can be described now as Jesus's kingdom citizens. Those whose ransom payment has been actualized enjoy the benefits that the victor has supplied—preeminently to live as forgiven and free citizens under the king's banner, "to reign on the earth" with him.

This explains why Paul doesn't say that the Christ's righteousness is credited for a person's righteousness. Instead, Paul says that "faith" is credited for a person's righteousness. Although liberty has already been purchased for humanity as a whole by King Jesus's ransom payment, *declared allegiance is how an individual person actualizes the benefits of the ransom payment—including forgiveness, liberation, and right-standing with the victorious king—and then persists in these benefits.* A person comes to enjoy all the benefits that a victorious king can offer by giving him allegiance.

In sum, Jesus's life and death are certainly of incalculable value for releasing those in bondage. That is not debatable. Traditionally, this has been called the meritorious or material cause of justification (see chap. 8). However, in the end, we can't claim that Scripture intends to assert that Jesus's ransom covers *an accrued debt in a person's merit ledger without nuancing how that happens through a group dynamic.* It is likely that the merit associated with the Christ's substitutionary suffering and victorious loyal obedience over the enemy paid the non-debt price to ransom *a group* that had been taken captive by an oppressive power. Righteousness is not credited for righteousness in Scripture. Rather, faith is credited for righteousness, because sworn allegiance (*pistis*) to the Christ is how an individual personally taps into the ransom payment that the king made for all, and in so doing becomes part of his liberated people.

The Record of Debt in Colossians

In Colossians, Paul states that the "handwritten record [*cheirographon*] of decrees that was opposed to us" was nailed to the cross and erased (Col. 2:14 AT). Does this involve personal "crediting" or "imputation" of Jesus's merit to erase individualized sin *debt*? No. Such a construal is unlikely for several reasons.

First, yes, it is possible that the handwritten record could be a statement of personal financial debt, but this is highly unlikely. At issue in context are, specifically, *legal trespasses* (*paraptōmata*) against God's law (Col. 2:13). A strictly personal-debt financial metaphor is less probable than a broader list of accusations for transgressing.

Second, this "handwritten record" is said to be "erased" (*exaleiphō*) and "taken away" (*airō*) when it is nailed to the cross; it is not said to be *paid* (Col. 2:14). It is remotely possible that payment is behind the scenes as the means that causes erasure, but that is merely to cheerlead for a preferred theological solution by speculating beyond the text. The text itself indicates neither a personal debt nor a debt-erasing payment.

In Colossians 2:14 Jesus's death is certainly effective in eliminating personal human transgressions. It is of meritorious value in the sense that it can and does erase legal violations. Moreover, the erasure disarmed the powers that opposed the Christ, so that he triumphs through the cross (2:15). On its own, however, the metaphor of the erasure of the handwritten record does not suggest that Jesus's merit was applied personally *to pay* the sin debt that various individuals had accrued by actively crediting his merit to each person's account.

Clothed in Christ's Righteousness Alone?

But doesn't Scripture say that we are personally clothed in or otherwise covered by Christ's righteousness? No. The New Testament does not say that Christ's righteousness is imputed *to cover* human unrighteousness. That idea was popularized by Luther, not by Scripture.[7]

Righteousness as clothing is indeed a metaphor in Scripture, but it is never applied in ways that match imputation. The righteousness-as-clothing metaphor is derived from texts such as Job 29:14, Isaiah 51:8, and Isaiah 61:10, and, negatively, Isaiah 64:6. Meanwhile, Christians are commanded, "Clothe yourselves with the Lord Jesus Christ" (Rom. 13:14 NIV) and are told that baptism into the Christ involves clothing themselves with him (Gal. 3:27). But these texts are not combined. *None of these texts say that God's or Jesus's own righteousness is "reckoned" as if it were a garment covering a person's unrighteousness.* Despite a great many hymns and popular Christian songs, the New Testament never uses the clothing metaphor to indicate that the Christ's righteousness *covers* our unrighteousness.

In short, the reason folks cling to imputed righteousness is not that the concept has a clear biblical warrant. Rather, it has become a traditional benchmark of Protestant orthodoxy within some denominations, confessions, and systematic theologies. If we want a more precise theology that remains true to what Scripture actually says, we should be eager to leave language of "imputed righteousness" behind.

Human Lack and Recovery

If Scripture does not frame personal justification as *merit* regained through Jesus's accomplished work when his *righteousness* is *imputed* or *credited* to each person's bankrupt account, then how is the issue framed? Humans collectively are unrighteous and disobedient, yes. One needs only to read Romans 1:18–33, 3:9–20, and Ephesians 2:1–3 to discover how true this is. Or to scan today's headlines. But individual unrighteousness in Scripture is not conceptualized as a *personal* debt owed.

Scripture prefers to frame personal lack and recovery in terms of the *glory* that attends image-bearing. Through the foolish exchange of sin and idolatry, individuals experience a *glory* deficit that prevents us from meeting God's righteous requirements: "they exchanged the glory" (Rom. 1:23) and "all have sinned and *lack the glory* of God" (3:23 AT). Sin causes a lack in glory that attends personal unrighteousness.

As glory is restored through the Holy Spirit, liberated humans are transformed so they are able to fully meet God's requirements (e.g., Rom. 8:4; 2 Cor. 3:18). Justification is not about Jesus's righteousness being credited to a personal sin debt on a ledger. To be more precise, although all humans are unrighteous, *the deficit is not simply unrighteousness but lost glory*. Sinful humans are unrighteous and are lacking the glory of God, but human fidelity to King Jesus is credited for righteousness, leading to a right-standing with God and to *glory's recovery* as allegiance unites us to King Jesus, his reign, and his benefits.

All this said, although imputed righteousness is inaccurate, it aims in the right direction. It urgently wants to affirm that the previously unrighteous people of God are now saved because they somehow possess or share in the Christ's righteousness. I agree that this is true. How can we best speak of that somehow beyond imputation? That is the key question.

Does God Share His Own Righteousness?

Drawing on others, I have a proposal for how we share in the Christ's righteousness that does not rely on imputation. Before discussing it, we first need to meet a challenge not only to imputed righteousness but to the idea that God shares his own righteousness with humans *at all*. The traditional Protestant position is that we share in God's own righteousness in the Messiah. The traditional terminology is "imputed righteousness." I am in the processes of arguing that we should use more precise language than that of imputed righteousness.

But when we are talking about "the righteousness of God," can we be certain that it is a right-standing that God shares with his people? Maybe it is better to say that it refers to God's own intrinsic righteousness but that God's own or Christ's own righteousness is not communicated to his people perpetually in justification. That is the Catholic position (see chap. 8). This is also the argument of N. T. Wright, whose treatment of the gospel and Christian origins has informed my own work on the gospel and salvation in countless ways. Indeed, I can't think of a scholar who has positively impacted the development of my overall gospel-allegiance proposal more. Wright has done the church an enormous service. But on this specific point I think that Wright is incorrect.

N. T. Wright on the righteousness of God. Wright claims that "the righteousness of God" means "God's covenant faithfulness," and therefore it is not a status in which the people of God can participate:

> If and when God does act to vindicate his people, his people will then, metaphorically speaking, have the status of "righteousness."
> . . . *But the righteousness they have will not be God's own righteousness.* That makes no sense at all. God's own righteousness is his covenant faithfulness, because of which he will (Israel hopes) vindicate her, and bestow upon her the status of "righteous," as the vindicated or acquitted defendant. But God's righteousness remains, so to speak, God's own property. It is the reason for his acting to vindicate his people. It is not the status he bestows upon them in so doing.[8]

Wright does not consider the righteousness of God to be a status that God bestows, but rather it is God's own activity as the righteous judge. God's own righteousness is the basis for his judging activity. It causes him to condemn wickedness while rescuing and vindicating his beleaguered people within the boundaries of justice. For Wright, God is indeed righteous, and he does decree that his people are righteous in the king, but God does not share his own righteousness with humans as part of that process.

Let me use an analogy to explain where I think Wright goes astray. A savanna is a context in which we might see giraffes, but when we see giraffes strolling on a savanna, we should not say that the savanna simply *is* giraffes, or vice versa. The savanna is a general setting closely associated with giraffes, but we can detect more specific referents, like lions and zebras, along with giraffes within that setting. This is akin to what Wright has done in asserting that the righteousness of God simply *is* God's covenant faithfulness.

Wright is correct that God's covenant faithfulness is the appropriate context for locating the righteousness of God. Yet Wright's analysis does not encourage us to spot more specificity within God's covenant faithfulness. In particular, contra Wright, we can see that in Scripture the righteousness of God can refer to God's righteous judging activity *and also* to a status of righteousness that God has opted to share with all humans who are united to the king by *pistis*, so that we can become God-like and Christ-like in our righteousness.

Wright's limited construal of "the righteousness of God" is difficult to square with a detailed reading of Paul's letters. Paul uses the phrase "the righteousness of God" ten times in his letters.[9] Contrary to Wright, Paul probably refers to a received status through union with the Christ in at least four of those passages (Rom. 1:17; 3:22; 2 Cor. 5:21; Phil. 3:9–11). So I disagree on this point with Wright, siding instead with Luther, Calvin, and their theological heirs. Luther was correct that "the righteousness of God" can refer at least in part to a status that belongs to God and to the Christ, *and that this status is shared* by all those who are united to the Christ by giving *pistis* to him. Let's briefly explore why.

In Romans 3:21–22 Paul says several things about "the righteousness of God," but he concludes by declaring it to be "*for* [*eis*] all those who perform the *pistis* action." This "for" is enormously important. It indicates purpose and suggests that "the righteousness of God" is a *benefit* that those who perform the *pistis* action somehow *enjoy* or *receive*. This also remains the most probable meaning of Paul's statement that "the righteousness of God" is revealed in the gospel "by allegiance *for allegiance*" (*ek pisteōs eis pistin*) in Romans 1:16–17 (see chap. 2). What is revealed is not merely God's covenant faithfulness but a benefit of received righteousness, because the Christ's *by pistis* action is *for* the purpose of human *pistis* resulting in human righteousness. The Christ acted in a loyal fashion so others can be righteous and live too when they respond to the king with loyalty. In 1:16–17 "the righteousness of God" is described as God's very own, but it is a benefit that the people of God come to enjoy when *by loyalty* they are *righteous* and *live*. All those who respond to the gospel by giving loyalty to Jesus the king receive the benefit of the righteousness of God and enter into his resurrection life.

That the righteousness of God is a benefit that humans can enjoy is confirmed in Philippians. Paul speaks of "not having my own righteousness from the law" but "the righteousness through the *pistis* of the Messiah." Then he further clarifies what he means by that, calling it "the righteousness *from* [*ek*] God based upon *pistis*" (Phil. 3:9 AT). Since Paul's *own* status of righteousness is in view negatively with his "*not* having *my own* righteousness," Paul's *own* is almost certainly still in view when he describes it positively as the righteousness connected with the Messiah's actions and as the righteousness that comes from God. So *"the righteousness from God" is that righteousness associated with the Messiah's faithful actions that God has given to Paul.* "The righteousness from God" is a status of righteousness that Paul now possesses personally through his participation in the Messiah's fidelity.

Paul's possession of the righteousness that comes from God via the faithfulness of the Christ is described here not by using the language of imputation or crediting; it is *by inclusion within the Messiah's loyalty framework.* It is a sharing in righteousness that comes from God and that is through the loyalty of the Messiah but that is accessed by our partnership in the Messiah's loyalty. This accords with Paul's "by the allegiance" of the Christ "for the allegiance" of other humans in Romans 1:17. Thus, in Philippians 3:9 God's own righteousness has devolved onto the Messiah in his vindication, and it is possessed by any individual who is united to him through loyalty.

Sharing in the Messiah's righteous status is also the best way to make sense of 2 Corinthians 5:21: "For our sake God made him to be sin who knew no sin, so that in him we might become the righteousness of God." That is, the status of the people of God is that once we were not in the right, but *in him*, in the king, we now are. We have become "the righteousness of God." This suggests that when we are first united with the Christ, we are united to his perfect righteousness, so that we share in it immediately, fully, and effectively (not gradually or based on our past merit or present disposition, as Catholic doctrine teaches). Although there is no mention of the imputation of the Christ's righteousness to individuals in this text, nevertheless the Christ's own righteousness has been shared with his *collective* people somehow, because *in him* they have become "the righteousness of God." Individuals share in this righteousness if and only if they are part of the Messiah's people, which suggests that it is a group benefit.

I hope that I have demonstrated sufficiently why I think that "the righteousness of God" is a *benefit* that those who are united to the Messiah enjoy. While I reject imputation—the personal crediting of the Messiah's righteousness to the bankrupt individual—as the best explanation for how the righteousness of God is possessed, nevertheless I agree that it is indeed a benefit humans can enjoy. In identifying the righteousness of God as a benefit humans can possess, the gospel-allegiance model sides with Luther, Calvin, and contemporary writers who favor imputation—for example, John Piper and Michael Horton—over against Wright and the Catholic position.[10]

Thus far I've focused on the positive side of the righteousness of God, but there is also a negative side. The righteousness of God is a positive status that the people of God share with the Christ, but there is a darker aspect to this language. "The righteousness of God" is also connected to the outpouring of God's wrath on human wickedness in Romans 1:17–18 and 3:5 and on the Christ as the sin-bearing atoning sacrifice in 3:25. So—and this is where Wright's view remains helpful—the righteousness of God is more than simply a gift of right-standing; God's justifying activity also includes judgment against sin.

We can't lose either pole—justifying activity or judgment against sin—in seeking to trace Paul's understanding of "the righteousness of God." Presently, I don't think I can improve on my previous definition of *the righteousness of God*:

> The righteousness of God is God's resurrection-affirming verdict that Jesus the wrath-bearing, sin-atoning, allegiant king is alone righteous—a verdict that all who are united to Jesus the representative king share.[11]

This articulation of the righteousness of God includes God's judging activity with respect to the righteous and the wicked within the bounds of his covenant promises and obligations, but it indicates that this judging activity has culminated in the vindication of Jesus the king—and by extension those who are united by pledged allegiance to the king. This explains why "the righteousness of God" is repeatedly *for* those who perform the *pistis* action: it is a benefit we receive when we are united to the righteous king by joining his Spirit-filled body through our professed allegiance. But it remains the Christ's righteousness first and foremost as the extrinsic source; it is ours only derivatively, when we join the group that is united to him and Spirit-infused.

In the end, what are we to make of Wright's proposal that would restrict the righteousness of God to God's covenant faithfulness? We can accept Wright's claim that the righteousness of God can refer to God's own righteous disposition and behavior in seeking to uphold his covenant promises (see esp. Rom. 3:25). We can do this while agreeing with Wright that imputed righteousness is not strictly a biblical idea. The traditional Protestant language of imputation does not track Scripture accurately, because it suggests a personal "righteousness" transaction—the Christ's righteousness in place of each person's unrighteousness—rather than collective benefits that can be personally realized.

However, Wright denies that God shares his own righteousness with those who respond to the gospel, and we must conclude against Wright on this point—and against Catholicism as well. Certainly, God is faithful to his covenant promises and that faithfulness is on stunning display in the Christ events. But this doesn't exclude a participatory construal of God's own righteousness for the Messiah's people via the Messiah's loyalty that resulted in his justification. We share in the righteousness of God as that is found in Jesus the king.

Catholic Ingrafted/Infused Righteousness

The basic Catholic model of imparted righteousness has already been discussed. Catholics believe, under ordinary circumstances, that justification is automatically imparted at baptism by virtue of the act of baptism itself. It has already been shown that this view contradicts the biblical witness (see chaps. 5 and 8).

Yet from the standpoint of Scripture, the secondary Catholic metaphors are more promising—ingrafting and infusion. This language appears in §7 of Trent's decree. Because the decree as a whole (esp. portions of §7 and canon 10 as specified above) makes it explicit that the formal cause does not involve a perpetual righteousness union with God or Christ, but instead imparted separation, it is fair to say that ingrafting and infusion are indeed secondary, not primary.

That impartation is primary and ingrafting/infusion secondary also follows from Trent's rejection of *duplex iustitia* (double justification). After weighing it at length, Trent rejected *double justification* as a formal cause—that justification is *extrinsically* sourced perpetually in Christ's own righteousness (as within classic Protestantism) and *intrinsically* sourced as a having-been-made righteousness by the Holy Spirit within the baptized person.[12] Catholicism rejects extrinsic righteousness and accepts only intrinsic righteousness as imparted by the Holy Spirit as the sole formal cause. For both these reasons, we are forced to conclude that ingrafted and infused righteousness are secondary metaphors for justification within Catholicism and cannot be accepted presently as stand-alone descriptions for how justification works.

These secondary metaphors are in tension with the primary metaphor, for on their own they would seem to suggest the maintenance of a *continuous organic link* between the Christ and the justified person, so that Christ's righteousness remains the source, but it trickles over to the person. Unlike the primary metaphor of impartation, which fronts momentary contact followed by separation, these secondary metaphors emphasize Christ as the ongoing source of human righteousness through perpetual union.

Analogies might help clarify Catholic ingrafted and infused righteousness. Regarding *ingrafted righteousness*, consider a tree with branches. The Christ is the tree and individuals are ingrafted branches. Christ-the-tree supplies sap to each ingrafted branch, so the branch receives nutrients and flourishes. Think about righteousness as one of those nutrients. As long as the graft is in place, Christ supplies the individual person righteousness through a perpetually open channel. Righteousness is maintained through a perpetual unbroken union, extrinsically sourced in Christ.

Now let's shift the imagery slightly. For *infused righteousness*, consider a swimming pool with a giant sponge sticking out onto an adjacent concrete pad. Christ's righteousness is the water in this swimming pool. Water infuses the sponge. Even when you are on the dry concrete pad beside the pool, if you opt to lay on the giant sponge, you become infused with the pool's wetness/righteousness, because water from the pool permeates the whole sponge and seeps into your skin. Even though the wetness is sourced in and properly belongs to the pool rather than to you, you are infused with its wetness. But the wetness/righteousness is not yours intrinsically or necessarily permanently. You must remain on the sponge to enjoy it. Wetness/righteousness is maintained through ongoing contact with the pool's water (via the sponge) as the extrinsic source of the infusion.

There is hope that Catholicism is beginning to emphasize its secondary metaphors of ingrafting and infusion for justification beyond its primary metaphor of impartation. Indeed, some of our finest Catholic biblical scholars are now articulating a theology of justification that fronts perpetual union with the Christ as the source of justification while seeming to downplay baptismal impartation as momentary contact followed by separation. They appear to affirm, at least tacitly, that human righteousness remains continually sourced in God's and Christ's righteousness extrinsically while also speaking of the intrinsic work of the Spirit.[13]

My reading of Trent suggests that when Catholic scholarship fronts participation in Christ as the source of righteousness (rather than the Spirit's initial impartation of righteousness through baptism followed by a separation between divine and human righteousness), it has affirmed what Trent rejects—double justification—and may have inadvertently adopted a Protestant position.

Whatever the case, this new Catholic scholarship is an exceedingly hopeful sign, for it offers a much better reading of Scripture than Trent does. Moreover, this improved Catholic scholarship may eventually steer the magisterium toward better models when Trent's theology is finally revisited by the bishops. In remodeling justification, the best way forward for Catholicism is to opt for a new model that can supersede Trent's model by affirming what was true within it.

Incorporated Righteousness

Because we must reject Catholic impartation as contrary to Scripture and can accept Protestant imputation and Catholic infusion/ingrafting only in qualified ways, I think that Catholic-Protestant dialogue can most fruitfully advance by adopting a new model entirely. "It is far more appropriate to speak of *incorporated righteousness*," as Michael Bird explains, for righteousness is not "somehow abstracted from Christ and projected" onto believers "but is located exclusively in Christ as the glorified incarnation of God's righteousness."[14] I concur with Bird that *incorporated righteousness* better describes Paul's theology at the exegetical level.

251

In agreement with him, I propose that we model justification as *incorporated righteousness.*

If Catholics can prioritize their secondary metaphor of ingrafting/infusion while ignoring previous teaching on impartation, and if Protestants can look back to collective union with the king as the true source of their ideas about imputation, then this language has the potential to bring Catholics and Protestants together. *Incorporated righteousness* or *in-the-Christ righteousness*—I use these phrases synonymously—has the potential to correct and reconcile Protestant and Catholic positions regarding justification.

When saving faith is construed as allegiance to Jesus the king, works are seen to play an appropriate role in final justification. Accordingly, the dominant Catholic and Protestant models both preserve valid insights into justification and encounter difficulties. *Incorporated righteousness* or *in-the-Christ righteousness* overcomes these obstacles by staying closer to the Bible's own language. It fronts group union with the Messiah using the imagery of location. Justified individuals are positioned amid other justified humans in the king rather than in Adam.

Incorporated righteousness further capitalizes on Scripture's frequent description of the church as a body with the Christ as its head, making it clear that he is the source of the righteousness and that our own righteousness depends on staying in organic union with him. The Christ as the kingly head has already been declared righteous; individuals within the church, as his Spirit-filled body parts, are righteous too if they remain part of the body via connection to the head. Within the metaphor of incorporated righteousness, any righteous standing that we presently enjoy derives perpetually from the Christ as the kingly head and is conditioned upon maintaining a fidelity union that bonds us to the Christ's own fidelity unto righteousness with the Spirit's help. Martin Bucer, one of the earliest Protestants, identified justification's primary cause as extrinsic in Christ but its secondary as intrinsic via the Spirit.[15] As part of the gospel-allegiance model, incorporated righteousness includes Protestant double justification (as proposed by Bucer and others) within its imagery, but it describes this doctrine differently, since key soteriological terms are redefined and realigned.

Why Better?

Why is incorporated righteousness a better model? First, beyond remaining close to Scripture's own language and imagery, the most helpful feature of *incorporated righteousness* is that it retains the community-first or collective emphasis on justification that we find in Scripture and have traced throughout this book. *Individuals are never justified on their own.* God justifies a community first at Pentecost. Subsequently, individuals are justified only when they are integrated into the justified body that already exists prior to their entrance into it.

Second, incorporated righteousness is a stronger model because it includes past, present, and future dimensions of justification per Scripture, while allowing good works to be properly integrated into justification. Both Protestant imputed righteousness and Catholic imparted righteousness struggle as holistic models of justification because they focus excessively on justification as an initial faith or baptism event that is soon in the past tense for a person. But justification is still a present happening for a person who is persisting in the Jesus-is-the-Christ faith declaration (Rom. 3:21–26; Phil. 3:9–11). Justification also has a future dimension for these same allegiant confessors, when each person will be justified on the basis of his or her own works as performed with the assistance of the Spirit (Rom. 2:13–16; 2:25–29; 8:4, 10–14). Because they draw the eye to initial justification, imputed and imparted righteousness struggle to portray justification's past, present, and future in Scripture accurately. However, incorporated righteousness correctly models justification's past, present, and future with respect to the individual.

Third, incorporated righteousness explains how the righteousness that attends justification can have a genuine moral rather than merely legal reality. This overcomes one of the fundamental objections that Catholicism has always had with Protestant imputation. The key is to see that personal justification involves more than initial justification, because it also has a present and future horizon within incorporated righteousness. Each Christian's human righteousness is always extrinsically sourced in the Christ's own righteousness through incorporation. But as each persists in confessing allegiance to King Jesus, that person grows in genuine human moral righteousness with the Spirit's help—and this genuine human righteousness will be vindicated in the future when that person's justification is completed at the final judgment.

Thus, Catholicism is correct that final justification includes actual moral righteousness within the human who is being justified.[16] Yet Catholicism falsely declares that this moral righteousness is necessarily imparted at the moment of initial justification at baptism in a seed-like form and then grows with human cooperation, and that baptism is the only way a human can receive justification. We have already discussed problems with the Catholic theology of baptism (see chaps. 5 and 8). But these problems should not obscure that Catholicism correctly maintains that an individual's final justification includes that individual's actual moral righteousness within the boundaries of the Spirit's liberating and transforming work (see chap. 8).

Protestantism is correct that human righteousness is never imparted but remains externally sourced in the Christ's own righteousness in an ongoing fashion. It errs when it declares that a person's moral righteousness has no bearing whatsoever on his or her justification because Christ's righteousness has been "reckoned" to the individual instead. This is false because in Scripture Christ's righteousness is not described as imputed to individuals in this bookkeeping sort of way. Moreover, it reduces the process of justification to the moment of initial entrance into Christ's body, missing how justification includes Spirit-led liberation and transformation in the present and future (see chap. 8).

Scripture teaches that our declaration of loyalty to the king causes us to enter into his justified body and that as we continue to confess loyalty within the bounds of that body, *we share in Christ's righteousness while coming to be conformed to the king's moral righteousness*. This coming to be conformed is not called "sanctification" in Scripture within an order of salvation but is part of justification's present and future horizon for the individual. Therefore, incorporated righteousness correctly includes not just repentant entrance into the justified community (past) but an individual's genuine moral transformation (present) and final moral right-standing (future) within justification.

In sum, *incorporated righteousness* or *in-the-Christ righteousness* is preferable as a model for justification because it can overcome problems with the traditional categories. We must reject Catholic *imparted righteousness* and the reduction of the righteousness of God to merely God's covenant faithfulness. Meanwhile, we can accept classic Protestant *imputed righteousness* and Catholic *ingrafted/infused righteousness* with qualifications, although in so doing we depart from Scripture's preferred descriptions.

Incorporated righteousness is better because it stays near to the Bible's pervasive "in the Christ" imagery and language. It fronts the primacy of the *corporate union*, not merely the personal union of individuals with the Messiah as the kingly head. Personal justification is conditioned on an ongoing allegiant response to Jesus as king (the gospel) and is about entering and remaining within the king's justified community.

King Jesus has already been justified. We can share in his justification fully right now when our allegiance forges a union with him, so that we are incorporated into his righteousness. Our final justification awaits the day of judgment, but if we as members of the body remain united to our kingly head by professing allegiance, that final judgment is secure. The righteousness of God is more than a benefit, but it is not less than one. The righteousness of God is a conditional, primary, and externally sourced benefit that each allegiance-professing person enjoys in and through the Messiah. The Holy Spirit is at work in each justified individual, including each individual's flesh, so that our allegiance includes good deeds and growth in actual moral righteousness.

10

Beyond the Salvation Wars

This book has affirmed that both Catholics and Protestants have responded to the gospel in a saving fashion. It has simultaneously drawn from Scripture and earliest Christian history to show why both nevertheless need to reimagine how salvation works holistically. Let me consolidate this book's vision about how the gospel, faith, baptism, and justification interface by summarizing how the gospel-allegiance model for salvation differs from classic Protestantism and Catholicism.

Classic Protestantism. Although Protestantism's rich history is diverse, the dominant Protestant traditions have tended to believe the following:

- On the basis of Jesus's merit, faith (*pistis*) is the sole instrumental means by which a person is declared righteous—that is, justified.
- Faith means personal interior trust that God's promise of salvation through Jesus's death and resurrection is true.
- Justification by faith is part of the gospel.
- The cross is the center of the gospel.
- Grace means a person can do nothing to merit salvation.

- Good works are entirely excluded as the basis for justification.

- Good works are required within sanctification as evidence that justification has really transpired.

- Justification and sanctification are inseparable but distinct.

- Justification logically comes prior to sanctification in an individual's order of salvation.

- An individual is justified by God when Christ's righteousness is imputed, so that Christ's righteousness is exchanged for her or his unrighteousness or otherwise covers it.

- Christ's imputed righteousness means a person is legally reckoned as righteous and declared innocent in God's sight even while that person remains a sinner.

- A person's justification is perpetually sourced in Christ's righteousness as an external (alien) source.

Catholicism. Official Catholic theology teaches that on the basis of Jesus's merit, baptism alone is the instrumental cause by which we are justified and apart from which it is impossible to be justified. Catholics hold the following beliefs:

- Faith is two-part, consisting of the essential dogma to be believed and the personal act of believing it.

- The formal cause of a person's justification is not a perpetual sharing in God's own or the Christ's own righteousness as an external (alien) source; rather, at baptism the Holy Spirit gives each person their own righteousness by renewing their mind.

- An individual is made righteous at baptism, but only to the extent that previous merit and present cooperative disposition allow.

- An individual is made righteous, not just declared righteous, at baptism by the impartation of morally superior qualities that impact behavior.
- Imparted righteousness, involving brief baptismal contact followed by a separation in righteousness between the divine and the human, is the dominant metaphor for explaining how justification happens.
- Infused righteousness and ingrafted righteousness, suggesting continuous union, are secondary metaphors explaining how justification happens.
- Since after baptism a person's righteousness (justification) is her or his own rather than perpetually sourced in God's or Christ's extrinsic righteousness, each person must nurture and grow in justification by performing good deeds in cooperation with the Holy Spirit to receive final justification.
- If a person commits a serious and intentional sin, they have forfeited their baptismal grace and whatever baptismal justification they had initially received.
- The restoration of baptismal justification occurs only via successful completion of sacramental reconciliation—penance and absolution—by a priest.

The gospel-allegiance model. The gospel-allegiance model seeks to recover the biblical and apostolic witness as a freshly nuanced form of Protestantism, but it does not embrace all that Catholics or Protestants have regularly taught. In agreement with classic Protestantism, the gospel-allegiance model affirms that on the basis of Jesus's merit, faith (*pistis*), not baptism, is the primary instrumental cause of justification. The model proposes the following as a truer account than that of classic Protestantism or Catholicism:

- Saving faith (*pistis*) is relational, outward-facing, embodied, and best understood as declared allegiance to the Christ.

- The gospel can be summarized: Jesus is the saving king.
- Jesus's justification by his *pistis* is part of the gospel, since his allegiance in taking the path of the cross resulted in his resurrection, proving that God justified him.
- Subsequently, each person's justification by *pistis* is not part of the gospel but rather a conditional benefit and required response.
- Justification by *pistis* includes works as an embodiment of allegiance but cannot require universally mandated works, including the sacrament of penance or obligatory holy days.
- An individual is declared righteous by allegiance alone, but this includes a liberating new-creation change connected to resurrection life as one participates in the Holy Spirit community.
- Justification and sanctification are not biblically distinct portions within a personalized order of salvation.
- In considering a personal order of salvation, it is best to speak of initial, present, and final justification, not sanctification.
- In the past, present, and future, the individual who is justified perpetually shares in the righteousness of God through an externally sourced union with the righteous king and his body as intrinsically facilitated by the Holy Spirit.
- A person's initial justification involves entering the Holy Spirit community in such a way that the individual's flesh is colonized by the Holy Spirit.
- A person is justified not when the Christ's righteousness is imparted or imputed but when a person is incorporated into the Christ's righteousness.
- Baptism is the ordinary way for an individual to enter into Holy Spirit union with the Christ and his body but is not the necessary or exclusive way.

- Baptism is a complex, multipart event, and its subparts must be appraised when describing how baptism relates to personal salvation.
- What causes Holy Spirit union for an individual—justification's precise instrument—is voluntary and repentant allegiance to King Jesus, and its premier form is a declared oath of fealty during a baptism.
- The baptismal process does not contribute to the initialization of salvation when the person undertaking baptism is personally insincere in pledging loyalty, unrepentant, or an involuntary participant, and baptism is not effective *ex opere operato* (i.e., by virtue of the baptismal action itself).
- Justification's present horizon involves imperfect but ongoing allegiance (*pistis*) to Jesus the forgiving king.
- This ongoing allegiance includes embodied good works and growth in virtues, such as genuine moral righteousness, as we are transformed into the image of the king.
- Final justification for an individual in the future requires perseverance and includes Spirit-led good works as part of its basis as the embodiment of a declared and active *pistis* (allegiance), for this is what it means to be incorporated into the Christ's righteousness.

Beyond Wars

Where does this leave the Catholic-Protestant discussion? I am persuaded that the gospel-allegiance model can help move the church toward unity in the truth. This book is a *theological proposal*. As such, it is concerned primarily to articulate a true theological description of how salvation works.

A Long-Term Hope

The theological proposal offered in *Beyond the Salvation Wars* expresses a long-term hope for the church. This can only be a long-term hope because the model suggests that certain cherished Catholic and Protestant dogmas and confessions are wrong and require change. Because it is united in the truth at the end, we know that the church will inevitably make progress toward reconciliation. So we should joyfully begin to work for greater unity today.

Since Scripture and early Christian history remain the unshakable standard in describing how salvation works for both Catholics and Protestants—and because it is impossible to suggest that Jesus and the apostles were mistaken in their descriptions of how a person is saved—whatever *truths* I've managed to synthesize about salvation here will inevitably reshape the church's soteriology.

I am bold to contend that this book offers a truer synthesis than do the models of classic Protestantism and Catholicism that presently dominate, so to the degree that this book's theological vision happens to inform the ongoing dialogue, it will help the church make progress toward a truer more unified future. I say *to the degree* for a reason. I am realistic in knowing that this book's particular impact probably will be modest.

This book is a theological proposal. It is not a practical handbook for how to implement its theological vision. Nevertheless, as we conclude, it is fitting to ponder what we might do to foster unity in the truth.

Toward a Gospel-Allegiance Culture

Here are three ways to help accelerate toward a gospel-allegiance culture: (1) intentionally network with others who affirm the gospel-allegiance model; (2) work toward symbolic and practical unity; (3) re-aim spiritual disciplines so they become allegiance opportunities.

261

Intentionally Network for Gospel Allegiance

Join with others in affirming an allegiance-based King Jesus gospel. If you see the gospel-allegiance model as better capturing the truth, then seek to build alliances with those who are like-minded. I am calling not for a new denomination—God knows we have far too many of those—but for networks and coalitions.

Transdenominational work. You who are pastors, priests, and elders and are already part of an established denomination, reach out to discover who else in your denomination can affirm this model. Seek to build alliances and coalitions with others within your denomination. Then work with them across denominational lines to create material and facilitate experiences that will promote a nonpartisan King Jesus framework and an allegiance response.

Join an established network. For leaders in independent churches or leaders who decide their current denomination cannot support this model and desire to start somewhere else afresh, there are many established church networking and planting groups that are using the gospel-allegiance framework. (This is not to say that associated leaders will agree with everything I've written—I'm speaking about broad contours.) I don't have a comprehensive list of networks—perhaps an innovative reader will create one and post it on the web—but renew.org, discipleship.org, Missio Alliance, the Bonhoeffer project, Nexus, and Ikon come immediately to mind.

Create Symbolic and Practical Unity

When we define the church in ways that depart from allegiance to King Jesus so as to receive the Spirit, we create false divisions in the church. Those who embrace the gospel-allegiance model can express symbolic unity while working toward practical unity.

Symbolic unity. The single bread loaf is a symbol of the unity of the one true church (1 Cor. 10:17). Are there ways to show through art that the bread's *boundary* is the *gospel-allegiance confession*? Or through liturgical action? Likewise, the human body is a symbol of the unity of the whole church as an organism

(Rom. 12; 1 Cor. 12). How can we display not merely Christ as the head but Christ as the *loyal* head, and many members entering and remaining in the body through *acts that share in his loyalty*? Images of individuals bowing the knee to King Jesus and yielding fealty to him so as to become one can be attached to art and action.

Practical unity. One of the best steps that Catholics, Orthodox, and Protestants alike can take is to advocate for *open Communion* for all willing to publicly yield allegiance in response to the one true Father-Son-Spirit gospel. Churches with closed Communion refuse to celebrate the Eucharist with those who disagree with their tradition's dogma or confession. Churches with open Communion welcome all who have responded to the gospel to partake, although some restrict it to the baptized.

Remembering that God "desires all people to be saved and to come to the knowledge of the truth" (1 Tim. 2:4), we should enjoy Christian fellowship—preeminently to share the Lord's Supper—with all those who uphold the content of the one true gospel and respond to it with a decisive oath of repentant allegiance. Both repentance from sins and fidelity to King Jesus, per Scripture's standards, are key boundary markers that set the Spirit-filled community apart from false churches that inaccurately claim Jesus's name. The gospel's express purpose is "allegiant obedience" (Rom. 1:5; 16:26) to Jesus as the Christ. So the *aim* to manifest loyal obedience is the hallmark of the true church. Beyond that, God can capably weigh whether we are responding with authentic saving allegiance no matter our denominational preference.

Let's welcome one another at the Lord's table while working toward full unity in the truth. Most Protestant churches and denominations today already have open Communion. I hope that closed-Communion denominations—Catholics, Orthodox, and the few Protestant holdouts—will reverse this policy in the future. *If the church is going to be what it is—one and only one body in the Messiah—then allegiance to Jesus the king as a summation of the one true gospel, even when it has been less than fully understood, must always form the essential boundary for shared Communion.*

RE-AIM SPIRITUAL DISCIPLINES AS ALLEGIANCE OPPORTUNITIES

To accelerate the church toward unity in the truth, nothing is more urgent than an emphasis on allegiant discipleship to King Jesus as part of everyday life. In short, we need to create and foster opportunities for people *to practice allegiance* routinely. In this regard, the church does not need new tools, but it does need to help re-aim the *why* with regard to the classic spiritual disciplines.

As disciples of Jesus, we need to regularly pray, read Scripture, serve others, fast, enjoy Sabbath rest, and above all else love God and our neighbors well. Yet the *why* driving these tasks is often blurry. We are often told we should do these things in order to move into a closer personal relationship with Jesus, or to learn how to better trust his promises, or simply to become more spiritual—whatever that might mean.

What is needful is to pray as a disciple of Jesus *in a way that is mindful of the mandate to persist and grow in allegiance*. What is needful is to read Scripture not merely to gain head knowledge or a word of encouragement but to grasp what it means *to live under the authority of King Jesus*. What is needful is to serve others not simply because it is good to help others out but because to do so is *to enter into the cruciform life for Jesus's sake and for his gospel*. What is urgent is formative practices that will accelerate and deepen our allegiance.

Jesus has become the king. We are saved as we profess and live out our allegiance to him.

The *gospel* is that the Son was sent by the Father to become the Christ, the forgiving king—with the emphasis on his ruling office. Although inclusive of trust that Jesus died for our sins, saving *faith* primarily intends embodied allegiance to him as king. Saving faith excludes rule-based approaches to meriting salvation, such as *works of law*, but includes *good works* performed as an embodiment of allegiance with the Spirit's assistance. *Baptism* is the premier event for decisively declaring allegiance to King Jesus, so as to receive the Holy Spirit—although God can and has justified humans apart from baptism. *Grace* is an unmerited free gift, but saving grace, the Christ gift, can be effectively received by us only when we give allegiance back in response initially and persistently.

Justification is best modeled as *incorporated righteousness*. A person is first *justified* when they enter the king's justified body, as the Holy Spirit envelops that individual. That person's present justification must *persevere* through an ongoing allegiance declaration so that justification can be ratified at the final judgment. It is possible to have initial justification but to lose that status by committing apostasy and becoming detached from the Christ and the Holy Spirit's community. The king's resurrection life is already at work in each person who is justified in the present, so they have actual human righteousness that is sourced perpetually in King Jesus when they persist in professing loyalty. Final justification depends on maintaining allegiance to King Jesus, so that we perform good deeds with our bodies and are morally righteous in and through him.

Embodiment matters now and forever. God's final vision for human salvation is *resurrection into a new creation*. United in the truth, we will rule alongside Jesus in resurrected bodies over the new creation. All of this leads us to the heart of the Christian *disciple-making mission*: worldwide allegiance to Jesus the king.

Acknowledgments

When I finish writing a book, a dazed fog surrounds me. It lasts for a few days or a couple weeks. Yes, it is exhaustion, but it is also an overwhelming sense of wonder and gratitude. Wonder because I have the privilege to write about salvation. Gratitude because I couldn't do this alone. Although I may be an inadequate tool, nonetheless I am honored to serve King Jesus and his church in this astonishing way.

I am grateful for my wonderful wife, Sarah, and my seven children: Tad, Zeke, Addie, Lydia, Evie, Anna, and Nate. Yes, we have a busy house. They are the fire that delights, refines, and energizes me. Sarah, Tad, and Zeke also supplied feedback on portions of the manuscript.

The team at Brazos deserves high praise. Thanks to Bryan Dyer for continuing to believe in the importance of this work and in me as an author. I'm also grateful for Eric Salo's excellence in production and for Jeremy Wells's in marketing. This is now my third book with Bryan, Eric, and Jeremy. Thanks also to Paula, Kara, and Erin—and doubtless other names could be added.

Two institutions helped facilitate my scholarship: Quincy University and Northern Seminary, my new home. My graduate assistants at Northern, Benjamin McDonald and Taylor Terzek, gave valuable feedback on the book. Benjamin also helped with proofreading while Taylor produced an index and had creative ideas for marketing. Thank you.

A number of people gave feedback, advice, or special assistance: I'd like to single out Leland Vickers, Eric Rowe, Aubrey Brady, and Michael Gorman. Leland volunteered to assist with some Scripture references and notes when I was under a time crunch. He also commented on the entire manuscript. Eric and Aubrey commented on the whole manuscript. Michael gave helpful remarks that led me to revise several sections. A few students endured preliminary chapters, including Joseph Siemer, Joseph Niemerg, and Nick Seibert. Three pastor-scholars gave feedback or advice: Darren Seitz, Jonathan Miles, and Chuck Sackett. Thank you all for your generosity!

Finally, I'm grateful to every reader of this book. Thanks for opting to read, for spreading the word about my books, for encouragement in reviews, and for interacting on social media. But thank you most of all for partnering with me in serving Jesus. Let's keep pursuing our Lord and his mission together.

Appendix

Guide for Further Conversation

Introduction

1. Were you raised non-Christian, Catholic, Protestant, or Orthodox? Describe the view you held of the "other" groups when growing up.
2. Have you ever witnessed or participated in a disagreement about the *how* of salvation? What was the content of the discussion and the tone?
3. Describe your past experiences with specific church denominations or organizations.
4. How are denominations like and unlike a marketing brand?
5. Do you tend to feel positive or negative about the future of the church? What do you understand the term *the church* to mean?

Chapter 1: Entering the Combat Zone

1. Zwingli's death reminds us of the reality of past salvation wars. Do you think certain Christian groups will ever again fight violently for a specific understanding of salvation?
2. Catholic and Protestant observers described Zwingli's death diversely. What are some events or practices today

that would be described differently by Catholics and Protestants? Why?

3. "We declare our passion for the gospel but then wear out
our couch cushions" (p. 9). What prevents you from telling
others the good news about King Jesus? Think especially
about your habitual practices and emotions.

4. The author gives five reasons for optimism regarding the
long-term unity of the church (pp. 10–14). Which reason
do you find most compelling? Can you think of additional
reasons?

5. Why is a premium placed on the New Testament and the
earliest history of the church when studying the mechanics
of salvation?

6. When studying salvation, why is it useful to study not just
the New Testament and the earliest history of the church
but the whole of Christian history? What risks attend the
study of the whole of Christian history when seeking the
truth about the *how* of salvation?

7. When you hear the term *Protestant*, what convictions or
understandings come to mind? What is the essence of
Protestantism?

8. What gains made through the Protestant Reformation
should be celebrated? What losses should we mourn?

9. What agreements create the strongest common ground between Catholics and Protestants today? What are the most
significant differences?

10. The author contrasts classic Protestantism with the gospel-allegiance model using five points: the gospel, its purpose, saving faith, works, and saving grace. Which point
did you find most surprising or challenging, and why?

Chapter 2: The More Explicit Gospel

1. Does the gospel change your everyday life? How?

2. The author describes three types of readers of this chapter (pp. 27–28). Which type do you most readily identify with?

3. The author seeks to overcome gospel imprecision by approaching it from seven angles (pp. 28–29). What angle do you find most essential? Least essential? Are there angles you think should be added?

4. Why might it be helpful to study ancient occurrences of *euangelion* ("gospel") and *euangelizomai* ("to gospel") outside the Bible?

5. What is the most common way to summarize the gospel in Scripture? Why is this significant for the church today?

6. Had you previously considered that Jesus had to move through *a process within history* in order to become the Christ? How does attending to that process clarify the gospel?

7. The author asserts, "The climax of the gospel is enthronement, not atonement" (p. 38). What happens to the church and its mission when atonement is emphasized over enthronement?

8. In summarizing the royal gospel, the author lists ten events but indicates that "one could package the content accurately in different ways or expand on these elements" (p. 39). If you were asked to expand on three of these, how would you do so?

9. How many of the ten events can you identify in Peter's speech in Acts 2? In Paul's speech in Acts 13?

10. What are some of the purposes of the gospel?

11. Why is it imperative to recognize that the gospel is not simply a true story with specific content but also a power-releasing event?

Chapter 3: Right and Wrong about the Gospel

1. The author claims that "all major streams and Christian denominations agree about the actual biblical, apostolic gospel" (p. 48). Do you agree or disagree?

2. In your understanding, what is a sacrament?

3. Describe your previous experience with sacraments or with people or groups who emphasize participation in the sacraments.

4. The author claims that "the gospel is eclipsed by the sacraments" within Catholicism (p. 52). A Catholic might counter that the sacraments are the greatest instrument for proclaiming and experiencing the gospel in the history of the church. What are the strengths and weaknesses of such a claim?

5. Read the Apostles' Creed (a version can be found at www .usccb.org/prayers/apostles-creed). How is it similar to the definition of the gospel's content on page 49? How does it differ?

6. The author pinpoints a number of "*wrong ways* of describing the gospel within classic Protestantism" (p. 55). Which of these do you think is most common? Which do you personally find to be the most troubling?

7. Can you summarize what is at stake in the Wright-McKnight-Bates versus Piper-Gilbert debate about the gospel? Why is this debate of practical significance for the church?

8. The author gives three reasons why it is better to see the *personal* receipt of forgiveness as a benefit of the gospel rather than as a required definitional component of the "good news" (pp. 60–64). Can you reexpress one of those reasons in your own words?

9. Name a few groups or associations to which you belong. What benefits does membership offer you? What conditions define or control entrance and departure from the group?

10. Why does it matter whether the gospel is social and political?
11. Think of the last sermon or public speech you heard. How did nonverbal communication pertaining to the messenger, the mode of delivery, and the setting affect the message's meaning? Why does this matter for a study of the gospel?

Chapter 4: Retooling the Protestant Critique of Catholicism

1. Based on your past encounters with Paul's letter to the Galatians, why do you think Protestants have used it to criticize Catholicism?
2. The author compares a party and a gift to nuance the relationship between the gospel and justification in Scripture. What is the point of that analogy? Can you think of your own analogy?
3. What was your understanding of "faith" prior to reading this chapter?
4. The author lists five faulty ideas about saving faith. Which do you think is the most prevalent? Which poses the greatest danger to the church and its mission to the world?
5. What is the difference between denying the essential content of the gospel and "not walking straight toward the truth of the gospel" (Gal. 2:14 AT)?
6. What steps can we take today to overcome the disconnect between justification's practical purpose in Scripture and how it has tended to function in Protestant-Catholic debates?
7. What is the difference between works and works of the law in Scripture? Why does this matter for an appraisal of ongoing Catholic-Protestant disagreements?
8. The author proposes a "better reading of Galatians." In what ways does this critique of Catholicism differ from that offered by classic Protestantism?

9. The author offers three critiques of Catholicism based on a reading of Galatians. Which do you think poses the greatest challenge for the future of Catholic-Protestant reconciliation?

10. This chapter seeks to rethink traditional Protestant criticisms of Catholicism as it pertains to salvation in the hope that this will promote future unity. What topics beyond salvation also need attention? Are there ways that you can work toward unity in the truth with respect to these topics?

Chapter 5: Is Baptism Saving?

1. How does your church (or tradition) perform baptisms? What specifically happens?

2. When the meaning of the baptismal event is described by the pastor or priest in your current church context, what is emphasized when speaking to the candidate, the family, and the congregation, respectively?

3. Do you know anyone who has been baptized more than once? What do you think motivates the desire for rebaptism?

4. What scriptural evidence suggests that baptism is either saving or not saving?

5. The author gives three reasons why the question "Is baptism saving?" is too imprecise. Which of the three do you find to be the most convincing, and why?

6. What were some purposes of baptism in pre-Christian Judaism? How are ritual impurity, contagious holiness, and water baptism connected in pre-Christian Judaism?

7. What is the importance of Simon the Magician's example for interpreting the meaning of baptism in the New Testament?

8. What exact features of the baptismal process in the New Testament and earliest Christianity (prior to the third

century) suggest that it was not intended for infants or young children?

9. How specifically do repentance, faith, justification, and baptism coordinate in the New Testament?

10. What does Justin Martyr emphasize in his description of baptism and his interpretation of its meaning? Why does this matter?

11. The author advocates for a *loyalist baptism* or *allegiant baptism* rather than infant or believer's baptism. How could baptism more clearly express allegiance to King Jesus in your current church context?

Chapter 6: Why Election and Regeneration Are False Starts

1. Have you ever participated in or witnessed a debate about whether God predestines humans for salvation or damnation? Was the debate based more on Scripture or philosophical reasoning?

2. In considering scriptural passages that mention God's eternal decrees, why is it important to consider that "the Christ" is a title, not a name?

3. What is the difference between corporate and individual election?

4. The Bible prefers group language for election. The author gives four reasons why it is unlikely that individual election is intended. Can you put some of these reasons in your own words?

5. What specifically do we learn about predestining election from Ephesians 1:11–13?

6. How do the examples of Paul, Pharaoh, Jacob, and Esau illustrate the difference between *vocational* election and *soteriological* election?

7. In Romans 9–11, what is the exact identity and purpose of the vessels of mercy and wrath?

8. How have you previously modeled God's sovereignty alongside human free will? The two most popular models are briefly sketched in this chapter. What model do you currently favor?

9. If Paul does *not* compare water baptism with physical circumcision within a covenantal framework in Colossians 2:11–13, then what is his actual comparison and framework? What does physical circumcision actually correspond to in Paul's theology?

10. What does Scripture say about human bondage of the will? How does the grace of the gospel change the human situation?

Chapter 7: Once Saved, Always Saved?

1. All the major Protestant denominations teach that works are required for salvation. Why do you think this Protestant teaching is so often misunderstood or forgotten, even by members of those denominations?

2. What is the difference between believing that perseverance is required for salvation (a view held by nearly all Christians) and believing "once saved, always saved" (a view held by a minority of Christians)?

3. What role should feelings (emotions) about personal assurance play in the debate about eternal security?

4. How much faith is necessary for salvation? What might it mean to have inadequate faith? What do you understand the word *faith* to mean?

5. John 15 speaks of the necessity of abiding or remaining in Jesus for eternal life, with detachment resulting in utter condemnation. What practices help you remain rooted in Jesus, strengthening your connection each day and for the long term?

6. Conditional statements ("if . . . then" type statements) in Scripture warn believers (those who share the Spirit) not to

commit apostasy, lest they be condemned. Why, according to the author, is it improbable that such conditionals are purely hypothetical?

7. With regard to eternal salvation, does the Spirit seal or guarantee? How should this be nuanced?

8. What evidence is there in the New Testament that the personal abiding presence of the Holy Spirit can be lost for an individual who previously had experienced that presence?

9. The author speaks of the directional flow of the Spirit. When we consider how the Spirit comes to indwell an individual today in a saving fashion, do you think it matters that the Spirit indwelt a saved community first at Pentecost?

10. What is the relationship between the Holy Spirit and church discipline? What can it teach us about the "once saved, always saved" debate?

Chapter 8: Disrupting the Order of Salvation

1. Prior to starting this book, how would you have defined *justification*? What about *sanctification*? What is your current understanding of these terms?

2. What is the difference between the history of salvation and the order of salvation? Why are they both worth studying?

3. Justification and sanctification quickly became a normal part of the Protestant order of salvation, even though their ordering is not taught in Scripture in a straightforward fashion. How and why did this come about?

4. The author gives three reasons why the justification-sanctification distinction is invalid (pp. 206–15). Which of the three reasons is the most challenging for you as you wrestle with these ideas?

5. Why is it important to establish from Scripture that justification is not merely declarative but also includes personal liberation and transformation?

6. What is imputed righteousness? Why did Luther value it so highly?

7. To understand Catholic justification, it is necessary to grasp five different kinds of causation (pp. 220–25). Describe the five causes with a sentence or two about each.

8. Regarding the instrumental cause of justification, what do Protestants and Catholics agree on? Why is there still disagreement?

9. Protestants and Catholics disagree sharply about the formal cause of justification. Give at least three reasons why.

10. According to the author, why is Catholic justification best described as *imparted* righteousness?

Chapter 9: Justification Remodeled

1. Why must Catholicism make its case from Scripture (not merely tradition) in articulating a theology of justification? (For further review, see chap. 4, under the heading "Scripture, Tradition, and Authority in Catholicism," pp. 91–93.)

2. How does the gospel-allegiance model describe the relationship between the gospel, faith, grace, and works?

3. Scripture does not clearly say that the Christ's righteousness is credited (imputed) for a person's unrighteousness. Something else is credited for righteousness. What is it, and why does this distinction matter?

4. With regard to salvation, what is meant by merit? In what way does a merit framework help us understand salvation? In what ways might it be misleading?

5. How does the ransom metaphor fit within the gospel-allegiance model?

6. A major purpose of the gospel in Scripture is to recover human glory (e.g., 2 Thess. 2:13–14; 2 Tim. 2:8–10)—all of which redounds to God's glory (e.g., Eph. 1:13–14). According to Scripture, how was glory lost and how is it being recovered?

7. According to N. T. Wright, what does Paul mean by "the righteousness of God"?

8. How is "the righteousness of God" understood within the gospel-allegiance model? Why?

9. What is Catholic infused/ingrafted righteousness? Why is it a secondary rather than primary way of describing the Catholic model?

10. What is incorporated righteousness? Why is it felt to be better than Protestant imputed or Catholic imparted righteousness?

Chapter 10: Beyond the Salvation Wars

1. This book's subtitle is "Why Both Protestants and Catholics Must Reimagine How We Are Saved." How would you describe this book's method and boundaries with respect to the process of reimagining?

2. In your own words, what are the main distinctives of the gospel-allegiance model compared to classic Protestantism on the one hand and Catholicism on the other?

3. The author suggests three ways to help accelerate a gospel-allegiance culture (pp. 261–64). Which of the three do you find most helpful? Can you think of other ways to help advance the conversation about the *how* of salvation in the church, locally or globally?

4. What are some common symbols of Christian unity? Are there ways—in thought, word, or deed—to emphasize for yourself and others that allegiance to King Jesus is the source and boundary of that unity?

5. What are three Christian activities you regularly practice (e.g., prayer, service)? Can you think of some specific ways to make each a more robust opportunity to bolster your allegiance to King Jesus?

Notes

Chapter 1 Entering the Combat Zone

1. The Catholic version (Johannes Salat) and the Protestant version (Heinrich Bullinger) have been conveniently reprinted in Denis R. Janz, ed., *A Reformation Reader: Primary Texts with Introductions*, 2nd ed. (Minneapolis: Fortress, 2008), 198–99. The quotations and details in this section herein rely on this source.

2. "It is only those who have neither fired a shot nor heard the shrieks and groans of the wounded who cry aloud for blood, more vengeance, more desolation. War is hell." William Tecumseh Sherman, speech to graduating class of the Michigan Military Academy, June 19, 1879.

3. Heb. 12:22–29; 2 Pet. 3:12–13. See J. Richard Middleton, *A New Heaven and a New Earth: Reclaiming Biblical Eschatology* (Grand Rapids: Baker Academic, 2014), 155–210.

4. See Irenaeus, *Against Heresies* 3.4.

5. Robert M. Grant, *The Apostolic Fathers: A New Translation and Commentary*, vol. 1, *An Introduction* (Camden, NJ: Nelson, 1964), 2. "Practically none of these writings [the Apostolic Fathers] was available. Latin versions of a spurious collection of Ignatius' letters and the Shepherd of Hermas had been published. . . . But 1 and 2 Clement, the genuine Ignatius, Polycarp, the Didache, and Barnabas were practically unknown. . . . This is to say that the documents which could have made church history and the development of early Christian theology intelligible were not in existence, as far as the Reformers—and their opponents—were concerned" (5–6). The Apostolic Fathers were essentially unavailable in the East or West until the various publications of James Ussher, Isaac Voss, Patrick Young, and others in the 1640–50s.

6. See Robert M. Grant, *Greek Apologists of the Second Century* (Philadelphia: Westminster, 1988), 197–202, esp. 201.

7. For developments after the Council of Trent, such as the Joint Declaration on Justification (1999), issued by the Lutheran World Federation and the Pontifical

Council for Promoting Christian Unity, see my remarks in chap. 8. For a fuller discussion, see Anthony N. S. Lane, *Justification by Faith in Catholic-Protestant Dialogue: An Evangelical Assessment* (London: T&T Clark, 2006).

8. John MacArthur, *Faith Works: The Gospel According to the Apostles* (Dallas: Word, 1993), 87, citing R. C. Sproul, "Works or Faith?," *TableTalk* (May 1991), 6.

9. See Thomas H. McCall, Caleb T. Friedeman, and Matt T. Friedeman, *The Doctrine of Good Works: Reclaiming a Neglected Protestant Teaching* (Grand Rapids: Baker Academic, 2023).

10. John Piper, *What Is Saving Faith? Reflections on Receiving Christ as a Treasure* (Wheaton: Crossway, 2022), 81.

11. Piper does correctly nuance the Catholic position (*What Is Saving Faith?*, 43).

12. "Decree Concerning Justification," in *Canons and Decrees of the Council of Trent: Original Text with English Translation*, trans. H. J. Schroeder (St. Louis: Herder, 1941), 42. In this context a "canon" is an authoritative theological statement that summarizes the teaching in the document.

13. On grace, the gospel-allegiance model largely depends on John Barclay, *Paul and the Gift* (Grand Rapids: Eerdmans, 2015). For my attempt to nuance and apply Barclay's six categories for grace, see Matthew W. Bates, *Gospel Allegiance: What Faith in Jesus Misses for Salvation in Christ* (Grand Rapids: Brazos, 2019), chap. 4.

14. Ulrich Gäbler, *Huldrych Zwingli: His Life and Work*, trans. Ruth C. L. Gritsch (Philadelphia: Fortress, 1986), 49–61, esp. 56.

15. Samuel Macauley Jackson, ed., *Ulrich Zwingli (1484–1531): Selected Works* (Philadelphia: University of Pennsylvania Press, 1972), 56–57.

16. Jackson, *Ulrich Zwingli*, 57.

17. Jackson, *Ulrich Zwingli*, 58.

18. Jackson, *Ulrich Zwingli*, 108.

19. Jackson, *Ulrich Zwingli*, 108.

20. Jackson, *Ulrich Zwingli*, xxi.

Chapter 2 The More Explicit Gospel

1. See N. T. Wright, *Simply Good News: Why the Gospel Is News and What Makes It Good* (New York: HarperOne, 2015); Scot McKnight, *The King Jesus Gospel: The Original Good News Revisited* (Grand Rapids: Zondervan, 2010); Michael Bird, *Evangelical Theology: A Biblical and Systematic Introduction*, 2nd ed. (Grand Rapids: Zondervan Academic, 2020); and Michael J. Gorman, "Paul's Gospel," in *Apostle of the Crucified Lord: A Theological Introduction to Paul and His Letters*, 2nd ed. (Grand Rapids: Eerdmans, 2017), 120–39.

2. For these ancient uses of "gospel" (*euangelion*), see Aristophanes, *Equites* 647, 656 (fish sale); Diodorus Siculus, *Bibliotheca historica* 15.74 (drama victory); and Cicero, *Letters to Atticus* 2.3.1 (lawsuit), 13.40.1 (political alliance). For a convenient collection of texts, see Glen Davis, "Pre-Christian Uses of 'Gospel,'" Glen Davis (blog), February 25, 2010, https://glenandpaula.com/wordpress/archives/2010/02/25/pre-christian-uses-of-gospel.

3. Aeschines, *Against Ctesiphon* 160.

4. Plutarch, *Agesilaus* 33.4, in *Agesilaus and Pompey; Pelopidas and Marcellus*, trans. Bernadotte Perrin (Cambridge, MA: Harvard University Press, 1917), 93.

5. 2 Sam. 4:10; 18:20, 22, 25, 27; 2 Kings 7:9.

6. The verb *euangelizō* is more common than the noun *euangelion* in the Greek Old Testament. Important passages include 1 Sam. 31:9; 2 Sam. 4:10; 18:19–20, 26, 31; Nah. 2:1 (1:15 in English Bibles); Isa. 40:9; 52:7; 60:6; 61:1.

7. Josephus, *Jewish War* 4.656, in *The Jewish War, Books IV–VII*, trans. H. St. J. Thackeray (Cambridge, MA: Harvard University Press, 1961), 195 (emphasis added). See also *Jewish War* 4.618 (p. 183).

8. For Jesus's kingship as the actualization of God's rule on earth as in heaven, see N. T. Wright, *How God Became King: The Forgotten Story of the Gospels* (New York: HarperOne, 2011).

9. For expanded treatment, see Matthew W. Bates, "A Christology of Incarnation and Enthronement: Romans 1:3–4 as Unified, Nonadoptionist, and Nonconciliatory," *Catholic Biblical Quarterly* 77 (2015): 107–27.

10. On "Christ" as an honorific title rather than a personal name, see Matthew V. Novenson, *Christ among the Messiahs: Christ Language in Paul and Messiah Language in Ancient Judaism* (Oxford: Oxford University Press, 2012).

11. This chart appears verbatim in Matthew W. Bates, *Gospel Allegiance: What Faith in Jesus Misses for Salvation in Christ* (Grand Rapids: Brazos, 2019), 86–87, except the words "as promised" have been added to line 2. The addition reflects the emphasis in Rom. 1:2; Acts 2:30; 3:21; 13:23, 32, among other gospel texts.

12. See Matthew W. Bates, *Salvation by Allegiance Alone: Rethinking Faith, Works, and the Gospel of Jesus the King* (Grand Rapids: Baker Academic, 2017), 47–75; and Bates, *Gospel Allegiance*, 86–104.

13. For a fuller treatment, see Bates, *Gospel Allegiance*, chaps. 1–3.

14. Michael J. Gorman, *Becoming the Gospel: Paul, Participation, and Mission* (Grand Rapids: Eerdmans, 2015), 297.

15. An inscription is generally at the top of our ancient Gospel manuscripts— e.g., *euangelion kata Maththaion*, or abbreviated to *kata Maththaion*. For details, see David Trobisch, *The First Edition of the New Testament* (Oxford: Oxford University Press, 2000), 38, 126n142.

16. The first ten uses of *pistis* in Romans (1:5, 8, 12, 17 [3×]; 3:3, 22, 25, 26) lean in the direction of externalized, embodied "faithfulness" or "fidelity" rather than "trust in," although it would be methodologically problematic to exclude mental trust. See Matthew W. Bates, "The Recent External-Relational Shift in *Pistis* (Faith) in New Testament Research: Romans 1 as Gospel-Allegiance Test Case," *Currents in Biblical Research* 18 (2020): 176–202.

17. Matthew W. Bates, *Why the Gospel? Living the Good News of King Jesus with Purpose* (Grand Rapids: Eerdmans, 2023).

18. "Prince of Wales Proclaimed King Edward VIII," United Press International Archives, January 21, 1936, https://www.upi.com/Archives/1936/01/21/Prince-of-Wales-proclaimed-King-Edward-VIII/7807693511214.

19. For discussion, see Bates, *Gospel Allegiance*, 73–81.

Chapter 3   Right and Wrong about the Gospel

1. John MacArthur, *The Gospel according to Paul: Embracing the Good News at the Heart of Paul's Teachings* (Nashville: Nelson, 2017), 60, 55.

2. R. C. Sproul, *Faith Alone: The Evangelical Doctrine of Justification* (Grand Rapids: Baker, 1995), 19; cf. Sproul, *Getting the Gospel Right: The Tie That Binds Evangelicals Together* (Grand Rapids: Baker, 1999), 100–103.

3. John Piper, *God Is the Gospel: Meditations on God's Love as the Gift of Himself* (Wheaton: Crossway, 2005), 44.

4. A scholarly movement called the "new perspective on Paul" includes this reappraised soteriology. See Michael B. Thompson, *The New Perspective on Paul* (Cambridge: Grove Books, 2002); and Kent L. Yinger, *The New Perspective on Paul: An Introduction* (Eugene, OR: Cascade Books, 2010).

5. On the inadequacy of traditional proof texts for justification by faith as part of the gospel (e.g., Acts 13:39; Rom. 1:16; Gal. 3:8; Phil. 3:9), see my discussion under the "2. Clarifying 'Our'" section in this chapter and my further discussion of justification in chaps. 4, 8, and 9.

6. N. T. Wright, *What Saint Paul Really Said: Was Paul of Tarsus the Real Founder of Christianity?* (Grand Rapids: Eerdmans, 1997), 129.

7. John Piper, *The Future of Justification: A Response to N. T. Wright* (Wheaton: Crossway, 2007), 86.

8. Greg Gilbert, *What Is the Gospel?* (Wheaton: Crossway, 2010), 140, 141.

9. For his critique of Gilbert, see Scot McKnight, *The King Jesus Gospel: The Original Good News Revisited* (Grand Rapids: Zondervan, 2011), 58–61.

10. Michael F. Bird, *Introducing Paul: The Man, His Mission and His Message* (Downers Grove, IL: IVP Academic, 2008), 74–91; N. T. Wright, *How God Became King: The Forgotten Story of the Gospels* (New York: HarperOne, 2011); Wright, *Simply Good News: Why the Gospel Is News and What Makes It Good* (New York: HarperOne, 2015); and Michael J. Gorman, *Becoming the Gospel: Paul, Participation, and Mission* (Grand Rapids: Eerdmans, 2015).

11. Greg Gilbert, "A T4G 2020 Sermon: What Is and Isn't the Gospel," 9Marks, April 15, 2020, https://www.9marks.org/article/a-t4g-2020-sermon-what-is-and -isnt-the-gospel. All quotes are taken from the published version.

12. Matthew W. Bates, "Good News? Are T4G/TGC Leaders Starting to Change Their Gospel?," *Jesus Creed* (blog), April 20, 2020, https://www.chris tianitytoday.com/scot-mcknight/2020/april/good-news-are-t4g-tgc-leaders-start ing-to-change-their-gosp.html.

13. Scot McKnight, "King Jesus Gospel: Mere Kingship? No," *Jesus Creed* (blog), April 20, 2020, https://www.christianitytoday.com/scot-mcknight/2020 /april/king-jesus-gospel-mere-kingship-no.html.

14. Greg Gilbert, "A Response to Scot McKnight and Matthew Bates," 9Marks, April 22, 2020, https://www.9marks.org/article/a-response-to-scot-mcknight-and -matthew-bates.

15. Matthew W. Bates, "Why T4G/TGC Leaders Must Fix Their Gospel," *Jesus Creed* (blog), April 29, 2020, https://www.christianitytoday.com/scot-mc knight/2020/april/why-t4gtgc-leaders-must-fix-their-gospel.html.

16. For further discussion of group priority and the Spirit's directional flow, see chaps. 6 and 7.

17. "The Statement on Social Justice and the Gospel," under section 6, "Gospel," https://statementonsocialjustice.com.

18. Graham H. Twelftree, *The Gospel According to Paul: A Reappraisal* (Eugene, OR: Cascade Books, 2019), 199. Twelftree's book describes how the gospel is an event that includes signs and wonders as part of its liberating message. On how the gospel inescapably creates a just community, see Gorman, *Becoming the Gospel*, 213–60.

19. "Statement on Social Justice and the Gospel," under section 6, "Gospel."

20. John MacArthur describes the relationship between faith and works this way: "Faith is an *internal* reality with *external* consequences. . . . Faith itself is complete before one work of obedience ever issues forth." *Faith Works: The Gospel According to the Apostles* (Dallas: Word, 1993), 99.

21. Twelftree, *Gospel According to Paul*, 199.

Chapter 4 Retooling the Protestant Critique of Catholicism

1. For this basic logic and specific passages cited, see Martin Luther, *Commentary on Galatians* (Wheaton: Crossway, 1998), xvi–xxi. Although they draw from more than Galatians in their respective treatments of justification, both John Murray (*Redemption, Accomplished and Applied* [Grand Rapids: Eerdmans, 1955], 125–28) and R. C. Sproul (*Getting the Gospel Right: The Tie That Binds Evangelicals Together* [Grand Rapids: Baker, 1999], 153–65) are informed by the surface logic of Galatians described here.

2. See, e.g., Sproul, *Getting the Gospel Right*, 21–22.

3. The broadest study is Teresa Morgan, *Roman Faith and Christian Faith: Pistis and Fides in the Early Roman Empire and Early Churches* (Oxford: Oxford University Press, 2015). The importance of covenant fidelity is highlighted in Nijay K. Gupta, *Paul and the Language of Faith* (Grand Rapids: Eerdmans, 2020).

4. See Matthew W. Bates, *Salvation by Allegiance Alone: Rethinking Faith, Works, and the Gospel of Jesus the King* (Grand Rapids: Baker Academic, 2017), esp. 77–100; Bates, *Gospel Allegiance: What Faith in Jesus Misses for Salvation in Christ* (Grand Rapids: Brazos, 2019), 57–83, 149–75; and Bates, "The External-Relational Shift in Faith (*Pistis*) in New Testament Research: Romans 1 as Gospel-Allegiance Test Case," *Currents in Biblical Research* 18 (2020): 176–202.

5. R. C. Sproul, *Faith Alone: The Evangelical Doctrine of Justification* (Grand Rapids: Baker, 1995), 19.

6. Vatican II, *Lumen Gentium* §15. The Council of Trent's "Decree on Justification" makes it explicit that the sacraments of baptism and penance (or the desire for them) are absolutely required for personal salvation (for evidence, see "Mandatory Activities among Catholics" section in this chapter and "Catholic Justification" in chap. 8). On the softening of this sacramental absolute, see the dogmatic decree of Vatican II, *Lumen Gentium* §§15–16, issued by Pope Paul VI (1964).

7. See James D. G. Dunn, *The Theology of Paul the Apostle* (Grand Rapids: Eerdmans 1998), 354–71.

8. See Bates, *Gospel Allegiance*, 197–200, 212–19.

9. See Matthew J. Thomas, *Paul's "Works of the Law" in the Perspective of Second-Century Reception* (Downers Grove, IL: InterVarsity, 2020). By exploring how second-century Christian writers (e.g., Ignatius, Justin Martyr, Irenaeus) interpreted Paul's letters, Thomas shows that the basic interpretation of "works" and "works of law" put forward by the so-called new perspective on Paul (pioneered by E. P. Sanders, James D. G. Dunn, N. T. Wright, and others) accurately recovers the ancient church's interpretation.

10. See Thomas H. McCall, Caleb T. Friedeman, and Matt T. Friedeman, *The Doctrine of Good Works: Reclaiming a Neglected Protestant Teaching* (Grand Rapids: Baker Academic, 2023), chap. 1. E.g., they show evidence that scholastic Reformed theologians Girolamo Zanchi, Samuel Rutherford, and Gisbertus Voetius give works instrumental causal power in justification, whereas Johannes Piscator and John Davenant make works an efficient cause (while offering caveats and qualifications).

11. Vatican II, *Dei Verbum*, November 18, 1965, 2.9, https://www.vatican.va /archive/hist_councils/ii_vatican_council/documents/vat-ii_const_19651118_dei -verbum_en.html.

12. Vatican II, *Dei Verbum*, 2.10.

13. Vatican II, *Dei Verbum*, 2.10.

14. Council of Trent, "Decree on Justification," canon 29.

15. All quotes in this paragraph are taken from the most essential official Catholic teaching tool, the Catechism of the Catholic Church (United States Conference of Catholic Bishops, 2000), §§1459–60 (pp. 366–67) (emphasis added).

16. See Khaled Anatolios, *Retrieving Nicaea: The Development and Meaning of Trinitarian Doctrine* (Grand Rapids: Baker Academic, 2011); and Matthew W. Bates, *The Birth of the Trinity: Jesus, God, and Spirit in New Testament and Early Christian Interpretations of the Old Testament* (Oxford: Oxford University Press, 2015).

17. See the Council of Trent's "Decree on Justification." According to canon 29, if a person commits a mortal sin after baptism, it is impossible to recover the state of justification apart from receiving the sacrament of penance. Canon 30 indicates that initial justification does not remove the guilt of subsequent sins in such a way that penance or purgation is unnecessary.

18. What might appear to be an exception proves the rule. In Mark 1:44 (cf. Matt. 8:4; Luke 5:14) Jesus commands that a priest certify a healing. However, this involves a priest of the old covenant under the laws of Moses, not a priest of the new covenant under the sacrifice of Jesus and his unique high priesthood.

19. See the Code on Canon Law, canons 1245, 1247–48, available at https:// www.vatican.va/archive/cod-iuris-canonici/eng/documents/cic_lib4-cann1244 -1253_en.html.

20. Mary's immaculate conception was a minority view within Catholicism— it was even rejected by Thomas Aquinas—until after Dun Scotus's views gained ascendancy in the late Middle Ages. It became dogma (required Catholic belief) in 1854.

21. The Protoevangelium of James contains numerous historical errors and impossibilities. E.g., Mary as a child lives for years in the holy of holies in the

Jerusalem temple. In actuality, women were not even allowed in the innermost courts of the temple, and even priests could not normally enter the holy of holies. The document does not explicitly articulate Mary's immaculate conception but hints in that direction, treats Mary as sinless, and indicates that her virginity remained intact physically (no ruptured hymen) even after completing the process of delivering the baby Jesus.

22. See the Code on Canon Law, canon 1364, available at https://www.vatican .va/archive/cod-iuris-canonici/eng/documents/cic_lib6-cann1364-1399_en.html.

Chapter 5 Is Baptism Saving?

1. George Blaurock, "The Hutterite Chronicle," in *Readings in the History of Christian Theology*, vol. 2, *From the Reformation to the Present*, ed. William C. Placher and Derek R. Nelson, rev. ed. (Louisville: Westminster John Knox, 2017), 15.

2. Blaurock, "Hutterite Chronicle," 16.

3. Contrary to Catholic claims, when Jesus gives the keys to Peter in Caesarea Philippi (Matt. 16:19), this does nothing to establish after Peter a unique and perpetual Petrine office in Rome. We know this because, as Matthew continues, *the power to bind and loose associated with the keys belongs also and equally to any "two or three" who gather in Jesus's name apart from Peter, and certainly apart from any purported successor to Peter* (18:18–20). These retaining and relinquishing powers grant *any* two or three gathered in Jesus's name *in that moment* the authority to determine the community's behavioral norms, standards, and boundaries. Any two or three can do this in Jesus's name not because of Peter's name, presence, or authority but because Jesus says, "I am in their midst" (18:20 AT).

4. See John 1:41–42 on Peter's involvement with John's baptism. Peter's baptism by John *might* be referenced obliquely by Jesus: "Those who have had a *bath* need only to wash their feet; *their whole body is clean*" (John 13:10 NIV). But baptism specifically into Jesus's name is unlikely here because next Jesus says to his disciples, "And you are clean," and then adds with reference to Judas Iscariot, "though not every one of you" (13:10 NIV). Since we have no indication that any of the disciples received baptism into Jesus's name, let alone *all* of them, "you are *all* clean" probably does not intend their personal baptisms. Nor does a baptismal reference explain Jesus's singular emphasis on Judas's present uncleanness compared to the others, since in context Jesus knows that both Judas and Peter are about to deny him, so both would be sinfully unclean if that was the intention. Only Judas is singled out (13:11). Later Jesus clarifies that his *word* (not water) has cleansed his disciples (15:3), so "bath" (13:10) appears to be a metaphor for holistic repentance and is not restricted to baptism as initiation.

5. See, e.g., Luke 16:24; Rev. 19:13. See also Henry George Liddell, Robert Scott, and Henry Stuart Jones, *A Greek-English Lexicon*, 9th ed. (Oxford: Clarendon, 1996), s.v. *baptizō*.

6. See Jonathan D. Lawrence, "Washing, Ritual," in *The Eerdmans Dictionary of Early Judaism*, ed. John J. Collins and Daniel C. Harlow (Grand Rapids: Eerdmans, 2010), 1331–32.

7. See, e.g., Matt. 23:25; Mark 7:4; Luke 11:38; John 2:6; 1QS 5:16; 4QMMT 4:55–58, 65–68; 4Q514 frag. 1.

8. Josephus, *Jewish War* 2.137–38.

9. 1QS 5:13.

10. 1QS 5:14.

11. Josephus, *Jewish Antiquities* 18.117–18, in *Jewish Antiquities, Books XVIII–XIX*, trans. Louis H. Feldman (Cambridge, MA: Harvard University Press, 1965), 81–83 (emphasis added).

12. 1QS 8:13–14, in Michael Wise, Martin Abegg Jr., and Edward Cook, *The Dead Sea Scrolls: A New Translation* (New York: HarperCollins, 1996), 138. See also 1QS 9:18–20.

13. Josephus, *Jewish Antiquities* 20.97–98, in Richard Horsley and John S. Hanson, *Bandits, Prophets, and Messiahs: Popular Movements in the Time of Jesus* (San Francisco: Harper & Row, 1988), 164.

14. See Josephus, *Jewish Antiquities* 18.116–19.

15. See Bruce J. Malina, *The New Testament World: Insights from Cultural Anthropology*, 3rd ed. (Louisville: Westminster John Knox, 2001), 58–80; and David A. DeSilva, *Honor, Patronage, Kinship, and Purity: Unlocking New Testament Culture* (Downers Grove, IL: IVP Academic, 2000), 178–93.

16. For examples of calling upon a name as an oath invocation, see Isa. 48:1; Jer. 44:26; Acts 19:13; Eph. 1:21.

17. In the New Testament, justification's instrument is once Jesus's blood (Rom. 5:9), once works (James 2:24), and twice grace (Rom. 3:24; Titus 3:7), but otherwise it is always *pistis* ("faith" or "loyalty") (Rom. 3:30; 5:1; 9:30; 10:6; Gal. 2:16; 3:8, 11, 24).

18. "Now that *pistis* [allegiance] has come"—i.e., now that the Christ has proven to be loyal to the Father and to us through his actions in the events that together constitute the gospel.

19. See Robert M. Grant, *Greek Apologists of the Second Century* (Philadelphia: Westminster, 1988), 201.

20. Justin Martyr, *First Apology* 61.2, in Denis Minns and Paul Parvis, ed. and trans., *Justin, Philosopher and Martyr: Apologies* (New York: Oxford University Press, 2009), 237, 239.

21. Justin Martyr, *First Apology* 61.3, in Minns and Parvis, *Justin*, 239.

22. Justin Martyr, *First Apology* 61.4, in Minns and Parvis, *Justin*, 239.

23. Justin Martyr, *First Apology* 61.9–13, in Minns and Parvis, *Justin*, 241, 243 (emphasis added).

24. Justin Martyr, *Dialogue with Trypho* 13.1, in *St. Justin Martyr, Dialogue with Trypho*, trans. Thomas B. Falls (Washington, DC: Catholic University of America Press, 2003), 22; see also 14.1.

25. Justin Martyr, *Dialogue with Trypho* 13.1 (trans. Falls, 22, slightly modified); see also 14.1; 19.2.

26. Justin Martyr, *First Apology* 65.1.

27. Justin Martyr, *First Apology* 65.2–3.

28. For these descriptions, see Tertullian, *On Baptism* 6–8; *The Crown* 3.

29. Tertullian, *On Baptism* 18.4–11.

30. Tertullian, *On Baptism* 18.9, in Alexander Roberts and James Donaldson, eds., S. Thelwall, trans., *Latin Christianity: Its Founder, Tertullian*, vol. 3 of *The Ante-Nicene Fathers: Translations of the Writings of the Fathers down to A.D. 325* (Peabody, MA: Hendrickson, 1994), 678.

31. Tertullian, *On Baptism* 18.8 (*ANF* 3:678).

32. Tertullian, *On Baptism* 18.4–5 (*ANF* 3:678).

33. Apart from the voluntarist evidence already reviewed, see Everett Ferguson, *Baptism in the Early Church: History, Theology, and Liturgy in the First Five Centuries* (Grand Rapids: Eerdmans, 2009), 196–98, 340–45, esp. 361–66, 853–57. Archaeological evidence—e.g., the standard size of baptismal founts—in early versus later Christianity also supports the claim that the baptism of adults was normative in earliest Christianity only to be eclipsed by infant baptism in late antiquity.

34. Origen, *Commentary on Romans* 5.9.11; *Homilies on Leviticus* 8.3.

35. Council of Trent, "Decree on Justification," §7 (emphasis added).

Chapter 6 Why Election and Regeneration Are False Starts

1. See Matthew V. Novenson, *Christ among the Messiahs: Christ Language in Paul and Messiah Language in Ancient Judaism* (Oxford: Oxford University Press, 2012).

2. Rom. 8:29–30 will be discussed in chap. 8.

3. On Jacob and Esau, see the section in this chapter titled "God's Vocational Election of Individuals."

4. On voluntary associations, see Everett Ferguson, *Backgrounds of Early Christianity*, 2nd ed. (Grand Rapids: Eerdmans, 1993), 131–36.

5. See Bruce J. Malina, *The New Testament World: Insights from Cultural Anthropology*, 3rd ed. (Louisville: Westminster John Knox, 2001), 58–80.

6. See E. Randolph Richards and Richard James, *Misreading Scripture with Individualist Eyes: Patronage, Honor, and Shame in the Biblical World* (Downers Grove, IL: IVP Academic, 2020).

7. Robert L. Shank, *Elect in the Son* (Bloomington, MN: Bethany House, 1989); William W. Klein, *The New Chosen People: A Corporate View of Election*, rev. and exp. ed. (Eugene, OR: Wipf & Stock, 2015); and A. Chadwick Thornhill, *The Chosen People: Election, Paul, and Second Temple Judaism* (Downers Grove, IL: IVP Academic, 2015).

8. Thornhill, *Chosen People*, 254.

9. For possible individual election texts, see Sirach 33:10–14; 1QS 4:26 (cf. 4:12–13); 1QH[a] 7:27–28; 9:20–22 (cf. 9:10–11). Robert J. Wiesner shows that there might be a couple counterexamples that manifest individual election amid the multitudinous texts that Thornhill analyzes as part of his "never" ("Predestinarian Election in Second Temple Judaism and Its Relevance for Pauline Theology," *Westminster Theological Journal* 82 [2020]: 36). However, given the overwhelming evidence that exclusively corporate election is normal in the New Testament era, whatever few counterexamples that perchance exist are not sufficient to make individual election probable for Paul. Wiesner shows how desperate the case against individual election truly is when he proposes that Paul, even though he

is a self-identified Pharisee, must have had his allegedly predestinarian teachings "formed under Essene influence" (36).

10. Thornhill, *Chosen People*, 254 (emphasis added).

11. For an extensive exegetical treatment of Rom. 9:1–24 that focuses on election, see Brian J. Abasciano, *Paul's Use of the Old Testament in Romans 9.1–9: An Intertextual and Theological Exegesis* (New York: T&T Clark, 2005); Abasciano, *Paul's Use of the Old Testament in Romans 9.10–18: An Intertextual and Theological Exegesis* (New York: T&T Clark, 2011); and Abasciano, *Paul's Use of the Old Testament in Romans 9.19–24: An Intertextual and Theological Exegesis* (New York: T&T Clark, 2022).

12. For discussion, see Jason A. Staples, *Paul and the Resurrection of Israel: Jews, Former Gentiles, and Israelites* (Cambridge: Cambridge University Press, 2024), 191–201.

13. For an overview of Augustine's soteriology and its reception, see Roger Olson, *The Story of Christian Theology: Twenty Centuries of Tradition and Reform* (Downers Grove, IL: InterVarsity, 1999), 255–77, 375–413. For a detailed treatment, see Alister E. McGrath, *Iustitia Dei: A History of the Christian Doctrine of Justification*, 4th ed. (Cambridge: Cambridge University Press, 2020), 42–58, 118–53, 156–68, 193–203, 221–26.

14. See McGrath, *Iustitia Dei*, 187–226.

15. See Kenneth Keathley, *Salvation and Sovereignty: A Molinist Approach* (Nashville: B&H Academic, 2010).

16. E.g., Louis Berkhof, *Systematic Theology*, 4th ed. (Grand Rapids: Eerdmans, 1979), 469.

17. Wayne A. Grudem, *Systematic Theology: An Introduction to Biblical Doctrine* (Grand Rapids: Zondervan, 1994), 702.

18. Grudem, *Systematic Theology*, 702–3.

19. Alister E. McGrath, *Iustitia Dei: A History of the Christian Doctrine of Justification*, 3rd ed. (Cambridge: Cambridge University Press, 2005), 34.

20. See Kenneth M. Wilson, *Augustine's Conversion from Traditional Free Choice to "Non-Free Free Will": A Comprehensive Methodology* (Tübingen: Mohr Siebeck, 2018).

21. See John Calvin, *Institutes* 4.16.11.

22. See discussion in Bruce Demarest, *The Cross and Salvation: The Doctrine of Salvation* (Wheaton: Crossway, 1997), 281–87.

23. Similarly, see Paul A. Rainbow, *The Way of Salvation: The Role of Christian Obedience in Justification* (Milton Keynes: Paternoster, 2005), 237.

24. As a representative example, see Berkhof, *Systematic Theology*, 472.

25. Libertarian freedom does not presume freedom from the consequences of previous decisions. All decisions have momentum-building consequences. Sometimes an initially free decision results in severely limited options subsequently. E.g., if I freely decide to jump from a cliff, I no longer have the freedom to undo that decision, and my future options are severely limited: I can only choose to smile, frown, or scream as I plummet toward death. The same is also true with respect to sin: the level of our entanglement in it carries an enslaving momentum that can affect our ability to repent as a consequence.

Chapter 7 Once Saved, Always Saved?

1. For an overview on works as saving within Protestantism, see Thomas H. McCall, Caleb T. Friedeman, and Matt T. Friedeman, *The Doctrine of Good Works: Reclaiming a Neglected Protestant Teaching* (Grand Rapids: Baker Academic, 2023).

2. E.g., John Piper states, "Our union with Christ and the enjoyment of these benefits is secure forever. Through faith alone, God establishes our union with Christ. This union will never fail, because in Christ God is for us as an omnipotent Father who sustains our faith, and works all things together for our everlasting good." Piper, *The Future of Justification: A Response to N. T. Wright* (Wheaton: Crossway, 2007), 184.

3. See Thomas R. Schreiner and Ardel B. Caneday, *The Race Set before Us: A Biblical Theology of Perseverance and Assurance* (Downers Grove, IL: InterVarsity, 2001).

4. For various statements and further conversation on this topic, see J. Matthew Pinson, ed., *Four Views on Eternal Security* (Grand Rapids: Zondervan, 2002).

5. For a thorough defense of this view, see Schreiner and Caneday, *The Race Set before Us*.

6. The verb *sōzesthe* is a present passive verb, and the otherwise unmarked present tense most often entails unfolding action ("being saved") rather than completed action ("saved").

7. John Barclay, *Paul and the Gift* (Grand Rapids: Eerdmans, 2015), 440.

8. Schreiner and Caneday, *The Race Set before Us*, 38–45, 142–213, 268–76.

9. See, e.g., Matt. 10:22; 24:13; Mark 13:13; John 8:31; Acts 13:43; 14:22; Rom. 2:7–8; 1 Cor. 10:12; Gal. 5:1–4; 1 Tim. 6:12; 2 Tim. 2:12; James 1:12; 2 Pet. 1:10–11; 3:17.

10. For evidence that authentic initial faith in Hebrews does not guarantee perseverance but rather can end in condemnation, see Scot McKnight, "The Warning Passages of Hebrews: A Formal Analysis and Theological Conclusions," *Trinity Journal*, n.s. 13 (1992): 21–59.

11. See Kyle R. Hughes, *How the Spirit Became God: The Mosaic of Early Christian Pneumatology* (Eugene, OR: Cascade Books, 2020).

12. My use of "from" is deliberately ambiguous but seeks to remain faithful to Scripture. The procession of the Spirit is in some way "from" both the Father and the Son—e.g., in John 15:26 and Acts 2:33. With regard to the Son, this "from" could involve ultimate sourcing and agency or merely secondary, and disputes about it have contributed significantly to Catholic and Orthodox schism (the *filioque* controversies). The gospel-allegiance model does not deem theological correctness about the *filioque* to be essential for salvation.

13. See Wayne A. Grudem, *Systematic Theology: An Introduction to Biblical Doctrine* (Grand Rapids: Zondervan, 1994), 797.

14. For *geuomai* ("tasting") as the sensory component of ordinary eating or drinking, note in the Septuagint Gen. 25:30; 1 Sam. 14:24; and in the New Testament Matt. 27:34; Luke 14:24, along with many other texts. Additionally, see Frederick W. Danker et al., *Greek-English Lexicon of the New Testament and Other Early Christian Literature*, 3rd ed. (Chicago: University of Chicago Press,

2000), s.v. γεύομαι, def. 1; and Paul Ellingworth, *The Epistle to the Hebrews: A Commentary on the Greek Text* (Grand Rapids: Eerdmans, 1993), 320.

15. See John 1:9; Eph. 1:18; 3:9; Danker et al., *Greek-English Lexicon*, s.v. φωτίζω, def. 3; and Gareth Lee Cockerill, *The Epistle to the Hebrews* (Grand Rapids: Eerdmans, 2012), 269.

16. Jesus states that he teaches in parables for a similar reason; see Mark 4:11–12, 24–25 (and parallels). Those who have open eyes and listening ears will discern the truth in Jesus's parables, so they will "turn and be forgiven." But those who do not want to repent will find the parables impenetrable, resulting in a deepening blindness and increased ripeness for judgment.

17. Dallas Willard, *Renovation of the Heart: Putting on the Character of Christ* (Colorado Springs: NavPress, 2002), 57.

18. I. Howard Marshall, *The Epistles of John*, New International Commentary on the New Testament (Grand Rapids: Eerdmans, 1978), 245–52, summarizes the "sin that leads to death," saying, "There is no doubt that when John wrote about it, he was thinking primarily of those who had left the church and whose lives were characterized by deliberate refusal to believe in Jesus Christ and to love their brothers" (249). Marshall goes on to conclude that John "did not altogether exclude the possibility that a person might fall away from his faith into apostasy" (250).

19. Gordon D. Fee, *The First Epistle to the Corinthians* (Grand Rapids: Eerdmans, 1987), 208–9.

Chapter 8 Disrupting the Order of Salvation

1. "Because if this article [of justification] stands, the church stands; if this article collapses, the church collapses." Martin Luther, WA 40/3:352.3, cited in Justin Taylor, "Luther's Saying: 'Justification Is the Article by which the Church Stands and Falls,'" The Gospel Coalition, August 31, 2011, https://www.thegospelcoalition.org/blogs/justin-taylor/luthers-saying.

2. For a detailed treatment of various orders within different denominational traditions, see Bruce Demarest, *The Cross and Salvation: The Doctrine of Salvation* (Wheaton: Crossway, 1997), 36–44.

3. On the golden chain, see Richard A. Muller, *Calvin and the Reformed Tradition: On the Work of Christ and the Order of Salvation* (Grand Rapids: Baker Academic, 2012), 161–201.

4. For this logic, see, e.g., Richard B. Gaffin, *By Faith, Not by Sight: Paul and the Order of Salvation*, 2nd ed. (Phillipsburg, NJ: P&R, 2013), 86–87.

5. John Calvin, *Commentary on the Epistles of Paul to the Corinthians*, trans. John Pringle (Grand Rapids: Baker, 1993), 93 (commenting on 1 Cor. 1:30). Cf. Calvin, *Institutes* 3.11.6, 3.16.1.

6. Calvin, *Institutes* 3.16.1, trans. Ford Lewis Battles (Philadelphia: Westminster, 1960), 2:798.

7. Calvin, *Institutes* 3.16.1 (trans. Battles, 2:798).

8. Calvin, *Institutes* 3.11.6 (trans. Battles, 2:732).

9. See, e.g., John MacArthur, *Faith Works: The Gospel According to the Apostles* (Dallas: Word, 1993), 90, 112–13; and Thomas Schreiner, *Faith Alone: The Doctrine of Justification* (Grand Rapids: Zondervan, 2015), 61–62, 175–78,

although Schreiner prefers the term *transformation* rather than *sanctification* in his discussion.

10. See discussion in Stephen Chester, *Reading Paul with the Reformers: Reconciling Old and New Perspectives* (Grand Rapids: Eerdmans, 2017), 218–64, esp. 240.

11. See Matthew W. Bates, *Gospel Allegiance: What Faith in Jesus Misses for Salvation in Christ* (Grand Rapids: Brazos, 2019), chap. 6.

12. See Michael J. Gorman, *Inhabiting the Cruciform God: Kenosis, Justification, and Theosis in Paul's Narrative Soteriology* (Grand Rapids: Eerdmans, 2009), 73–79.

13. Peter J. Leithart, *Delivered from the Elements of the World: Atonement, Justification, and Mission* (Downers Grove, IL: IVP Academic, 2016), 181–83.

14. See Rom. 1:17; 3:20–22; 4:25; 5:16–19; 8:4, 33–34; 2 Cor. 5:21. See Leithart, *Delivered from the Elements*, 212–96, 333–54; and Michael J. Gorman, *Becoming the Gospel: Paul, Participation, and Mission* (Grand Rapids: Eerdmans, 2015), 225–40, 277–86.

15. All quotes from Luther in this paragraph come from John Dillenberger, ed., *Martin Luther: Selections from His Writings* (Garden City, NY: Doubleday, 1961), 11–12.

16. Vatican II, *Lumen Gentium* §§15–16, issued by Pope Paul VI (1964).

17. Calvin, *Institutes* 3.14.17.

18. Calvin, *Institutes* 3.14.17.

19. Calvin, *Institutes* 3.14.17.

20. Calvin, *Institutes* 3.14.17.

Chapter 9 Justification Remodeled

1. See Matthew W. Bates, *Gospel Allegiance: What Faith in Jesus Misses for Salvation in Christ* (Grand Rapids: Brazos, 2019), chaps. 2, 5.

2. See Bates, *Gospel Allegiance*, chaps. 6, 7.

3. See Bates, *Gospel Allegiance*, chap. 4.

4. For a summary of recent criticisms of imputed righteousness from a biblical standpoint, see Michael Bird, *The Saving Righteousness of God: Studies on Paul, Justification, and the New Perspective* (Eugene, OR: Wipf & Stock, 2007), 61–70.

5. See, e.g., Lam. 5:8; Isa. 43:14; 1 Macc. 4:11; Luke 1:68; 2:38; Josephus, *Against Apion* 2.45; Philo, *Against Flaccus* 1.60.

6. For an exhaustive analysis of the atonement's scope, see David Allen, *The Extent of the Atonement: A Historical and Critical Review* (Nashville: B&H Academic, 2016).

7. On Luther's use of the clothing metaphor, see chap. 8, section "Protestant Righteousness." As an additional example, Luther states, "His righteousness stands for me before the judgment of God and against the wrath of God . . . for a foreign righteousness has been introduced as a covering." Martin Luther, "Lectures on Titus," in *Luther's Works*, vol. 29, *Lectures on Titus, Philemon, and Hebrews*, ed. Jaroslav Pelikan (St. Louis: Concordia, 1968), 41.

8. N. T. Wright, *What Saint Paul Really Said: Was Paul of Tarsus the Real Founder of Christianity?* (Grand Rapids: Eerdmans, 1997), 99. Wright reaffirms this position in *Paul and the Faithfulness of God*, 2 vols. (Minneapolis: Fortress, 2013), 2:945–47.

9. See Rom. 1:17; 3:5, 21, 22, 25, 26; 10:3–4 (2×); 2 Cor. 5:21; Phil. 3:9; cf. James 1:20.

10. See John Piper, *The Future of Justification: A Response to N. T. Wright* (Wheaton: Crossway, 2007); and Michael Horton, *Justification* (Grand Rapids: Zondervan Academic, 2018), 2.321–61.

11. Matthew W. Bates, *Salvation by Allegiance Alone: Rethinking Faith, Works, and the Gospel of Jesus the King* (Grand Rapids: Baker Academic, 2017), 191.

12. For discussion of how *duplex iustitia* was intimated at Regensburg and then fully weighed and rejected by the Council of Trent, see Alister E. McGrath, *Iustitia Dei: A History of the Christian Doctrine of Justification*, 4th ed. (Cambridge: Cambridge University Press, 2020), 293–300, 310–16.

13. E.g., Brant Pitre, Michael P. Barber, and John A. Kincaid, *Paul, a New Covenant Jew: Rethinking Pauline Theology* (Grand Rapids: Eerdmans, 2019), 162–210, esp. 167–69; and James B. Prothro, *A Pauline Theology of Justification: Forgiveness, Friendship, and Life in Christ* (Eugene, OR: Cascade Books, 2023), 76–107, esp. 83–87, 105.

14. Bird, *Saving Righteousness of God*, 85.

15. On Bucer's double justification, see Alister E. McGrath, *Iustitia Dei: A History of the Christian Doctrine of Justification*, 3rd ed. (Cambridge: Cambridge University Press, 2005), 251–53.

16. On the moral dimension of justification, see Michael J. Gorman, *Becoming the Gospel: Paul, Participation, and Mission* (Grand Rapids: Eerdmans, 2015), 222–58; and Pitre, Barber, and Kincaid, *Paul*, 162–201.

Scripture and Ancient Sources Index

Old Testament

Genesis

3:15 143
3:20 142
9:15–16 143
12:3 143
17:10–14 166
18:18 143
22:18 143
25:30 290n14
27:40 153
32–33 153
32:4 154
36 153

Exodus

4:21 154
7:3 154
7:13–14 154
7:22 154
8:15 154
8:32 154
9:12 154

9:34–35 154
10–14 154

Leviticus

1–7 87
15:31 110
16 87

Joshua

3 116
7:11–12 110

Judges

15:14

1 Samuel

14:24 290n14
31:9 282n6

2 Samuel

4:10 31,
  282nn5–6
7:12–16 143
18:19–20 282n6

18:20 282n5
18:22 282n5
18:25 282n5
18:26 282n6
18:27 282n5
18:31 282n6

2 Kings

7:9 282n5

Job

29:14 242

Psalms

110:1 32

Isaiah

40:1–5 115
40:9 31, 282n6
40:10 115
43:14 292n5
48:1 287n16
51:8 242
52:7 31, 32, 115,
  282n6

52:8 115
58:6 34
60:6 31, 282n6
61:1 31, 282n6
61:1–2 34
61:10 242
64:6 242

Jeremiah

1:5 152
18:4–6 155–56
44:26 287n16

Lamentations

5:8 292n5

Nahum

1:15 282n6

Habakkuk

2:4 46

Malachi

1:2–3 153

Old Testament Apocrypha

1 Maccabees
4:11 292n5

4 Maccabees
6:29 239
17:21 239

Sirach/ Ecclesiasticus
33:10–14 288n9

New Testament

Matthew
1:25 100
3:2 96
3:3 114
3:11 118, 185
7:21 162
8:4 285n18
10:22 290n9
16:15–16 105
16:17–18 105–6
16:19 286n3
16:27 87, 210
18:3 130
18:18–20 41, 286n3
20:28 238
21:32 169
22:43 185
23:25 287n7
24:13 290n9
26:24 178
26:52 103
27:34 290n14
28:19 123

Mark
1:1 41
1:3 114
1:4 112, 114, 118
1:8 117, 118
1:14–15 29, 34
1:44 285n18
3:11 112
3:21–31 100
3:35 100
4:11–12 291n16
4:16–17 176
4:24–25 291n16
7:3–4 110
7:4 287n7
7:14–23 110
8:29 35
8:34–35 35, 156
8:38 35
10:45 238
13:13 290n9
14:21 178
14:62 32

Luke
1:41 186
1:68 239, 292n5
2:25 186
2:26 185
2:38 239, 292n5
3:3 112, 114, 118
3:4 114
3:8 116
3:10–14 116
3:16 118
3:17–18 61
4:1 117, 185
4:16–21 69
4:18–19 29, 34, 60
4:29 60
4:37 60
4:43 35, 60
5:7 191
5:14 285n18
7:22 35, 69
9:6 60
10:9 60
10:10–16 60
11:38 287n7
14:24 290n14
16:24 286n5
18:25 162
20:1 60
22:3–6 178
22:47–48 178
23:42–43 106
24:21 239

John
1:9 291n15
1:12–13 168
1:26 112
1:29 112
1:33 117, 118, 185
1:41–42 286n4
2:6 287n7
3 196
3:3–8 168
3:5 130, 162
3:16 157
3:23–26 109
4:1–3 109
5:1–7 110
5:24 175, 196
5:28–29 87, 210
5:42 169
6:37 176, 178
6:44 162, 169
6:65 162–63
8:31 290n9
9:7 110
10:27–29 176
10:28–29 178
12:32 157, 163
12:36 132, 169
12:46 132, 169
13:10–11 177, 286n4
13:27–30 178, 196
14–17 178
14:26 185
15:1–6 177–78
15:3 286n4
15:26 185, 290n12
16:7 185

Acts
1:5 185
1:15 185
1:17 178
1:25 178
2:1–4 183–84
2:4 185
2:14–36 29, 38–39
2:17–18 185
2:17–28 184
2:30 282n11
2:33 290n12
2:33–36 32
2:38 96, 105, 123, 184
3:11–26 29, 38–39
3:21 282n11
4:8 185
5:27–32 29, 38–39
5:42 33
7:8 166
8:4–5 33
8:4–25 121
8:12 123
8:16 123
9:3–8 40
9:22 33
10:28–29 81
10:34–43 29, 38–39, 77
10:44–48 107
10:45 185
10:48 123
13:16–47 29, 38–39, 64
13:23 282n11
13:32 282n11

16:8–11 185
16:13 185
17:11 10–11
17:20–22 10–11
17:23 11
18:36 67
20:22 184

13:38–41 156
13:39 283n5
13:43 290n9
13:46 156, 169
14:22 290n9
15:8 119
15:8–9 107
16:14 163
16:15 120
16:33–34 120
17:2–3 33
17:22–31 29,
  38–39
18:5 33
18:8–9 120
18:28 33
19:2–6 118
19:13 287n16
19:17 123
22:6–10 40
22:16 123
26:12–18 40
28:24 169

Romans

1:1 36
1:2 282n11
1:2–4 29, 36, 76
1:3–4 36
1:4–5 43
1:5 66, 83, 234,
  263, 282n16
1:8 282n16
1:12 282n16
1:16 29, 43, 45,
  169, 283n5
1:16–17 67, 246
1:17 45, 46,
  76, 77, 83,
  216, 245–47,
  282n16,
  292n14, 293n9
1:17–18 247–48
1:18–33 242
1:21 169
1:23 243
1:28 169
1:32 169

2:6 87
2:6–8 210
2:7–8 290n9
2:13 87, 210
2:13–16 253
2:25 88
2:25–29 253
2:29 87, 165
3:3 282n16
3:5 293n9
3:9–20 239, 242
3:10–12 169
3:20–22 292n14
3:21 293n9
3:21–22 245–46
3:21–26 216, 253
3:22 46, 77, 245,
  271n16, 293n9
3:23 243
3:24 213
3:25 88, 247–48,
  282n16, 293n9
3:26 223,
  282n16, 293n9
3:27 86
3:27–30 86
3:30 287n17
4:5 236
4:9–11 236
4:11 166
4:22 236
4:25 62, 211,
  292n14
5:1 213, 287n17
5:2 234
5:5 185
5:9 287n17
5:16–19 292n14
5:17–19 46
5:18 238
5:21 234
6:3 123
6:3–4 105, 109
6:3–7 126
6:4 213
6:6 239
6:7 210
6:12 211
6:19 207–9

7:7–13 89
7:18 169
8:3–4 237
8:4 87, 243, 253,
  292n14
8:7 169
8:9–10 187, 189
8:9–11 198
8:10–14 253
8:12–13 210
8:13 87
8:13–19 108
8:17 213
8:29–30 175,
  189, 204, 207,
  212–14, 288n2
8:33–34 292n14
8:34 11
9:10–13 152
9:16–23 154
9:22–24 154–55
9:30 287n17
9:30–10:17 155
9:32 86
9:33–10:4 155
10:3–4 293n9
10:4 88
10:6 287n17
10:9–10 156–57
10:9–16 61, 106
10:10 106–7
10:15 32
11:7–15 156
11:26–36 156
12 263
13:14 242
14:9 35
14:9–12 210
14:12 145
15:2 145
15:4 88
15:18–19 43
15:19 33
16:25–26 40, 43
16:26 66, 83,
  234, 263

1 Corinthians

1:12 145
1:14–17 107
1:16 120
1:27 126
1:30 207, 209
2:4–5 67
3:16 184
3:16–17 197–98
5:5 198
6:9–11 78
6:11 119, 126,
  207–9, 213,
  220
6:14 175
6:18–20 184
6:20 239
7:18–19 165
7:19 89
7:23 239
9:1 40
9:9 88
9:12 33
9:22–27 181
9:27 152
10:12 290n9
10:13 159
10:17 262
12 263
12:3 68, 189
12:4–27 68
12:13 185
15:1–2 178–79
15:1–3 40
15:1–11 42
15:3 62
15:3–5 29, 36,
  37, 76, 197

2 Corinthians

1:21–22 183
2:3–11 199
2:12 33
3:3–6 89
3:12–18 89
3:6 89
3:7–11 213
3:17 198

3:18 188, 213, 243
4:4 41, 44, 66
4:4–6 132
4:5 41
4:6 213
4:13 46
5:5 183, 188
5:10 87, 210
5:17 89, 168
5:21 245, 247, 292n14, 293n9
8:1–5 234
8:23 213
9:13 33
10:14 33
13:5 188

Galatians

1:1 76
1:4 76, 88
1:6 179
1:6–7 80
1:6–9 74, 90
1:7 33
1:11–12 40
1:15 152
1:18 40
2:2–5 82
2:5 74, 82, 90
2:7 80–81
2:12 81
2:12–13 81
2:14 74, 81–82, 90
2:16 75, 81, 83–84, 86, 89, 90, 213, 287n17
2:18 89, 94
2:20 78
3:2 90
3:5 90
3:8 40, 83, 283n5, 287n17
3:10 75, 88, 90
3:11 75, 83, 287n17
3:13–14 40
3:14 83
3:16 83
3:16–17 89
3:24 287n17
3:24–27 126
3:27 123, 242
3:28 83
3:29 90
4:3 89
4:9 89
4:9–10 86
4:9–11 99
4:21–31 89
5:1–4 290n9
5:1–6 90
5:2–4 75
5:3 75, 88
5:3–7 181
5:4 179
5:6 75, 77, 165
5:19–21 78, 179
6:7–10 87
6:8 179
6:15 88, 89, 168

Ephesians

1:1 183
1:3–5 140–41
1:3–14 144, 148–51
1:4 34, 143
1:13 43
1:13–14 183, 220
1:18 291n15
1:21 287n16
2:1–3 239, 242
2:4–5 174–75
2:5 164
2:8 174–75
2:8–9 4
2:8–10 86
3:6 83
3:7–9 234
3:9 291n15
5:5–6 78
5:11–14 132, 169
5:18 185

Philippians

1:6 175
1:19 198
1:27 33, 41, 67
3:3–5 165
3:7–14 108, 181
3:9 63, 246–47, 283n5, 293n9
3:9–11 245, 253
3:11–14 152

Colossians

1:23 180
2:8 89
2:11–14 164–67
2:13 241
2:14 241
2:14–17 99
2:15 241
2:16 86
2:20 89

1 Thessalonians

1:5 67, 185
2:8–9 70
2:12 145
3:2 33
3:5 179
4:4 145

2 Thessalonians

2:14 213

1 Timothy

1:19–20 199
1:20 198
2:4 263
2:6 239
3:6 177
6:12 290n9

2 Timothy

1:1 43
1:9–10 141
1:10 143

1:14 184, 185
2:4 157
2:8 29, 36
2:12 12, 290n9
4:6–8 181
4:14 87, 210

Titus

2:14 239
3:5 105, 168
3:6 185

Hebrews

1:8–12 185
2:1–4 182
3:1–4:13 182
3:1 191
3:13 192
4:2 169
5:11–6:12 182
6:4 132, 193
6:4–6 190–92
6:9 191
7:25 11
9:12 239
9:15 239
9:26 239
10:10–14 98, 239
10:19–39 182
10:22 118, 125–26
10:26 192–93
10:26–27 190, 192, 199
10:29 193
10:32 132, 191
11:1 182
11:20 154
12:1–3 181
12:1–29 182
12:8 191
12:16–17 154
12:22–29 280n3

James

1:12 290n9
1:13 159
1:20 293n9

1:22–26 173
2:10 88
2:17 77, 79
2:21–24 210
2:22 79
2:24 77, 287n17
2:26 77

1 Peter

1:18–19 167
1:19–20 141
1:21 167
1:22 167
1:23 167
2:24 237
3:21 105, 125,
    193–94

2 Peter

1:10–11 290n9
2:20–21 193–94
3:9 157
3:12–13 280n3
3:17 290n9

1 John

1:8 173
2:18–19 194, 196
2:19 199
2:23–25 196
2:29 173
3:7 173
3:9 195
3:24 195
4:1 196
4:13 194–95
5:1 196
5:4 196
5:10–13 196
5:16 194
5:18 196

2 John

7–11 196
9 194–95, 196

Revelation

1:5–6 240
2:5 96
2:7–11 11
3:12 11
5:9–10 240
19:13 286n5
19:16 12
20:4–6 12
20:12–15 210
21:7–8 11
22:1 12
22:5 12
22:15 78

Other Ancient
Writings

Aeschines

*Against
Ctesiphon*
160 281n3

Aristophanes

Equites
647 281n2
656 281n2

Cicero

*Letters to
Atticus*
2.3.1 281n2
13.40.1 281n2

Dead Sea
Scrolls

1QHa
7:27–28 288n9
9:10–11 288n9
9:20–22 288n9

1QS
4:12–13 288n9
4:26 288n9
5:13 287n9

5:14 287n10
5:16 287n7
8:13–14 114,
    287n12
8:16 114
9:18–20 114,
    287n12

4Q514
frag. 1 287n7

4QMMT
4:55–58 287n7
4:65–68 287n7

Didache

7:1 128
7:2 128
7:3 128
7:4 128

Diodorus
Siculus

*Bibliotheca
historica*
15.74 281n2

Josephus

Against Apion
2.45 292n5

*Jewish
Antiquities*
18.116–19
    287n14
18.117–18
    287n11
20.97–98 287n13

Jewish War
2.137–38 287n8
4.618 283n7
4.656 282n7

Justin Martyr

First Apology
61.2 287n20
61.3 287n21
61.4 287n22
61.9–13 287n23
65.1 287n26
65.2–3 287n27

*Dialogue with
Trypho*
13.1 287nn24–25
14.1 287nn24–25
19.2 287n25

Origen

*Commentary
of Romans*
5.9.11 288n34

*Homilies on
Leviticus*
8.3 288n34

Philo

Against Flaccus
1.60 292n5

Plutarch

Agesilaus
33.4 30, 282n4

Tertullian

On Baptism
6–8 287n28
18.4–5 288n32
18.4–11 287n29
18.8 288n31
18.9 288n30

The Crown
3 287n28